This book is a much-needed DEI resource for strategic communication educators, students, and professionals. It's more than an introductory text, going beyond explanations by demonstrating how concepts can be applied to professional practice during the research, planning, and execution phases of the communication process.

Jennie Donohue, *University of Massachusetts Amherst, USA*

Diversity, Equity, and Inclusion in Strategic Communications

Taking a DEI-first approach, this book teaches students to become culturally proficient communicators by approaching diversity, equity, and inclusion (DEI) with intentionality in every aspect of strategic communications.

Those who work in strategic communications play a powerful role in shaping public perceptions and thus have a crucial responsibility to understand and practice the principles of diversity, equity, and inclusion in their work. This book introduces students to DEI theories and concepts and guides them through applying these concepts to communications research, planning, and execution. Chapters in the book align with the courses and competencies most often taught in advertising and public relations programs. It also includes chapters on "Inclusive Leadership" and "Working on Diverse Teams," as students will need these competencies when working on group class projects and in preparing for internships. The concluding chapter on "Communicating for Social Change" allows students to look beyond advertising and PR as corporate-centered disciplines and expand their understanding of the power of communications to advocate for social justice and change.

Ideal for students at the undergraduate level with relevance to graduate students as well, the book can be used as a stand-alone text in DEI communications courses, as a supplement to core advertising or public relations texts, or in modules in advanced communications courses.

Online materials for instructors include teaching tips, suggested discussions and activities, student assignments, sample quizzes, and video links. They are available at www.routledge.com/9781032533865.

Lee Bush is a professor of Strategic Communications at Elon University, USA.

Karen Lindsey is an assistant professor of Strategic Communications at Elon University, USA.

Diversity, Equity, and Inclusion in Strategic Communications

Becoming Culturally Proficient
Communicators

Lee Bush and Karen Lindsey

Routledge
Taylor & Francis Group

NEW YORK AND LONDON

Designed cover image: cienpies / © Getty Images

First published 2025
by Routledge
605 Third Avenue, New York, NY 10158

and by Routledge
4 Park Square, Milton Park, Abingdon, Oxon, OX14 4RN

Routledge is an imprint of the Taylor & Francis Group, an informa business

Library of Congress Cataloging-in-Publication Data
Names: Bush, Lee (Professor of strategic communications), author. | Lindsey, Karen (Professor of strategic communications), author.
Title: Diversity, equity, and inclusion in strategic communications : becoming culturally proficient communicators / Lee Bush and Karen Lindsey.
Description: New York, NY: Routledge, 2025. | Includes bibliographical references and index.
Identifiers: LCCN 2024021309 (print) | LCCN 2024021310 (ebook) | ISBN 9781032533872 (hardback) | ISBN 9781032533865 (paperback) | ISBN 9781003411796 (ebook)
Subjects: LCSH: Communication in organizations. | Public relations. | Advertising. | Discrimination. | Equality.
Classification: LCC HD30.3 .B85 2025 (print) | LCC HD30.3 (ebook) | DDC 302.2--dc23/eng/20240509
LC record available at https://lccn.loc.gov/2024021309
LC ebook record available at https://lccn.loc.gov/2024021310

ISBN: 978-1-032-53387-2 (hbk)
ISBN: 978-1-032-53386-5 (pbk)
ISBN: 978-1-003-41179-6 (ebk)

DOI: 10.4324/9781003411796

Typeset in Times New Roman
by SPi Technologies India Pvt Ltd (Straive)

Access the Support Material: www.routledge.com/9781032533865

Contents

List of Contributors   *ix*
Preface   *x*

Introduction   1

1 DEI Definitions, Theories, and Concepts   3
LEE BUSH

2 Understanding and Reaching Diverse Audiences   18
KAREN LINDSEY

3 Centering DEI in Strategic Writing   37
VANESSA BRAVO

4 Visual Storytelling: Reframing Diversity and Inclusion   50
K. MICHELE LASHLEY

5 Inclusive Digital and Social Media Strategies   65
QIAN XU

6 Designing Culturally Sensitive Research   79
LEE BUSH

7 Integrating DEI into the Campaigns Planning Process   94
LEE BUSH

8 Working on Diverse Teams   111
KAREN LINDSEY

 9 Inclusive Leadership   124
    KAREN LINDSEY

10 Reputation Management and DEI   135
    KAREN LINDSEY

11 Communicating for Social Change   145
    LEE BUSH

    Glossary   *162*
    Index   *170*

Contributors

Vanessa Bravo, Professor of Strategic Communications, Elon University, USA.

K. Michele Lashley, Assistant Professor of Strategic Communications, Elon University, USA.

Qian Xu, Professor of Strategic Communications, Elon University, USA.

Preface

In June 2020, after the murder of George Floyd by police officers in the United States, brand strategist Isis Dallis wrote an open letter to the industry on the power and responsibility of communications professionals. She wrote:

> As image-makers, platform builders, conversation managers, and story-tellers, we contribute to the images, messages, and perceptions that circulate within our society and culture. These images and messages have tremendous power. They have the power to influence the thoughts, feelings, and behaviors of our collective society today and for generations to come ... They have the power to make people see and recognize the humanity in others, or the power to objectify and dehumanize others.[1]

To use this power responsibly, Dallis called on members of the industry to learn about the history of racial stereotypes and systemic oppression; diversify our teams; amplify the work of people of color; understand culturally diverse audiences; and ensure our strategies, images, messages, and stories authentically reflect the culturally diverse world in which we live.

This book was written in part as a response to that call. It was also written in response to professional associations (World Federation of Advertisers, Association of National Advertisers, Public Relations Society of America) impelling the industry to drive global action on DEI, and to educational associations and accrediting bodies (the Commission on Public Relations Education, the Accrediting Council on Education in Journalism and Mass Communications) urging educators to develop courses and content to create culturally proficient communicators.

While much of the DEI focus in communications textbooks is on the workplace, we saw a need for a textbook that expands that focus, approaching DEI with intentionality in every aspect of strategic communications. Themes in the book align with the courses and competencies most often taught in advertising and public relations programs, filling a content gap in considering DEI at the forefront of research, planning, creative development, and execution.

In addition to being educators and scholars, the authors and contributors of this text have years of professional experience in the communications industry – as brand strategists, corporate communications managers, journalists, copywriters, visual storytellers, and digital/interactive technology experts. Each of us has experienced discrimination in our own way, be it against race, ethnicity, gender, sexual orientation, or the intersectionality of these identities. We are passionate about bringing a more inclusive and equitable approach to the field and preparing the next generation of communicators to carry forth the change that Dallis envisions.

Note

1 Dallis, I. (2020, June 4). *We need to talk about how media and creatives portray Black people.* Fast Company. www.fastcompany.com/90512750/we-need-to-talk-about-how-media-and-creatives-portray-black-people.

Introduction

Those who work in strategic communications play a powerful role in shaping public perceptions and thus have a crucial responsibility to diversity, equity, and inclusion (DEI). Through the research insights we uncover, the strategies we create, the stories we tell, the images we circulate, and the channels through which we disseminate our messages, our communications can mean the difference between presenting a narrow, stereotyped view of the world or one that is representative and inclusive of the diverse publics that make up our society. For the organizations with which we work, our communications can also mean the difference between connecting authentically with publics or potentially alienating audiences and negatively impacting an organization's reputation.

To become proficient communicators, we learn many skills and competencies, like how to effectively conduct research, strategize, develop content, and evaluate media channels. And we learn to problem-solve, effectively counsel clients, and work well with our teams along the way. When we add the word *culturally* to the term *proficient communicators*, it means we can do all these things through a DEI lens. In fact, we can't become effective communicators *without* becoming culturally proficient.

Being a culturally proficient communicator starts with being able to understand and effectively engage with people from a diversity of backgrounds, identities, and cultures. But it is more than that. It means our communications are representative and inclusive of the diverse cultures that make up our society and that we acknowledge the history and impact of systemic inequities. This textbook was designed to introduce you to DEI theories and concepts and help you apply these concepts at the forefront of every aspect of strategic communications.

DOI: 10.4324/9781003411796-1

- Chapters 1 and 2 review DEI definitions and theories and explore the intersectional identities that make up our audiences.
- Chapters 3 and 4 discuss how to create and produce inclusive written and visual storytelling that avoids stereotypes and authentically represents diverse audiences.
- Chapter 5 provides an overview of how digital and social media use differs across cultures and how to develop inclusive and accessible digital communications strategies.
- Chapter 6 explores how to design culturally sensitive research by putting DEI first in every phase of the research process.
- Chapter 7 reinforces DEI concepts learned in earlier chapters and provides guidance for putting them together in a coherent campaign planning structure.
- Chapters 8 and 9 address ways to work cohesively within culturally diverse teams and the complexities and communications behaviors of being an inclusive leader.
- Chapter 10 explores the realities of political consumerism and how increasing demands that organizations take a stand on sociopolitical issues can impact a brand's reputation.
- Chapter 11 investigates how strategic communications is employed by social justice advocates and activists to promote social change.

Each chapter aligns with the core skills and competencies most often taught in advertising, PR, or strategic communications majors. Thus, you can read the chapters in order or select the chapters that most relate to the courses in which you are currently engaged. The online instructor hub provides additional materials, videos, discussion questions, and activities for instructors to apply the content in their courses.

As you read the content, it's crucial to understand that DEI is not a one-off that you memorize and put away for use somewhere in the distant future. The content of the text should be applied throughout the semester to each of the skills and competencies learned in your strategic communications program and, ultimately, to your practice as a professional. DEI is as much a mindset as it is a competency. When you begin to look at your work – and the world – through a DEI lens, it changes your perspective on everything.

1 DEI Definitions, Theories, and Concepts

Lee Bush

As stated in the introduction to this book, those who work in strategic communications play a powerful role in shaping public perceptions and thus have a crucial responsibility for diversity, equity, and inclusion (DEI) (Dallis, 2020). Our communications can mean the difference between presenting a narrow, stereotyped view of the world or one that is representative and inclusive of the diverse publics that make up our society. Taking a DEI-first approach to strategic communications begins by understanding what we mean by the terms diversity, equity, and inclusion and the importance of DEI in our industry. While the industry has long sought to address diversity in the workplace, only in recent years has the industry turned its attention toward applying DEI principles to external communications.

In this chapter, we will review the terms, concepts, and theories most often associated with DEI. We use the initials DEI throughout this text, but it's helpful to know that the principles of DEI are referred to in a variety of ways by different entities and geographic regions. For example, some refer to it simply as D&I, while others put equity first in the initials EDI. In addition, our awareness and understanding of DEI principles are always changing and growing. In more recent years, the concept of belonging has been added in the initials DEIB. And, with an extended focus on systemic inequities, the term justice is often added for the initials JEDI.

In this chapter, we will begin to discuss what it means to be culturally proficient in communications by:

- Reviewing the definitions of diversity, equity, and inclusion
- Exploring the history and current state of DEI in the industry
- Recognizing the importance of DEI in strategic communications
- Exploring DEI theories and concepts
- Addressing the apprehensions many feel when applying DEI

DOI: 10.4324/9781003411796-2

DEI Definitions

The term ***diversity*** refers to *the range of differences in identities, experiences, and perspectives between people and groups.* Imagine you are sitting in a classroom right now. As you look around the room at your classmates, what do you notice? One of the first things you might notice is differences in outward appearance, like skin tone, age, how your classmates dress, or their physical abilities. These are often thought of as surface-level differences or those that can be observed.

Once you begin to talk or work with your classmates, you notice deeper-level differences in experiences, thoughts, and perspectives. You may learn that one classmate celebrates Hannukah in December while another celebrates Christmas. One classmate grew up in a large family while another grew up as an only child. One classmate approaches problem-solving from an individualist perspective while another considers the consensus of the group.

While surface-level differences can and do account for differences in cultural perspectives, where we can make mistakes in communications is relying *only* on surface-level differences when we engage with our audiences. For example, if we assume that all Latinx voters in the United States vote alike, we will get it wrong. Voting patterns can be impacted by multiple characteristics like differences in national origin, upbringing, or age. Making assumptions about social identity groups can lead to ***stereotypes*** or *applying uneducated judgements or generalizations to everyone in a group.*

The term ***equity*** refers to *fairness, with the goal of eliminating disparities in treatment, access, or opportunity.* For example, if a teacher assigned homework that required doing research on the internet, but not every child had access to the internet at home, this would not be equitable. The goal in an equitable society is to break down barriers to participation and success, like making sure every child has access to the same tools for doing homework.

It's important to understand that equity and equality are related, but not the same. Imagine, for example, you are invited to celebrate a friend's birthday at an expensive restaurant where each attendee is expected to split the cost of the meal equally. If you had a lower income than your peers and could not afford that restaurant, splitting the cost of the check evenly would be equal but not equitable. Equity recognizes that we start from different places in life, but all should have equitable opportunities to achieve success (Figure 1.1).

Barriers to equity can be, and often are, ***systemic***. That is, inequities are *embedded and reinforced in societal policies, systems, and structures.* For example, in the United States, Black women have significantly higher maternal mortality rates than White women (Centers for Disease Control, 2016). The reasons for this are both historical and complex and include inadequate

EQUALITY   EQUITY

Figure 1.1 An illustration of equality versus equity.

research on health issues affecting Black women, lack of access to health-care and health insurance, and disparities in how Black women are treated by the medical profession (Chinn et al., 2021). Thus, the barriers to Black women's health are systemic and structural and the solutions therefore must also be systemic.

Box 1.1 Brands Promoting Equity of BIPOC-owned Businesses

Due to systemic inequities, BIPOC-owned businesses are often finan-cially undervalued, lack equal access to capital and market recogni-tion, and face bias and harassment, among other challenges (Faster Capital, 2023; Perry et al., 2022). Several brands are working to address these barriers.

In 2023, the NBA and ESPN launched the fourth year of #ChampionBlackBusinesses. The initiative highlights businesses during the NBA Finals across ESPN and NBA platforms and gives them access to mentors from ABC's *Shark Tank* panel (Milner, 2023).

In 2022, Roundel, Target Corporation's internal media network, launched the Roundel Media Fund to offset marketing costs for BIPOC-owned brands and expand their reach to Target customers. Target plans to invest $25 million in the fund by the end of 2025 (Iboko, n.d.).

In 2021, restaurant chain El Pollo Loco launched the "For Your Consideration" campaign, nominating 11 Latinx chefs for the James Beard Award (QSR Magazine, 2021). Though the Latinx community plays an outsized role in the foodservice industry (and owns 18% of U.S. restaurants), Latinx chefs held only 2.4% of nominees for the coveted award as of 2018. El Pollo Loco used a variety of media activations to highlight the chefs and awarded a $5,000 scholarship to advance the culinary career of one of its employees.

The third piece of the DEI equation is inclusion. **Inclusion** refers to *the practice of creating an environment in which all voices within a society are included, respected, and supported.*

We often talk about inclusion in terms of *belonging*. Think about a group where you feel like you truly belong. Your needs are met, you are respected by your peers, you feel safe sharing your ideas, and your voice is welcomed and valued. Conversely, think about being in an environment where you felt *ex*cluded. Perhaps you were afraid to speak up for fear of being criticized, or the group favored only one way of doing something and you did it differently. The group may have had access to knowledge that you were not privy to, or the consensus of the group went against the experiences of your culture.

For example, plagued with decades of school shootings in the United States, one popular solution is to hire more police officers on school grounds. The thought is that everyone will feel safer with more police officers. What this solution doesn't consider, however, is the historic racial inequities in the U.S. criminal justice system. So, while *some* students may feel safer with more officers, students of color may feel *less* safe in such an environment.

The concepts of diversity, equity, and inclusion work together in strategic communications, allowing us to understand, listen to, and authentically engage with our audiences, and promote equity and social change. As Emily Graham, Chief Equity and Impact Officer at Omnicom, has said, "Diversity is a fact, inclusion is a practice, and equity is a goal" (Burrell, 2020).

There are many ways we can practice DEI in our communications. Using inclusive language, recruiting diverse participants when conducting research, making sure our content is representative of and accessible to the diversity of our audiences, and taking culture into consideration when crafting strategies and stories are just some of the ways we'll talk about applying DEI to external communications in subsequent chapters.

The Evolution and Importance of DEI in Strategic Communications

DEI in strategic communications started with a focus on diversity in the workplace. Historically, the advertising and PR fields began as mostly White and male professions. In the latter half of the 20th century, with advancements in civil rights, women's rights, and LGBTQ+ rights, agencies began to expand the range of employees hired to reach a growing number of diverse audiences. However, with a focus only on recruiting, the industry struggled to retain diverse employees due to a lack of inclusive policies and practices.

Today, the communications industry has evolved in its diversity for women. It now skews female with around 67% of both the advertising and PR fields comprised of those who identify as women (Association of National Advertisers, 2022; U.S. Bureau of Labor Statistics, 2023). However, racial and ethnic diversity in the industry is much lower. For example, Black participants comprised only 7.2% of the Association of National Advertisers member companies in 2022, and Hispanic/Latino participants made up only 10.9%, significantly lower than percentages in the U.S. population. Similarly, on the creative side, the graphic design field skews toward women (54.7%) and White people (77.9%) (U.S. Bureau of Labor Statistics, 2023). In the PR field, the Diversity Action Alliance (2023) found that only 29% of PR professionals are racially or ethnically diverse.

When it comes to inclusion, a Global DEI Census in 91 countries highlights several areas where the communications industry is falling short (WFA, 2023). The report shows that women, ethnic minorities, people with disabilities, and LGBTQ+ respondents feel less included in their organizations; people with disabilities are significantly underrepresented; and parents/caregivers feel their status hinders their careers. In addition, while the report indicates that 87% of U.S. and Canadian employees said their companies were addressing DEI, this percentage was lower in other countries (e.g., 60% in Sweden, 49% in Japan) (WFA, 2023, p. 8).

While the industry continues to work on improving its diversity and inclusion, these statistics underscore the need for building cultural competency. With much of the focus in past decades on DEI in the workplace, the communications industry has only recently turned to putting DEI first in external communications. This decision is being driven by both the business case and the moral case for DEI.

In the corporate world, there are often two rationales for practicing DEI: the business case and the fairness or moral case. The business case focuses on DEI as the means to a profitable outcome; the moral case justifies DEI because it's the right thing to do in a fair and just society (Georgeac &

Rattan, 2022). While the business case can exploit identity groups and lead to organizations scrapping DEI as business conditions change, the moral case ensures that DEI is embedded in an organization's values and policies (Beach & Segars, 2022). In fact, the Commission on Public Relations Education has called on the industry to move beyond the business case and "help create and convey cultural value for D&I to core stakeholders" (Mundy et al., 2018, p. 141).

In external communications, the numerous studies and statistics discussed throughout this book show the significant purchasing power of diverse audiences, consumers' desire for great representation in communications, and the competitive advantage DEI gives to brands and organizations (or the harm it can cause if DEI is lacking). On the moral side, a heightened awareness of social justice issues and an acknowledgement of the role organizations have historically played in perpetuating systemic injustices are driving organizations to reexamine their responsibility to society. Both scenarios propel strategic communicators to embed DEI into their programs and practices. In doing so, we become better, more effective communicators, build greater trust with our audiences, and help create a more equitable society.

DEI Theories and Concepts

Now that we've discussed the definitions and evolution of DEI in the industry, it would be helpful to understand some of the theories and concepts that can contribute to our knowledge of DEI in strategic communications. Below we outline a few of these theories. Others will be discussed throughout the book.

Cultural Reductionism

When we lack cultural proficiency, we can perpetuate what is known as cultural reductionism. *Cultural reductionism* is *being unable to view situations from a perspective other than our own* (Krownapple, 2016, p. 131).

A good example of this is a simple question posed on social media one day: When is the last time you took a *real* shower? For many people, this question might seem perplexing. "I took a shower this morning," you might think. But consider that this question was posed by a person with a disability. For people with mobility issues, showering is not as simple as walking in and turning on the water. If you do not have mobility issues, you may not have even considered this.

Cultural reductionism explains why people with disabilities are often represented in the media in a variety of ableist tropes. For example, as disability communications expert Rosemary McDonnel-Horita explains, "the viral videos that get spread around prom season of a high school football player asking a girl with Down syndrome to prom," exploit and infantilize people with disabilities instead of portraying them as having full, rich lives (Rajkumar, 2022).

To avoid cultural reductionism, it's important to understand that we don't know what we don't know. In other words, acknowledge where there are gaps in our understanding and center a variety of voices who can educate us and speak directly to the experiences and perspectives of a cultural group. This is particularly important given the statistics of the industry outlined earlier.

Intersectionality

Intersectionality originated as a legal concept, coined by legal scholar Kimberlé Crenshaw in 1989. At that time, she was concerned with how anti-discrimination doctrine favored mutually exclusive single-issue frameworks; for example, *either* racial discrimination *or* sex discrimination but not the intersection of the two. Further, these frameworks often focus on the most privileged members in a group. She outlined several legal cases where Black women faced discrimination in workplaces (Crenshaw, 1989). In these cases, not *all* Black people were discriminated against, and not *all* women were discriminated against. Instead, discrimination was based on the overlapping identities of being both Black *and* women. However, because the courts only recognized race or sex as single-issue frameworks, the unique challenges of Black women (separate from White women or Black men) were either marginalized or erased.

Since that time, the term intersectionality has been expanded to encompass a range of identities (such as race, class, ability, gender, sexual orientation, age, etc.). *Intersectionality acknowledges that individuals and groups experience discrimination differently based on their multiple, overlapping identities.* It helps us consider the impact and relationship of messages, systems, structures, and institutions on individuals or groups of people with multiple marginalized identities and how we communicate to and represent them in campaigns.

Theory of Corporate Responsibility to Race

The *theory of corporate responsibility to race* (CRR) was developed by public relations professor and corporate communications expert Dr. Nneka Logan. At the heart of the theory is the acknowledgement that corporations have historically "perpetuated and profited from racial oppression," and thus have a responsibility to "*communicate in ways that advocate for racial justice, attempt to improve race relations, and support achieving a more equitable and harmonious society*" (Logan, 2021, p. 1).

Some of the ways corporations in the United States have perpetuated and profited from racial oppression include the use of enslaved labor to fuel the economies for railroads, cotton, rice, and other industries; the housing and banking industries' participation in housing discrimination (e.g., redlining); brands perpetuating racial stereotypes in advertising; and the exploitation of low-income workers.

Logan outlines five communications principles for CRR that include drawing significant attention to racism; explaining its complexities and applications; advocating for racial justice and equity; expressing "a desire to improve race relations in an effort to achieve a more equitable and harmonious society," and, with its impetus in the moral case for DEI, prioritizing societal needs over corporate economic needs (Logan, 2021, p. 8). In practice, CRR can be applied to analyzing existing organizational policies and programs or to develop communications plans and campaigns that advocate for racial equity

Corporate Social Responsibility and Corporate Social Advocacy

Corporate social responsibility (CSR) has long been a global business practice rooted in the concept that organizations have a responsibility to be good citizens; that is, they are socially responsible not just for their organizations but for the larger society in which their organizations operate. CSR is manifested in many ways in organizations, such as through charitable giving, adopting sustainable practices, or partnering with nonprofit organizations.

In more recent years, CSR has evolved and expanded to include *corporate social advocacy* **(CSA)** (Gandiwa, 2022). CSA refers to *institutions taking a stance on and advocating for sociopolitical issues, like racial and social justice, gun violence, LGBTQ+ rights, or immigration issues.* In previous decades, organizations were counseled to remain neutral on often controversial issues for fear of angering members of their customer base. However, younger generations began demanding that organizations recognize their outsized role in society and be transparent in advocating for social change. In essence, consumers want to support businesses that share their values. It's worth noting that these values span across the political spectrum. For example, while companies such as Ben & Jerry's support more liberal values like refugee rights, LGBTQ+ rights, and voting rights, companies like Hobby Lobby and Chick-fil-A are transparent about their support for more conservative evangelical Christian values.

Criticism of both CSR and CSA is that organizations often "talk the talk" but don't "walk the walk." For example, an organization might promote Pride Month in their communications, but then fail to include LGBTQ+ individuals in their workplace parental leave policies. When organizations are more "performative" in their CSA communications rather than genuinely supporting a cause, it is often known as "rainbow-washing," "green-washing," or "diversity-washing."

Critical Theories

There are several ***critical theories*** that relate to DEI in strategic communications. First, it's helpful to understand what the oft-misunderstood word "critical" means in the realm of academic theory. Much like a "critic" would critique a play, movie, or artist's music, critical theory critiques systems of power and oppression. But critical theory goes a step further to propose solutions for dismantling structural inequalities. Thus, critical theory relates to *theories that analyze and critique societal systems and structures with an eye toward making them more just and equitable for all.*

At the core of critical theories is the acknowledgement that discrimination is embedded in our structures and systems, and not just the result of individual prejudices. Critical theories can be applied to an array of topics and fields and often elevate the intersectional voices and experiences of those who have been historically excluded from social science research. Some critical theories that relate to DEI in strategic communications are outlined below.

Critical Race Theory (CRT)

CRT originated in the 1970s and 80s to examine how legal systems and structures reproduce racial inequalities and has since expanded to other fields. It is often difficult to explain what CRT is because, as Kimberlé Crenshaw, one of the early scholars of CRT, has noted, CRT is a *verb* rather than a *noun* (Fortin, 2021). In essence, CRT is a practice – a lens through which we can study the role of race and racism historically, politically, and culturally in societal systems.

Some of the tenets of CRT include rejecting the notion of a colorblind society; acknowledging that race is socially, rather than biologically, constructed; recognizing that racism persists at a structural and systemic level; and, through storytelling and other experiential methods, exploring how these systems impact the lived experiences of people of color (George, 2021).

In strategic communications, CRT can be used to develop and examine public communications programs, corporate policies and practices, and corporate advocacy campaigns. For example, Logan (2016) used the theoretical framework of CRT to examine the Starbucks Race Together Campaign. By centering race, the campaign displayed a commitment to racial equality; elevated the voices and lived experiences of people of color; and took on an educational nature, raising public consciousness about the impact of racial inequality (Logan, 2016, pp. 104–105). Logan concludes that CRT can serve as an innovative tool for PR practitioners by integrating it into the planning process.

In the advertising industry, scholars have called on marketers to utilize CRT as a tool to increase diversity and inclusion in the industry; as a framework to understand consumers and marketplace dynamics; and as a lens to recognize, research, and address the automation biases inherent in artificial intelligence technologies (Casey, 2021; Poole et al., 2021).

Feminist Theory

Like CRT, feminist theory is a broad lens through which to study gender and the structural mechanisms that have created gender inequality around the globe. These could include structures in private spheres such as relationships and family structures, or those in public spheres such as political and organizational structures. In addition, feminist theory considers intersectionality (such as the intersection of gender with race or socioeconomics), and often integrates other theoretical lenses or concepts.

For example, in 2022, Schwarz looked at human trafficking through the lens of what Nixon (2011) calls "slow violence." While human trafficking is often framed as a criminal justice issue, with a focus on rescuing victims and capturing perpetrators, Schwarz suggests that human trafficking is instead the consequences of the gradual violence of structural inequities that accumulate over time (e.g., poverty, domestic violence, the stigmatization of LGBTQ+ youth, etc.). These inequities "must be eradicated if we are committed to ending human trafficking locally and globally" (Schwarz, 2022, p. 1).

It's important to note that, in practice, feminist theory is not always as intersectional as implied. The feminist movement has long been criticized for centering the issues of White women and ignoring or minimizing the experiences of Black women. For example, the passage of the 19th Amendment in the United States (the right to vote) wasn't a victory for all women (or men), despite the efforts of Black activists. Yet, Black women have an extensive history of feminist activism intermingled with movements such as the abolitionist and civil rights movements (Taylor, 1998).

Encompassing the intersection of race, gender, and socioeconomics, this standpoint has shaped feminist theory with a more intersectional lens. In 1989, sociologist Patricia Hill Collins discussed how Black feminist thought, rooted in both traditional African values (such as dialogue and empathy) and Black women's lived experience, leads to alternative knowledge-construction and knowledge-validation processes for feminist scholarship.

Queer Theory

Emerging as an area of study in the 1990s, queer theory challenges the assumption that heterosexual and cisgender identities are the norm (also called heteronormative), asserts that sexuality is fluid and gender expressions are socially constructed, and examines the power dynamics that privilege heteronormative identities while marginalizing queer identities (University of Illinois, n.d.). We can see these power dynamics at play in debates over same-sex marriage and adoption; LGBTQ+ rights in employment, healthcare, and housing; and in the numerous anti-LGBTQ+ bills that have been introduced across the United States (Peele, 2023).

In strategic communications, queer theory can inform audience analysis and understanding, help us avoid only heteronormative depictions in our communications, as well as contribute to policies and programs aimed at dismantling inequities. For example, Sampson et al. (2023) applied queer theory to targeted advertising and found that representation of queer identities was limited, lacked intersectionality, and perpetuated stereotypes. In addition, study participants communicated the emotional harms of heteronormative advertising and the potential risks of being identified and targeted as an LGBTQ+ person.

Building Intercultural Competence

Learning to be a culturally competent communicator starts with acknowledging where we are in our own cultural competence maturity. In her Cultural Competence for Equity and Inclusion framework, Goodman (2020) outlines five key components to living and working effectively in culturally diverse environments. These include self-awareness of our own social identities and biases; an understanding and appreciation of others' social identities and cultures; and knowledge of social inequities and their impact on individuals and structures. The last two components in the framework deal with skill building and include skills to adapt and work collaboratively with a diversity of people in different social contexts, and skills to transform society by being able to "identify and address inequities and choose appropriate interventions to create environments, policies, and practices that foster diversity and social justice" (p. 16).

In discussing how to put DEI first in strategic communications, this book will address several skills and competencies related to Goodman's model. For example, in Chapter 2, we discuss the myriad components that make up cultural and social identities, and how our own cultural perspectives can impact our decisions. In Chapters 8 and 9, we discuss how to work collaboratively with a diversity of people and become inclusive leaders. In Chapter 11, we explore how strategic communications can be used to dismantle social inequities and promote social justice. And, throughout the chapters in this book, we discuss ways to build culturally competent knowledge and skills in every aspect of strategic communications.

In building self-awareness, a good place to start is recognizing our own conscious and unconscious biases. Conscious biases are a little easier to recognize because we're aware of them. ***Unconscious biases*** (also known as implicit biases) are trickier because they are *prejudices that we may hold* *toward another person or group that we are unaware of.* These can be both internal (toward our own group) or external (toward other groups).

Unconscious biases are often developed from an early age, and can come from our families, educational institutions, the media, our own experiences, or the collective biases of the societies in which we live. For example, when someone asks a school-aged girl if she has a "boyfriend," they are displaying multiple unconscious biases about relationships, gender, and sexual orientation that were likely embedded in their upbringing. When creating advertising and PR campaigns, our own biases influence how we might portray an individual or group of people.

In addition, before you begin this work it's important to address another component of doing DEI work – fear. This is a common emotion experienced by both students and professionals. We fear saying or doing the wrong thing, exposing our biases, or having the focus be on us if we are from a marginalized community (Sivayoganathan, n.d.).

Workplace inclusion expert Kristy Ware (2022) says our fears can come from three places: misunderstanding, lack of knowledge, and lack of practice. We fear what we don't know or understand. If we let our fears rule us, however, we can't move forward in becoming culturally competent communicators.

The first step in addressing our fears is to acknowledge them. Name them and identify where they're coming from. Only then can we take steps to dismantle them. In doing this work, it's also important to acknowledge you *will* make mistakes. We all do. That's part of being human and how we learn and grow. The key is to understand the mistake, take responsibility for it, and display genuine intent in learning how you can do better next time.

Here are five ways you can address and overcome your fears in doing DEI work in strategic communications:

1. Acknowledge your apprehensions and identify where they're coming from.
2. Approach DEI with a mindset of curiosity and growth. Reid and Brown (2018) have found that intrinsically inclusive people are naturally curious about the world around them, internally motivated to connect with and learn from other people, and less likely to rely on stereotypes.
3. Be open to making mistakes and learning from them. Likewise, be open to feedback and respond with appreciation rather than defensiveness.
4. Listen to people's stories without centering yourself and with a genuine interest in better understanding their perspectives.
5. Expand your cultural knowledge by reading or listening to books, articles, blogs, and podcasts from people with a diversity of social identities. Likewise, expand your social media feed by following brands and people from social identities other than your own. In doing so, listen rather than interject your own perspective.

Doing DEI well also means practicing doing DEI. Like any new skill, the more we do it the better we get at it. When you begin to look at the world through a DEI lens, it changes your perspective on everything. As brand strategist Isis Dallis says, "This is about a way of being, not a list of doing" (Matter Unlimited, 2021).

Bibliography

Association of National Advertisers (ANA). (2022, November 7). *A diversity report for the advertising/marketing industry.* Alliance for Inclusion and Multicultural Marketing. www.ana.net/miccontent/show/id/rr-2022-11-diversity-advertising-marketing-industry

Beach, A. A., & Segars, A. H. (2022, June 7). How a values-based approach advances DEI. *MIT Sloan Management Review.* https://sloanreview.mit.edu/article/how-a-values-based-approach-advances-dei/

Burrell, V. (2020, August 13). DEI for media relations: Setting definitions, positioning efforts around revenue and understanding relevance. *Muck Rack blog.* https://muckrack.com/blog/2020/08/13/dei-for-media-relations

Casey, T. (2021, July 7). *Why critical race theory should be taught in schools: Ad agency edition.* Triple Pundit. www.triplepundit.com/story/2021/critical-race-theory-ad-agency/725286

Centers for Disease Control & Prevention. (2016). *Racial/ethnic disparities in pregnancy-related deaths – United States, 2007–2016.* www.cdc.gov/reproductivehealth/maternal-mortality/disparities-pregnancy-related-deaths/infographic.html

Chinn, J. J., Martin, I. K., & Redmond, N. (2021). Health equity among Black women in the United States. *Journal of Women's Health, 30*(2). https://doi.org/10.1089/jwh.2020.8868

Collins, P. H. (1989). The social construction of Black feminist thought. *Signs, 14*(4), 745–773. www.jstor.org/stable/3174683

Colvin, C. (2022, June 14). *How and why to move past the DEI 'business case'.* HRDIVE. www.hrdive.com/news/business-case-for-dei-2022/625330/

Crenshaw, K. (1989). Demarginalizing the intersection of race and sex: A Black feminist critique of antidiscrimination doctrine, feminist theory, and anti-racist policy. *University of Chicago Legal Forum,* Vol. 1989, Issue 1, Article 8. https://chicagounbound.uchicago.edu/uclf/vol1989/iss1/8

Dallis, I. (2020, June 4). *We need to talk about how media and creatives portray Black people.* Fast Company. www.fastcompany.com/90512750/we-need-to-talk-about-how-media-and-creatives-portray-black-people

Diversity Action Alliance. (2023, December). *Race and ethnicity in public relations and communications: 2022 benchmark report.* www.diversityactionalliance.org/reporting-tool/#report

Duren Conner, M. (2023, February 9). *PR has a diversity problem: 4 ways to start fixing it.* AdAge. https://adage.com/article/opinion/pr-has-diversity-problem-4-ways-start-fixing-it/2469826

Faster Capital. (2023, December 12). *Major challenges facing minority-owned businesses in today's economy.* FasterCapital.com. https://fastercapital.com/content/Major-Challenges-Facing-Minority-Owned-Businesses-in-Today-s-Economy.html

Fortin, J. (2021, November 8). Critical race theory: A brief history. *The New York Times*. www.nytimes.com/article/what-is-critical-race-theory.html

George, J. (2021, January 11). *A lesson on critical race theory*. American Bar Association. www.americanbar.org/groups/crsj/publications/human_rights_magazine_home/civil-rights-reimagining-policing/a-lesson-on-critical-race-theory/

Georgeac, O., & Rattan, A. (2022, June 15). Stop making the business case for diversity. *Harvard Business Review*. https://hbr.org/2022/06/stop-making-the-business-case-for-diversity

Gandiwa, R. (2022, January 8). *Exploring the growing trend of corporate social advocacy*. LinkedIn. www.linkedin.com/pulse/exploring-growing-trend-corporate-social-advocacy-gandiwa-mcipr/

Goodman, D. (2020). Cultural competence for equity and inclusion. *Understanding and Dismantling Privilege*, *10*(1), 41–60. www.wpcjournal.com/article/view/20246

Iboko, F. (n.d.). *Learn more about the Roundel Media Fund, one way we're championing BIPOC-owned businesses*. Roundel. https://roundel.com/insights/roundel-media-fund/

Krownapple, J. (2016). *Guiding teams to excellence with equity: Culturally proficient facilitation*. Corwin Press.

Logan, N. (2016). The Starbucks Race Together Initiative: Analyzing a public relations campaign with critical race theory. *Public Relations Inquiry*, *5*(1) 93–113. https://doi.org/10.1177/2046147X15626969

Logan, N. (2021). A theory of corporate responsibility to race (CRR): Communication and racial justice in public relations. *Journal of Public Relations Research*, *33*(1), 6–22. https://doi.org/10.1080/1062726X.2021.1881898

Matter Unlimited. (2021, February 22). *A Q&A with Isis Dallis*. https://matterunlimited.com/2021/02/22/a-qa-with-isis-dallis/

Milner, I. (2023, June 2). ESPN and the NBA continue to 'champion Black businesses' for a 4th year. *Black Enterprise*. www.blackenterprise.com/the-nba-and-espn-continue-to-champion-black-businesses-in-fourth-installment-of-initiative/

Mundy, D., Lewton, K., Hicks, A., & Neptune, T. (2018). Diversity: An imperative commitment for educators and practitioners. In *Fast Forward: The 2017 report on undergraduate public relations education* (pp. 139–148). Commission on Public Relations Education. www.commissionpred.org/wp-content/uploads/2018/04/report6-full.pdf

Nixon, R. (2011). *Slow violence and the environmentalism of the poor*. Harvard University Press.

Peele, C. (2023, May 23). *Roundup of anti-LGBTQ+ legislation advancing in states across the Country* [Press release]. Human Rights Campaign. www.hrc.org/press-releases/roundup-of-anti-lgbtq-legislation-advancing-in-states-across-the-country

Perry, A., Seo, R., Barr, A., Romer, C., & Broady, K. (2022, February 14). *Black-owned businesses in U.S. cities: The challenges, solutions, and opportunities for prosperity*. Brookings. www.brookings.edu/articles/black-owned-businesses-in-u-s-cities-the-challenges-solutions-and-opportunities-for-prosperity/

Poole, S. M., Martin, S., Grier, S. A., Thomas, K. D., Sobande, F., Ekpo, A. E., Torres, L. T., Addington, L. A., Weekes-Laidlow, M., & Henderson, G. R. (2021). Operationalizing critical race theory in the marketplace. *College of Communication*

Faculty Research and Publications, 564. Marquette University. https://epublications. marquette.edu/comm_fac/564

QSR Magazine. (2021, September 15). El Pollo Loco launched 'for your consideration' campaign to spotlight Hispanic community. www.qsrmagazine.com/news/ el-pollo-loco-launches-your-consideration-campaign-spotlight-hispanic-community

Rajkumar, S. (2022, August 8). *How to talk about disability sensitively and avoid ableist tropes*. NPR. www.npr.org/2022/08/08/1115682836/how-to-talk-about-disability-sensitively-and-avoid-ableist-tropes

Reid, J., & Brown, V. (2018, September 6). A new approach to diversity and inclusion. How to think and behave like inclusive people. *Psychology Today*. www.psychologytoday.com/us/blog/the-social-brain/201809/a-new-approach-to-diversity-and-inclusion

Sampson, P., Encarnacion, R., & Metaxa, D. (2023). Representation, self-determination, and refusal: Queer people's experience with targeted advertising. In *2023 ACM Conference on Fairness, Accountability, and Transparency (FAccT '23)*, June 12–15, 2023, Chicago, IL, USA (pp. 1711–1722). ACM. https://doi.org/10.1145/3593013.3594110

Schwarz, C. (2022). Theorising human trafficking through slow violence. *Feminist Theory*, Online first edition. https://doi.org/10.1177/14647001211062731

Sivayoganathan, S. (n.d.). *Fears of DEI: Working past them so we can move forward.* Lunaria. https://lunariasolutions.com/blog-post/common-fears-dei/

Taylor, U. (1998). The historical evolution of Black feminist theory and praxis. *Journal of Black Studies*, 29(2), 234–253.

U.S. Bureau of Labor Statistics. (2023). *Labor force statistics from the current population survey, 2023*. www.bls.gov/cps/cpsaat11.htm

University of Illinois Library. (n.d.). *Queer theory: Background*. https://guides.library.illinois.edu/queertheory/background

Ware, K. (2022, May 23). *The #1 fear stopping you from taking action towards diversity, equity, and inclusion*. KristyWare.com. https://kristyware.com/the-1-fear-stopping-you-from-taking-action-towards-diversity-equity-inclusion/

World Federation of Advertisers (WFA). (2023). *The Global DEI Census*. https://wfanet.org/knowledge/diversity-and-inclusion/the-global-dei-census/2023

2 Understanding and Reaching Diverse Audiences

Karen Lindsey

Understanding the intersections across identity categories and cultural preferences of a specifically defined audience is fundamental to building trust and the beginning of creating authentic relationships through advertising and public relations campaigns.

Central to reaching diverse audiences is demonstrating awareness, respect, and sensitivity to the multitude of practices and preferences within specific cultures and social identity groups. In this chapter, we explore how social identity, categorization, and cultural nuances help us frame and use our research. You will become familiar with key terminology and concepts including:

- Intersectionality as a strategic communications mindset
- Defining social identity and categorization
- Generalized insights for social identity groups
- Tips to effectively reach diverse audiences

Understanding the Bigger Picture

Intersectionality: A Strategic Communications Mindset

In Chapter 1 we introduced intersectionality as a key theory. The word is often used to describe the multitude of interconnected identities that an individual might possess including race, gender, ability, religion, age, and more. *Intersectionality acknowledges that individuals and groups experience societal discrimination differently based on their multiple, overlapping identities* (Crenshaw, 1989, 2013). For example, a person may identify as Latinx, Catholic, low income, and a woman. When we think about how this person might experience a social setting or workplace, each identity category comes with situational challenges and power dynamics that cannot be separated. In adopting an intersectional strategic communications mindset, we do not merely add together distinct identities. Instead, we consider the ways in

DOI: 10.4324/9781003411796-3

which we communicate to ensure we make choices that acknowledge power and privilege and demonstrate understanding of how lived experiences impact interactions with a product, service, issue, or idea.

Let's consider the American Heart Association's "The Heart Truth" public information campaign as an example. The campaign was directed toward women in the United States to increase awareness of heart disease and promote healthy eating. However, "women" are not monolithic. Researchers examined how women of different races and ethnicities perceived the campaign based on their intersectional identities and found that dominant American ideals of health often contradicted the everyday lived experiences of women within their cultures (Tindall & Vardeman-Winter, 2011). These contradictions were associated with cultural food preferences, perceived racial stigmas in the campaign, the time needed to prepare healthy meals, exercise availability, and financial barriers to purchasing healthy ingredients for meal preparation (Tindall & Vardeman-Winter, 2011). While the organization focused on women as the target audience, the intersectional nuances of the women within that audience reflected a wide range of experiences and perceptions.

Using an intersectional strategic communications mindset, the campaign messages would have reflected the differing experiences and needs of the identity category of "women" across a multitude of educational, financial, and cultural experiences. An intersectional strategic communications mindset focuses on gaining a deeper understanding of the circumstances that influence an individual or a collective and considers layers of lived experiences, historical realities, sociopolitical implications, and power dynamics to make meaning within a specific situational context that may be used for advertising or public relations campaigns. Through research we gain insight into identities and their interactions with systems in society, products, services, and even political ideas.

For the purposes of this chapter, we will learn through exploring generalized insights, examples, and situational contexts to help us begin to create communications that are meaningful, respectful, and resonate with the intersecting identities of your intended publics and audiences. Throughout this book, we use the term ***publics*** to refer to *a group of people who share common interests and actively engage with a product, service, or idea.* We sometimes interchangeably refer to publics as ***audiences*** – which generally means *those with whom you want to communicate.* Publics are thought to be more actively engaged with a product, service, or idea and audiences are considered more passive.

Understanding categorization, social identity, and broad insights about identity groups and their intersections provides the basis for developing inclusive creative communications.

Categorization: Why Do We Do It?

As human beings, our brains are wired to try to label people and objects quickly. The ability to determine what things are and what they are not while being able to process detail is central to human learning (Crisp & Hewstone, 2007; Van Knippenberg & Dijksterhuis, 2000). We typically learn how to categorize at an early age from personal experiences, family members, peers, teachers, and the media. Within social identity exploration, we recognize that **categorization** is *typically a spontaneous cognitive process that humans use to identify and label groups, individuals, or objects based on observing or experiencing them* (Crisp & Hewstone, 2007). Researchers further describe categorization as a simplistic way to distinguish between similarities and differences, allowing the human brain to store information (Crisp & Hewstone, 2007; Van Knippenberg & Dijksterhuis, 2000). For communicators, social identity categorization can lead to false assumptions, discrimination, and stereotyping because we rely on our own perceptions, memory, experiences, and inferred knowledge rather than researching, asking, and listening. The knowledge of a social identity is often processed based on what is understood through our own experiences or deemed acceptable by the dominant culture of Whiteness in American society. When we use traditional approaches to categorize or segment audiences, we risk bias and activating stereotypes about a culture.

What Is a Culture?

Researchers have asked the question, "what defines a culture?" for decades. To put it simply, **culture** is *a set of shared meanings, norms, values, beliefs, symbols, and traditions among a specific social identity group*. These shared meanings can influence (but not determine) our behavior and how we interpret others' behavior (Spencer-Oatey & Kádár, 2021). Culture is commonly manifested through **traditions**, where we focus on *social customs, religious practices, celebrations, and habits passed from generation to generation within a shared community*. For example, in many parts of India, Diwali, "the festival of lights," is celebrated. One tradition of Diwali is for celebrants to light candles and clay lamps (called *diyas*), placing them throughout their homes and in the streets to light up the night. The word Diwali comes from the Sanksrit *dipavali*, meaning "row of lights" (Burnett, 2023).

Learning about a culture and cultural traditions assists advertisers and public relations practitioners in authentically centering meaningful narratives about a specific community featured in a campaign. Using an intersectional strategic communications mindset, we recognize that identity categories overlap, are interconnected, and cannot be communicated with monolithically.

What Is Social Identity?

In recent years, we've increasingly heard the term *social identity*. For our purposes, we use this broad term to refer to *a person's self-concept that is derived from belonging to a group or category with similar beliefs, characteristics, experiences, or physical traits.* Social identity affiliation suggests that an individual has adopted or been born into a set of shared values, beliefs, or behaviors.

Belonging to a specific social identity group can provide individuals with a sense of pride and self-esteem. *Belonging suggests that individuals have a need to form meaningful relationships, social attachments, and experiences by being part of a group or community* (Baumeister & Leary, 1995; Yuval-Davis, 2006). Belonging gives members of a group shared practices around appearance, collective actions, language, and other outward demonstrations of membership within the larger group category.

For example, on college campuses across the United States, members of sororities and fraternities might wear specific colors, have secret handshakes, hold special rituals, and espouse belief in the same set of values. Individuals who partake in these practices often feel a sense of belonging. If we encounter an individual who has publicly or privately expressed their membership in a certain sorority or fraternity, we might also make certain assumptions about their socioeconomic status, their values, and more.

When we are tasked with implementing advertising or public relations campaigns, inclusive strategic communicators must research audiences taking an intersectional and situational approach. While this may sound complex, this approach provides useful insights into identity categories as well as how and when they overlap. These categories might include gender, ethnicity, race, religion, sexual orientation, and socioeconomic class. Recognizing that there are inseparable connections between social identity, let's explore insights about social identity categories.

Identity Insights

Gaining insight into defined social identity categories is a useful starting point to reach specific audiences. In strategic communications, the most often used social identity categories refer to race, ethnicity, ability, gender, sexual orientation, religion, and age. As we use insight-related data for social identity categories, we recognize that these categories do not fully acknowledge the intersections and nuances that affect interest, trust or acceptance of a brand and its messages. Let's look at some generalized insights and examples to consider how we might more effectively reach diverse audiences.

Race and Ethnicity

We often use these words interchangeably, but they have distinct meanings. So, what's the difference? *Race* refers to the *historic, socially constructed categories assigned to a group of individuals based on observable physical characteristics*. When inclusive communicators refer to race as being socially constructed, it refers to the fact that racial categories are not scientific or biological and were the early creations of colonists to assign physical descriptions to groups of people. The idea of categorizing groups of people by race reflects specific beliefs imposed on populations in the wake of the 15th-century Western European conquests (Gannon, 2016). The colonists believed that individuals belonged to a certain "race" purely because of their skin tone or other externally observed physical features. Scientists have since proven that race is not biological even though humans have different skin tones, eye color, facial features, and hair textures (Gannon, 2016; Smedley & Smedley, 2005).

When we use the term *ethnicity*, we are writing or speaking about *a group of individuals who share the same cultural traditions, language, and ancestry*. For example, after living in southwestern China for thousands of years and then migrating to countries like Laos, Thailand, and eventually Western countries like the United States, the Hmong people have carried many of their ethnic traditions with them. These include elaborate embroidered costumes, cooking traditions, and funeral rituals (Yang, 2015).

Racial and ethnic groups have been underrepresented or misrepresented in many aspects of modern communications. Many people believe it is respectful or a way to evade dealing with the historical and societal challenges by saying, "I don't see color." When a person claims this, it indicates that you are choosing to erase power hierarchies and the historically unjust experiences of racial groups due to their "color." The website of the National Museum of African American History & Culture (https://nmaahc.si.edu/learn/talking-about-race/topics/race-and-racial-identity) offers a perspective on talking about race and understanding the history of race and racial identity development. As communicators, it is necessary to learn as much as possible about how to discuss race and matters of culture to help brands find their authentic positionality and voice when it comes to diversity, equity, and inclusion (DEI).

Racial/ethnic categories are still used by many agencies, corporations, governments, and healthcare entities. There are five racial categories that have been used since 1997 and remain listed on the U.S. Census today: American Indian or Alaska Native; Asian; Black or African American; Native Hawaiian or Other Pacific Islander; and White. There is ongoing debate about racial categories and U.S. government officials are proposing changes to the 2030 Census that would affect how certain populations are categorized and counted. In recent years, the U.S. Census added, "Some Other Race" (SOR) for those identifying as multiracial – two or more races.

Given the ongoing conversation about the social construction of race, the U.S. Census Bureau offers a disclaimer on their website: "The census categories used in the census questionnaire generally reflect a social definition of race recognized in the United States and is not an attempt to define race biologically, anthropologically, or genetically" (U.S. Census, 2023). By 2060, the U.S. Census Bureau projects that non-Hispanic White residents will dip below 50% for the first time (to around 44.9%). At the same time, the Hispanic population will increase to around 26.9% (from 19.1% in 2022), the Black population will remain about the same at around 13%, and the Asian population will grow to 8.6%, up from the current 6.2% (U.S. Census, 2023; Schneider, 2023). Alongside the Census Bureau categories, there are acronyms and abbreviations used in society to describe racial identities. Here are a few you may encounter:

- AAPI (Asian American Pacific Islander)
- API (Asian Pacific Islander)
- APA (Asian Pacific American)
- BIPOC (Black, Indigenous, People of Color)
- Latinx (a gender-neutral, nonbinary term used instead of Latina or Latino)
- POC (People of Color)

Despite the availability of these acronyms and abbreviations, there is not universal agreement on when to use an acronym or abbreviation. Whenever possible, strategic communicators should conduct formal focus groups and informal conversations with members of a specific audience to determine which acronym, abbreviation, or identifier the individual or group prefers. For example, while Latinx is a gender-neutral term (and one we use in this text), some members of this identity category still prefer to be referred to by the more traditional, gendered terms Latino or Latina. Inclusive communicators recognize the complex lived experiences within racial identity categories. There is no singular acronym, abbreviation, or terminology to reach all audiences within a racial identity group. Your research for every campaign and message will help you determine the best one to use.

In recent years, brands, celebrities, and social media creators have been criticized for **cultural appropriation**, *where appearance, traditions, behaviors, languages, or cultural practices from diverse communities are used or profited from by those not belonging to those communities without giving proper acknowledgement or credit to the original diverse identity group.*

For example, in 2021 TikTok dancer Addison Rae appeared on *The Tonight Show with Jimmy Fallon* to teach host Jimmy Fallon how to perform viral dances. Both Rae and Fallon were criticized on social media for not crediting the original creators, many of whom were Black. After backlash exploded across social media platforms, Black creators called for a ban on sharing any new dances on TikTok. Fallon eventually invited the original creators to appear on the show and later provided credit using captions on all YouTube video clips from the original show. While many argued that copying the dances was an innocent mistake, Rae financially profited from performing the dances on TikTok (Mitchell, 2021).

Appropriating cultural behaviors or traditions is often the biggest mistake advertisers, influencers, and entertainers make. Some brands that have used social media influencers to represent their products have been accused of **blackfishing**, a term that *describes the phenomenon of non-Black influencers, celebrities, entertainers, or public figures who change their appearance to look like what society considers Black identifying* (Stevens, 2021; Thompson, 2018). This may include injections to enlarge lips, cosmetic surgery to increase the fullness of the buttocks, bronzers to darken the skin, or excessive photo editing to achieve these looks. Whether it is cultural appropriation or said to be imitating a look they admire, it commodifies the Black culture (Washington-Harmon, 2023).

Advice about Using Slang

Strategic communicators are greatly encouraged to stay informed about **slang** or *informal words associated with race, ethnicity, gender, ability, or other cultural traditions.* Many slang words are restricted to use by those who belong to a specific social or cultural identity group. When referring to or engaging with an identity group to which you do not belong, avoid using the slang of that group. Using the slang of an identity group to which you do not belong is insulting and may be perceived as mocking. Advertisers, marketers, and public relations practitioners using slang for a humorous effect are often viewed as disrespectful.

In some social identity groups, there is a trend to *reclaim derogatory words to diminish the power of the word*, known as **reappropriation**. Examples are words like "hapa" or "queer." Using reclaimed words is acceptable when a person from that identity group uses the word to describe themselves and in a context which isn't discriminatory.

Ability

In 1990, the Americans with Disabilities Act (ADA) was passed as the first U.S. civil rights law to encourage equal opportunities for employment and housing. The ADA was designed to help ensure economic self-sufficiency for those with physical or mental impairments. The ADA defines a ***person with a disability*** as *a person who has a physical or mental impairment that limits one or more life activities.* The word disability was developed as a legal term rather than a medical one to provide clear mandates to eliminate discrimination in employment and housing. Disabilities can be visible and non-visible. The types of disabilities covered include developmental, emotional, physical, and sensory (ADA.gov, 2023).

The World Health Organization (2023) reports that an estimated 1.3 billion people experience significant disability. This represents 16% of the world's population. Approximately 42.5 million Americans identify as having one or more conditions that would categorize them as a disabled person. While some brands have been celebrated for their efforts to reach disabled people, disability activists often use the phrase, "Nothing about us without us." This refers to ensuring that when ads, messages, and images are developed, there should be a disabled person contributing to the development of authentic creative concepts. Strategic communicators should test images and messages with individuals who identify as disabled, since not all disabilities are the same. Always recognize the many other social identity intersections such as age, race, gender, LGBTQ+, religion, and more.

When brands create content where disabled persons are depicted as wanting to be "normal" or are celebrated for doing basic tasks, it can be viewed as ableism. ***Ableism*** is *a type of social prejudice that devalues or ignores disabled people through normalizing ability.* When someone is described as ableist, it often refers to the inappropriate use of humor or actions that underrate a person's disability. Common examples of ableist language are words or phrases like "lame," "dumb, "blind as a bat," "idiot," "nuts," "psycho," or "spaz." In 2020, entertainers Lizzo and Beyoncé received backlash for using the offensive term "spaz" in song lyrics when referring to a person who was out of control (Zimmer, 2022). The word is a derivative of a medical condition, spastic, and implies that the way a person with the condition functions is abnormal. Misusing words associated with a disabled person's challenges is insulting and hurtful. Many words and phrases are used so casually that we often don't realize they are part of ableist language. As inclusive strategic communicators, it's important to be aware of how our private and public use of certain words or phrases can perpetuate ableism.

In the United States, July is Disability Pride Month to commemorate the passage of the previously mentioned ADA. Many in the disabled community suggest that brands should prioritize accessibility over advertising during this month. For example, Sony created a customizable game controller for its PlayStation that allows gamers with disabilities to play more comfortably. The controller affords disabled players the options to change the shape and size of the buttons and even change the overall position of each stick for improved comfort and ease. In 2023, the make-up brand Lancôme released HAPTA, a motorized device that stabilizes hand and arm movements when applying lipstick or mascara (Bitmead, 2023). These brands demonstrate understanding of living life with a disability while prioritizing accessibility.

Age

Another way to consider audiences for advertising or public relations campaigns is to segment by age. To do this, we might use generational categories. Simply put, a **generation** is *a group of people born and living within a 15 to 20-year period*. Generational theory began in the 1920s and 1930s when sociologists suggested that categorizing groups by generations would help us understand how historical and age-related experiences influence behaviors and opinions. Depending on the resource, the beginning and end years of the generational categories can be fluid. The following are typical categories:

- The Greatest Generation – born 1901–1924
- The Silent Generation – born 1925–1945
- Baby Boomers – born 1946–1964
- Generation X – born 1965–1980
- Millennials or Generation Y – born 1981–1996
- Generation Z – born 1997–2012
- Generation Alpha – born 2013–2025

Historic events and life experiences of each generational group increases the likelihood of similar views on family, politics, societal issues, and technology (Howe & Strauss, 1991). However, when we assume all behaviors, beliefs, or preferences are the same solely based on the age of a person, it can create **ageism**, which refers to *discrimination, stereotypes, and prejudices that occur due to assumptions made about a person based on their age or generational category.*

Ageism is usually directed toward adults over 50 years old related to their technological literacy, physical ability, or social awareness. For example, the phrase, "Okay, Boomer" is a dismissive response used when a Baby Boomer's comments are perceived to be out of touch with modern culture. Studies have shown that older adults can feel 13 years younger than their chronological age. Most older adults view themselves younger and feel subjectively younger than they are (Kleinspehn-Ammerlahn et al., 2008). So, instead of ignoring older adults, it would make sense to do your research and create campaigns that reflect how older adults want to be seen. Occasionally, reverse ageism affects younger adults. Reverse ageism occurs when we use tropes like "Millennials want a trophy for everything they do," or "Gen Z is lazy." Ageism in any form means that there is a missed opportunity to reach a viable audience.

Generational theory suggests that generations go through cycles typically marked by a historic crisis. It is believed that the crisis and societal response shapes views and values of the next generation (Howe & Strauss, 1991). Think about how the topic of social justice was greatly debated in the United States after the murder of George Floyd in 2020. The resulting political and social discourse involved disagreements across multiple generations and identity categories. People began to use the word *woke* to describe *awareness of systemic injustices and prejudices, especially involving the treatment of historically oppressed individuals.* Brands began to include diversity statements on their websites and even turned their social media avatars and logos Black to show support. *When brands try to capitalize on social justice and identity themes in their advertising and social media campaigns without ongoing, identifiable support or immediate action*, it is known as **woke-washing**. The word "woke" was later weaponized by politicians to label and refer to anyone with liberal beliefs or who spoke out and supported racial equity and inclusion (Robinson, 2022).

Gender "Norms"

Earlier in this chapter, we discussed race as a social construct. Gender is also considered a social construct in that societal "norms" and expectations influence how we think about gender. For example: Boys are strong; girls are weak. Pink is for girls; blue is for boys.

Gender categorizations are typically established within the socially constructed binaries of male or female, man or woman. For many people, however, gender is more fluid. In a glossary of terms created by NPR and GLAAD, **gender identity** is defined as *one's own internal sense of self and their gender, whether that is man, woman, neither or both* (Wamsley, 2021). People who do not define their gender within the man/woman binary may refer to themselves as nonbinary or gender queer, among other terms. Likewise, transgender describes people "whose gender identity differs from the sex assigned at birth" (Wamsley, 2021).

Western culture has historically influenced the world with binary thinking about gender. However, the Bugis people in South Sulawesi, Indonesia recognize five genders. Since the pre-Islamic era, they have embraced gender flexibility and divided the society into *man (oroane)*, *woman (makkunrai)*, *male woman (calabai)*, *female man (calalai)*, and *androgynous priest (bissu)* (Hidayana, 2018). Notions of gender are evolving. For example, in the United States, 50% of millennials consider gender as a spectrum rather than a binary (Wong, 2016). In addition, brands like Nike, Old Navy, and Asos are creating non-gender specific lines of clothing and embracing statistics suggesting that 61% of Gen Z think brands could be doing more to prove that "style should not have a gender" (Kelly, 2022).

Every culture has established beliefs about gender roles and behaviors. These beliefs can turn into stereotypes, especially when humor is intended. On International Women's Day in 2021, Burger King UK wanted to highlight the lack of women chefs in the restaurant industry. From their corporate Twitter account, they tweeted, "Women belong in the kitchen." The humor fell flat, and they were flooded with complaints across social media. The company followed up with a tweet indicating that only 20% of chefs in the culinary industry were women and that they were "on a mission" to change the gender ratio by encouraging women to pursue a culinary career (Molina, 2021). A day later they apologized and deleted the tweet. Gender-related humor in advertising can easily become sexist. Sexism occurs when we create stereotyped images and messages about the way culture perceives women and their expected roles in society.

Using an intersectional strategic communications mindset, communicators can avoid stereotyping by being thoughtful about gender roles, using humor, and avoid making broad assumptions.

LGBTQ+

The abbreviation **LGBTQ+** refers to *people who identify as one or more of these categories: lesbian, gay, bisexual, transgender, queer, and the plus sign is also used to signify inclusion of other identities (i.e., intersex, asexual) and orientations that words cannot yet describe.* The abbreviation was originally used to show unity. At the same time, each identity category represented has unique concerns across a range of issues from threats to safety to freedom of expression to discriminatory state laws. In 2023, the Human Rights Campaign issued a national warning for LGBTQ+ Americans traveling across the United States due to an increase in violence and discrimination against individuals who identify as LGBTQ+ (Human Rights Campaign, 2023).

In the United States, Pride Month is celebrated in June of each year to honor the historic Stonewall uprising of the 1960s. The rainbow symbol and colors are used to signify pride in the spectrum of identities represented across the community. Brands often conduct advertising and public relations campaigns during June to cash in on the lucrative LGBTQ+ audience, which represented $1.4 trillion in spending power in the United States in 2022 (LGBT Capital, 2022). This problematic approach is known as *rainbow-washing, when brands use rainbow-themed symbolism in advertising, merchandise, or on social media, to support LGBTQ+ people during Pride Month, but do not offer active, long-term support of their rights or identities beyond Pride Month.*

It's not enough to use the rainbow flag during Pride Month, as people in this identity category want to do business with brands that demonstrate a long-term commitment to LGBTQ+ consumers and the employees inside their companies too. An example of a brand that seeks to consistently demonstrate internal and external support for the LGBTQ+ community is Levi Strauss & Company, a global leader in denim jeans. In 1992, the company was the first to offer domestic partner benefits to employees. In 2019, the brand began to promote gender-neutral clothing and created a guide to embrace unisex style (Levi Strauss & Company, 2019).

Like other identity categories, the LGBTQ+ community has intersections of racial, educational, financial, age, and religious backgrounds that influence their motivation to engage with a product, service, or issue. They are parents and grandparents, live in rural areas and cities, and are of every race, ethnicity, religion, political affiliation, and socioeconomic status. Brands can earn trust by understanding the many intersections of this identity group.

Religion

Religion and faith traditions bring individuals together around their shared values and beliefs. Identifying with a specific religion or faith tradition provides another way to understand how groups and individuals engage with a product, service, or idea. Using an intersectional strategic communications mindset helps us avoid generalizing and prevents avoidable mistakes. For example, in 2017, organizers of the North Carolina Pride organization scheduled a parade on Yom Kippur (Jewish Telegraphic Agency, 2017). This meant that a Jewish person identifying as LGBTQ+ wouldn't be able to attend since the faith tradition requires fasting and prayer until sundown. Organizers eventually cancelled the parade.

To respect religious inclusivity, review a calendar or religious organization's website or contact a local religious organization for a list of their holidays. If you decide to show inclusivity by using celebratory language, be aware of what's appropriate to say for each religious holiday. For example, it is not appropriate to wish a Jewish person, "Happy Yom Kippur!" since the holiday is one of atonement and reflection. A more informed acknowledgement might be "Have a good Holy Day" or "Have a good fast."

From Muslims to Christian Evangelicals to Judaism, individuals who belong to organized religions and faith practices want strategic communicators to acknowledge and respect their interconnected social identities (i.e., age, gender, race, religion, etc.). Strategic communicators who are adept at using their research to recognize how a person's age, gender, race, and other interconnected identities exist within a religious or faith community practice gain greater trust and support for their product, service, or idea.

Language Considerations

The number of languages and frequency with which they are spoken regularly fluctuates with worldwide population numbers. There are more than 7,000 languages spoken around the world. English, Mandarin, Hindi, and Spanish are the top four languages most spoken (Linguistic Society.org, 2023). In the United States, we often use words and phrases derived from other languages. For example, the word apartment comes from the Italian word *appartamento* and shampoo from the Hindi word *champo*, meaning "to massage." The English language has a complicated history. The origin and meaning of words, symbols, and phrases can be traced back to many other cultures.

Language is a central component of culture and the fundamental way strategic communicators connect with our audiences. But language isn't just about speaking Italian or Mandarin or Farsi. It's about understanding how different cultures use language, symbols, and images to create meaning, as we describe below.

Translation and Localization

Global advertising and public relations communications are vital to brands. To create a comprehensive campaign aiming to be successful in international markets, translation and localization techniques should be used to ensure a brand's messages are clear and images are respectful. Let's look at the differences.

Translation primarily focuses on *interpreting and communicating spoken or written words into a different language.* Once translated, dialects and the meaning of words can change dramatically. For example, when Mercedes-Benz entered the Chinese market using the brand name Bensi, they quickly found that in one Chinese dialect, the word translated as *rush to die.* Another famous campaign was the American Dairy Association's "Got Milk?" campaign. When the campaign was extended to Mexico, a literal Spanish translation for "Got Milk?" is "Are you lactating?" Clearly, not a polite question to ask.

Translation is not the only consideration for an international audience. The meaning of logos, colors, and images differs by country and region. **Localization** helps us *effectively adapt messages, images, and behaviors to meet both the linguistic and cultural needs of the audience.* An example of localization involves Starbucks. The U.S.-based multinational coffee company is famously known for its green mermaid logo. In Saudi Arabia, the logo was deemed too racy because it portrayed what was considered full frontal nudity according to Muslim beliefs and cultural traditions. Out of respect, Starbucks adjusted its logo to feature only the crown portion of the mermaid in advertising and on signage in Saudi Arabia (Walker, 2011).

For international projects, include agencies and resources in the country for help with translation and local cultural traditions. Build relationships with major media outlets, influencers, and other local representatives in the countries where you are doing business. A commitment to linguistic matters and cultural traditions will save a brand from embarrassment. With proper research, critical thinking, and sensitivity, global campaigns can be highly successful.

Normalization

When creating advertising or public relations content, your dominant ideologies influence what you consider humorous, beautiful, or respectful. *Normalization occurs when we try to conform people or places to what we believe is an acceptable societal standard.* These ideologies are formed over time because of your own personal identity, cultural traditions, religious practices, geographic location, life experiences, and more. In the United States, standards of what is normal are typically based in White, Eurocentric behaviors, beliefs, standards of beauty, and customs. As strategic communicators, it's important to consistently use tools to check our biases throughout the research, creative, and communication process (see Box 2.1).

Conducting in-depth research, applying insights about social identities, and creating messages that demonstrate care and awareness of intersectional identities increases the likelihood of building trust and respectfully reaching diverse audience members.

Strategic communicators who adopt an intersectional strategic communications mindset typically do the following:

1. Challenge your own assumptions about identity categories, geographic regions, and what you perceive to be their history, values, or traditions. Decenter Westernized thinking and be aware that images, words, and humor translate differently across cultures.
2. For international projects, use local agencies and resources for translation and to research cultural traditions. Build relationships with major media outlets, influencers, and other local representatives in the countries where you are doing business.
3. Make sure individuals working on advertising and public relations campaigns are representative of various social identities for a voice-centered perspective or use focus groups for feedback on appropriateness and respectful use of language, humor, and images in campaigns.

Box 2.1 The IDEA Wheel

One tool that may help in considering intersectional identity and culture is the Luttrell and Wallace IDEA Wheel developed by the research team of Regina Luttrell and Adrienne A. Wallace (2021). The IDEA Wheel is a tool designed to help strategic communicators formulate campaigns that consider diversity at every step of campaign development, from research to implementation to evaluation. The wheel includes social and behavioral identity categories that assist in integrating cross-cultural and multicultural approaches through a series of discovery questions (Figure 2.1).

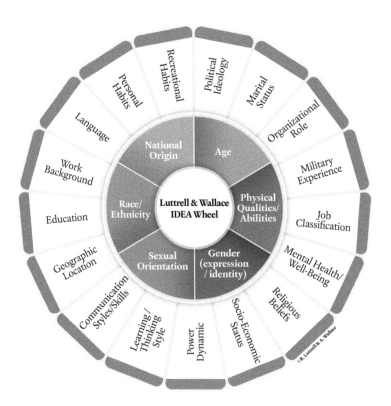

Figure 2.1 The Luttrell and Wallace IDEA Wheel. Copyright Luttrell and Wallace.

4. Keep in mind that no single person or group speaks for nor defines an entire identity group's experiences, opinions, behaviors, values, or preferred nomenclature. Conduct in-depth, campaign-specific research at every stage of your creative process.
5. Recognize that there is rarely one universally agreed-upon identity description or abbreviation. Always ask how a person or group prefers to be identified. Terminology may change. If you get it wrong, acknowledge it, take responsibility, and apologize publicly and privately. Correct your mistake even if it means recalling or redoing an entire campaign.

Bibliography

ADA.gov, U.S. Department of Justice and Civil Rights Division. (2023). www.ada. gov/

Bankrate. (2023). *The rising purchasing power of women: facts and statistics*. www. bankrate.com/loans/personal-loans/purchasing-power-of-women-statistics/ #purchasing

Barnett, D. (n.d.). *What is blackfishing?* Influencer Intelligence. www.influencer intelligence.com/blog/Trn/what-is-blackfishing

Baumeister, R. F., & Leary, M. R. (1995). The need to belong: Desire for interpersonal attachments as a fundamental human motivation. *Psychological Bulletin*, *117*(3), 497–529.

Bitmead, C. (2023, January 6). Lancôme debuts new motorised makeup application device to help those with limited mobility. *Cosmopolitan Magazine*. www. cosmopolitan.com/uk/beauty-hair/makeup/a42415614/lancome-hapta-motorised-makeup-application-device/

Burnett, C. (2023, November 16). *Diwali 2023: What is Diwali?* Almanac. www. almanac.com/content/diwali

Crenshaw, K. (1989). Demarginalizing the intersection of race and sex: A Black feminist critique of antidiscrimination doctrine, feminist theory and antiracist politics. *University of Chicago Legal Forum*, Vol. 1989, Article 8. https://chicagounbound. uchicago.edu/uclf/vol1989/iss1/8

Crenshaw, K. W. (2013). Mapping the margins: Intersectionality, identity politics, and violence against women of color. In M. A. Fineman & R. Mykitiuk (Eds.), *The public nature of private violence* (pp. 93–118). Routledge.

Crisp, R. J., & Hewstone, M. (2007). Multiple, social categorization. *Advances in Experimental Social Psychology*, *39*, 163–254.

Demangeot, C., Adkins, N. R., Mueller, R. D., Henderson, G. R., Ferguson, N. S., Mandiberg, J. M., Roy, A., Johnson, G. D., Kipnis, E., Pullig, C., Broderick, A. J., & Zúñiga, M. A. (2013). Toward intercultural competency in multicultural marketplaces. *Journal of Public Policy & Marketing*, *32*(1_suppl), 156–164.

Gannon, M. (2016). Race is a social construct, scientists argue. *Scientific American*, *5*, 1–11.

Hidayana, I. M. (2018, September 18). On gender diversity in Indonesia. *The Conversation*. https://theconversation.com/on-gender-diversity-in-indonesia-101087

Howe, N., & Strauss, W. (1991). *Generations: The history of America's future, 1584 to 2069*. William Morrow & Company.

Human Rights Campaign (HRC). (2023, June 6). *For first time ever, Human Rights Campaign officially declares 'State of Emergency' for LGBTQ+ Americans*. www.hrc.org/press-releases/for-the-first-time-ever-human-rights-campaign-officially-declares-state-of-emergency-for-lgbtq-americans-issues-national-warning-and-guidebook-to-ensure-safety-for-lgbtq-residents-and-travelers

Jewish Telegraphic Agency. (2017). *North Carolina Pride organizers alter event schedule to avoid Yom Kippur conflict*. www.jta.org/2017/08/08/united-states/north-carolina-pride-organizers-alter-event-schedule-to-avoid-yom-kippur-conflict

Kelly, C. (2022, March 4). *Nike, Asos, Old Navy are most inclusive brands for Gen Z, study says*. RetailDive. www.retaildive.com/news/nike-asos-old-navy-are-most-inclusive-brands-for-gen-z-study-says/619805/

Kleinspehn-Ammerlahn, A., Kotter-Grühn, D., & Smith, J. (2008). Self-perceptions of aging: Do subjective age and satisfaction with aging change during old age? *The Journals of Gerontology: Series B, 63*(6), 377–385.

Leppert, R., & Schaeffer, E. (2023). *Facts about Americans with disabilities*. Pew ResearchCenter.www.pewresearch.org/short-reads/2023/07/24/8-facts-about-americans-with-disabilities/

Levi Strauss & Company. (2019). The Levi's® guide to unisex style. *Off the Cuff blog*. www.levi.com/US/en_US/blog/article/the-levis-guide-to-unisex-style

LGBT Capital. (2022). *LGBT market statistics*. www.lgbt-capital.com/index.php?menu_id=2

Linguistic Society of America. (2023). *How many languages are there in the world?* www.linguisticsociety.org/content/how-many-languages-are-there-world

Luttrell, R. M., & Wallace, A. (2021). Shifting the paradigm – improving student awareness of diversity, equity, and inclusion efforts through public relations campaigns. *Journal of Public Relations Education, 7*(1), 200–209. https://journalofpreducation.com/wp-content/uploads/2022/12/8725f-jpre-71-6.21.pdf#page=200

Market Research Future. (2023). *Most languages spoken over the world in 2023*. www.marketresearchfuture.com/news/most-spoken-languages-over-the-world-in-2023

Mitchell, T. (2021, August 21). 'They take our dances': Black users demand TikTok combat cultural appropriation. *Business Insider*. www.insider.com/black-creators-call-out-tiktok-for-financial-loss-from-appropriation-2021-8

Molina, B. (2021, March 9). Burger King UK under fire for tweeting 'Women belong in the kitchen' on International Women's Day. *USA Today*. www.usatoday.com/story/money/2021/03/08/burger-king-uk-under-fire-women-belong-kitchen-tweet/4627505001/

National Museum of African American History and Culture. (2023). *Talking about race: Race and racial identity*. https://nmaahc.si.edu/learn/talking-about-race/topics/race-and-racial-identity

Pompper, D. (2007). The gender-ethnicity construct in public relations organizations: Using feminist standpoint theory to discover Latinas' realities. *The Howard Journal of Communications, 18*(4), 291–311.

Robinson, I. (2022, August 26). *How "woke" went from Black to bad*. Legal Defense Fund. www.naacpldf.org/woke-black-bad/

Schneider, M. (2023, November 9). The Census Bureau sees an older, more diverse America in 2100 in three immigration scenarios. *AP*. https://apnews.com/article/growth-population-demographics-race-hispanic-f563ebc4537f83792f3f91ba5d7cdade

Smedley, A., & Smedley, B. D. (2005). Race as biology is fiction, racism as a social problem is real: Anthropological and historical perspectives on the social construction of race. *American Psychologist*, 60(1), 16–26.

Spencer-Oatey, H., & Kádár, D. Z. (2021). *Intercultural politeness: Managing relations across cultures*. Cambridge University Press.

Stevens, W. E. (2021). Blackfishing on Instagram: Influencing and the commodification of Black urban aesthetics. *Social Media+ Society*, 7(3). https://doi.org/10.1177/2056305121103

Strauss, W., & Howe, N. (2000). *Millennials rising: The next great generation*. Vintage Books.

Thompson, W. (2018, November 14). *How White women on Instagram are profiting off Black women*. Paper. www.papermag.com/white-women-blackfishing-instagram-2619714094.html

Tindall, N. T., & Vardeman-Winter, J. (2011). Complications in segmenting campaign publics: Women of color explain their problems, involvement, and constraints in reading heart disease communication. *Howard Journal of Communications*, 22(3), 280–301.

Turner, J. C. (2010). Social categorization and the self-concept: A social cognitive theory of group behavior. In T. Postmes & N. R. Branscombe (Eds.), *Rediscovering social identity* (pp. 243–272). Psychology Press.

U.S. Census Bureau. (2023, November 9). U.S. Population projected to begin declining in second half of century [Press release]. www.census.gov/newsroom/press-releases/2023/population-projections.html

Van Knippenberg, A., & Dijksterhuis, A. (2000). Social categorization and stereotyping: A functional perspective. *European Review of Social Psychology*, 11(1), 105–144.

Vardeman, J., Tindall, N. T., Saad, N., & Smith, L. (2022). Revisiting intersectionality. In D. Pompper, K. R. Place & C. K. Weaver (Eds.), *The Routledge companion to public relations*. Routledge.

Vardeman-Winter, J., Tindall, N., & Jiang, H. (2013). Intersectionality and publics: How exploring publics' multiple identities questions basic public relations concepts. *Public Relations Inquiry*, 2(3), 279–304.

Walker, A. (2011, January 10). *New Starbucks logo too racy for some countries*. Good. www.good.is/articles/new-starbucks-logo-too-racy-for-some-countries

Wamsley, L. (2021, June 2). A guide to gender identity terms. *NPR*. www.npr.org/2021/06/02/996319297/gender-identity-pronouns-expression-guide-lgbtq

Washington-Harmon, T. (2023, June 1). *Blackfishing: What it is and why some people do it*. Health. www.health.com/mind-body/what-is-blackfishing

Wong, C. M. (2016, February 2). 50 percent of millennials believe gender is a spectrum, Fusion's Massive Millennial poll finds. *HuffPost*. www.huffpost.com/entry/fusion-millennial-poll-gender_n_6624200

World Health Organization. (2023, March 7). *Disability and health fact sheet*. www. who.int/news-room/fact-sheets/detail/disability-and-health

Yang, M. (2015, March 1). 10 things about Hmong culture, food, and language you probably didn't know. *MPR News*. www.mprnews.org/story/2015/03/01/10-things-hmong

Yuval-Davis, N. (2006). Belonging and the politics of belonging. *Patterns of Prejudice, 40*(3), 197–214.

Zimmer, B. (2022, August 3). The surprising history of the slur Beyoncé and Lizzo both cut from their new albums. *Slate*. https://slate.com/culture/2022/08/beyonce-renaissance-lizzo-spaz-ableist-slur-lyrics-history.html

3 Centering DEI in Strategic Writing

Vanessa Bravo

Writing is central to the human experience. In fact, humans have been writing for more than 5,400 years now (Getty Center, 2021). Writing is one of the main ways in which people all around the world share information, communicate ideas, persuade others, and educate different communities about issues of importance to them, either online or offline. ***Writing in the disciplines*** means *writing purposefully within the framework of specific professions/disciplines to practice formats and genres that are typical or popular in those areas* (WAC Clearinghouse, 2023). This means that the format and content that are appropriate for a news release, for example, are very different from those used for a strategic campaign's proposal, a TV show script, a biology lab report, the minutes of a stockholders' business meeting, or a company's annual report. Thus, strategic communication students need to understand and master the process of writing in the different formats and genres that are typical in our discipline and in our industries.

This chapter focuses on writing in the discipline of strategic communications, which includes professions such as public relations, advertising, and integrated marketing communications, among others. ***Strategic communications*** *explores the capacity of all organizations including corporations, not-for-profit organizations (including advocacy and activist groups), and government for engaging in purposeful communication* (Oxford Bibliographies, 2018, para. 1). The main purpose of strategic communications is to build and maintain mutually beneficial relationships with the stakeholders (or publics) that the organization interacts with and depends on (PRSA, 2023).

These stakeholders (or publics) are complex in many ways and embody multiple social identities that impact how they consume information, what their information needs are, and the best strategies to reach them in a manner that is sensitive, respectful, nuanced, culturally appropriate, and impactful. This is why centering diversity, equity, and inclusion (DEI) in strategic communications is essential to be an effective strategic communications professional. This chapter focuses on how to write strategically with DEI as a core part of the writing process. In this chapter, you will find the following:

DOI: 10.4324/9781003411796-4

- How to write strategically while centering the values of DEI
- Practical advice and examples of DEI in strategic writing
- A list of resources (websites and readings) where you can learn more about identity groups
- A short reflection on the potential – and the downsides – of using generative AI (artificial intelligence) for writing materials in the field of strategic communications

DEI at the Center of Strategic Writing

Corporations, nonprofit organizations, and other entities are seeking to reach diverse audiences and employees. From creating culturally relevant advertising campaigns to promoting a new health initiative, centering DEI in writing has become an imperative for strategic communicators.

Whether you are writing a PR plan, a news release, or advertising copy, writing well is essential, and it includes not only being accurate with your facts and careful with the mechanical aspects of your copy (grammar, punctuation, spelling, etc.), but also treating your audiences with respect and awareness of their lived experiences. In other words, good writing begins with good research, not only about the topic you are writing about, but also about the characteristics of your audiences and their information needs. Below we outline four steps for centering DEI in your writing.

Step 1: Learn about History and Social Identities

The first step to practice inclusive writing is to conduct research about your audiences, considering the purpose of the communication and the type of communication method that will be used to reach them.

As mentioned in other chapters of this book, your strategic writing research should consider the variety of social identities people have. Some of the social identity categories include age, socioeconomic status, education level, gender and gender expression, sexual orientation, ability, religious affiliation (if any), immigration statuses, race, ethnicity, political views, family structure, and geographical location, among others (Bush & Bravo, 2022). For insights into social identity categories, look at Chapter 2 in this book.

When writing for an audience, you need to understand the different social identities at play and the history of those communities. In many cases, the characteristics, issues, and struggles of a given community can be explained by contemporary contextual factors but also by historic realities that have impacted and shaped those communities today. What are, then, some aspects to which you should pay attention?

You need to understand how the history of a country, of a region, of a state, of a city and even of a neighborhood have impacted and shaped a given community. You also need to grasp the power dynamics at play in those locations; for instance, who has political power, who possesses wealth, and who makes key decisions that impact the community. To write, create, and deliver effective and responsible communication messages, you will also need to understand the social issues that matter to the community, the economic issues that affect the social group, the environmental issues that affect the way certain groups of people live, the perceptions that exist (accurate or inaccurate) about a community, and who are some leaders in those communities who can provide insight about these social groups.

For example, if you are writing for or about the Latinx immigrant community in the United States, you need to understand how the presence of the United States in Latin America has been often positive (through economic aid and cultural exchanges and programs), but also highly detrimental (through the support of coup d'etats, the extractive control of local economies, the tacit or direct backing of right-wing authoritarian regimes such as the Pinochet regime in Chile, and the ousting of democratically elected presidents such as Jacobo Arbenz in Guatemala) (Coastworth, 2005). This U.S. presence in Latin America has contributed to generating large immigration movements from Latin America to the United States (Gonzalez, 2022).

However, according to the U.S. Census Bureau (2020a, 2020b), 70% of the Latinx community is comprised of U.S.-born Latinos and Latinas. Another 10% is comprised of immigrants with legal documents of different sorts (residency, student visas, etc.), and about 20 percent is comprised of undocumented migrants (U.S. Census Bureau, 2020a, 2020b). The Latinx community is very complex and fragmented. For example, Cubans in Miami are very different from Mexicans in Arizona, but even older Cubans in Miami are very different from their children and grandchildren in many different ways (De Moya & Bravo, 2021). For that reason, the "Latino vote" does not exist because different members of the Latinx community vote depending on all of their intersecting social identity factors, including age, location in the United States, socioeconomic status, level of education, religious affiliation, gender identity, and more (Cadava, 2022).

If you are writing for or about the Black community in the United States, then you need to understand the history of racism in this country, including the process of forced migration through chattel slavery, segregation processes through Jim Crow laws, discrimination processes in housing through government-sanctioned redlining and racially restrictive covenants, etc. (Alexander, 2012; DuVernay, 2016; Jones, 2019). Before you start writing, do the research needed to make sure you are writing with knowledge of lived experiences, historic realities, and the ethics of care.

Using an intersectional strategic communications approach takes time, but it is essential to learn in depth so that you can write for and about these communities with enough knowledge to showcase thoroughness, depth, nuance, respect, and inclusiveness in your writing. There are many reputable online databases and resources to help you learn more. Two good starting points are the Pew Research Center's website and Chapters 1 and 2 in this book.

Additionally, even if you learn a lot about these topics and communities, it is essential to continually update your knowledge – for the rest of your life – through books, films, websites, podcasts, and other resources. You should also stay up to date with the news and read audience-specific media and social media outlets.

The bottom line is that inclusive language that considers identity and equity generates better content. As Farwell et al. (2022) explain, instead of thinking of your audiences as monolithic (i.e., "women") or considering only a few aspects about them ("women aged 18 to 35"), think of all the characteristics that impact the groups or communities you are trying to reach. Thus, ask yourself: Do our communications campaigns include content that resonates and is useful for women of color, women who are part of the LGBTQ+ community, women who have neurodiversity, women with different levels of education, women with other characteristics not mentioned before, and women for whom many of these categories intersect?

Step 2: Consider How Circumstances Affect Audiences Differently

When writing strategically, it is important to think about how societal issues and circumstances can affect different communities and social identity groups in very particular ways.

For example, in 2020 when COVID-19 hit the United States and businesses were closed for prolonged periods, issues of race, gender, geography, employment, and socioeconomic status affected how people were impacted by the pandemic. The shortage of items on supermarket shelves, the sudden transition to online education, and the exposure of essential workers to the virus were salient situations. Now, think how these situations could affect, differently, the following groups:

In the case of the shortage of items in supermarkets:

People with cars (who could drive around town easily to find products they needed) and savings (to buy what was required or to even buy items in bulk, to "weather the storm") versus people with no transportation and/ or people who lived paycheck to paycheck, who had little to no way to react to the shopping wave that ensued; or

People who were trying to buy items for their families versus people who were trying to stock up the food inventory of shelters, churches, daycares, community clinics, hospices, etc.; or

People who faced shortages of medicines that were essential for their survival (such as insulin in the case of patients with diabetes) versus people with relatively good health who maybe had difficulty finding certain commonly used medicines to treat colds or the flu.

In the case of the sudden transition to online education:

People with children (including teenagers) living in small apartments or small houses versus those living in large houses where each person could have their space to study and to work remotely; or

People with children (including teenagers) with a good internet connection at home and several electronic devices available versus those with a bad internet connection (or no internet at all) in their places of residence and maybe only one electronic device (a computer, for instance) for all the members of the family, or no device at all on which to try to work or study remotely.

In the case of access to vaccines and willingness to get vaccinated:

People from communities where access to healthcare services and healthcare insurance is more prevalent versus people with limited or no access to healthcare. This might include communities prone to distrust the medical establishment because of historical traumas from racist and unethical medical practices, such as the Tuskegee Experiments (Bajaj & Stanford, 2021; Gamble, 1997).

People with U.S. citizenship, resident status (Green Cards) or work visas versus people who are in the United States undocumented, trying to raise their families and provide opportunities for their children but without access to formal services and fearful of getting deported.

For each of these circumstances, the strategic writer needs to have awareness of the different situations people face in their daily lives, the factors that can potentially make each social group react to situations differently, the historical processes that can explain current realities, the situations going on internationally that can impact what happens at home, and best practices to communicate messages in ways that are appropriate and culturally sensitive for each audience. And all this needs to happen even before writing the first word.

In this example, once you have researched the audience, then you may start thinking of how to answer the following questions using an intersectional strategic communications mindset:

- How would you craft your messages about the transition to online education or the shortage of supplies in supermarkets or the availability of vaccines for each of these audiences or communities?
- What could be some key messages that would work for each case?
- What facts are you going to use to support your arguments?
- What additional research do you need to undertake?
- How are you going to make sure that these are the right key messages?
- Can you try, for example, to run your piece by some members of these communities (your "target audiences") to make sure that information is presented appropriately and is free of stereotypes or biases?
- If your writing piece will offer recommendations ("how-to" lists or step-by-step advice), have you considered how those lists or steps would look different for each audience?

The task of centering DEI in strategic writing requires learning purposefully about different communities and identity groups, and it necessitates understanding their circumstances and identity "intersections" (Cho et al., 2013; Crenshaw, 2017). Inclusive writing is about accuracy, raising your awareness levels, empathizing with the communities you write about, and caring about their lived experiences. Once you write, it is about testing/fact-checking your writing with knowledgeable sources, refining what you wrote, and then copy-editing and fact-checking again. Once you have done your due diligence you are ready to share your final piece with the audiences you are trying to inform, persuade, or educate.

The route to center DEI in strategic writing is not that different from what is taught to any good strategic communications writer: Know your audience and their identity intersections. Develop content that amplifies true narratives and lived experiences; in other words, write with your audience in mind. Now you are ready to move to the next step.

Step 3: Brainstorm Topics and Keep a Resource Library

To center DEI in your writing, it is important that you consider diversity at every level: in the topics and angles you use in your stories, the sources you cite and quote in your narratives (both expert sources and "regular" people), and the visual representations you use in your materials (Bush & Bravo, 2022). The variety of topics and angles will come from doing your research to know the communities you are writing about and the issues that matter to them. You can help yourself in this process by constantly brainstorming (MindTools, 2023) and idea-mapping different topics (MindManager, 2023).

Having diverse sources can be accomplished by identifying and keeping a list of leaders from underrepresented communities. Put those numbers in your list of contacts and update that list periodically. You can also use the snowball technique (Indeed Editorial Team, 2023) to grow your list, so that your initial set of contacts helps you find more people with similar characteristics that might be willing to talk to you. Do not use BIPOC people (Black, Indigenous, and people of color) as sources just for stories that are explicitly about race, or women just for stories that are explicitly about raising children or fashion, or White males just for stories about finances or the economy. Use a variety of sources for any topic and always consider using experts from a variety of social identities.

Have these materials ready to use (in the form of annotated bibliographies, online folders, and organized directories) and store them in a variety of formats. Along with a diverse library of topics, angles, sources, and visuals, make sure to improve your writing by using reliable sources of information to obtain background knowledge. The following are some resources to consider using in your approach to inclusive writing:

- The Pew Research Center website, which does a great job of providing U.S.-based, well-updated information about racial groups, ethnic communities, LGBTQ+ communities, generational categories, religious groups, immigrant populations, and more.
- The website of the Unstereotype Alliance (2024a), which is an industry-led initiative convened by UN Women to "unite advertising industry leaders, decision-makers and creatives to end harmful stereotypes in advertising" (Unstereotype Alliance, 2024b, para 1).
- The Micropedia of Microaggressions (The Micropedia, 2021), which helps students understand the different types of microaggressions that people in marginalized groups face daily, rooted in implicit (and sometimes, explicit) bias and stereotypes, and how these microaggressions impact their wellbeing. Here, you will also find important definitions (starting with what is a microaggression or tone-policing) and advice on how to avoid saying or doing something that constitutes a microaggression, how to respond to different situations where you are the recipient of a microaggression, and how to be accountable. This "Micropedia" includes sections ("volumes") about age, class, disability, ethnicity, gender, Indigenous communities, LGBTQ+ groups, race, and religion.
- The AP (Associated Press) Stylebook (Froke et al., 2020), which includes specific guidelines on how to write about minoritized groups, what terms to use and which ones to avoid (and why), strategies to become more

interculturally competent, and other practical knowledge. The most recent edition of the AP Stylebook, published in June 2022, also includes a new chapter on inclusive storytelling (Meir, 2022).

- The websites of specialized groups such as the National Association for the Advancement of Colored People (NAACP), the National Association of Black Journalists (NABJ), the National Association of Hispanic Journalists (NAHJ), the American Civil Liberties Union (ACLU), the American Association of Retired People (AARP), the Gay and Lesbian Alliance Against Defamation Media Institute (GLAAD), the nonprofit organization UnitedWeDream, the National Association of Latino Elected and Appointed Officials (NALEO), and the civic-engagement organization Voto Latino, among others.

Step 4: Avoid Stereotypes and Use Inclusive Language

Blatantly ignoring certain groups of people in our strategic writing materials is bad enough, but even worse is when we use stereotypes or language that harms or excludes communities. Some of these stereotypes happen in the descriptions, terms, and images we use to refer to some identity categories, which we should avoid. After conducting research on our audiences, developing a diverse resource library and establishing relationships with diverse people and groups in the community, we also need to confirm that we are using inclusive language.

Using inclusive language in external communications "demonstrates a conscious effort to communicate with respect for, and acceptance of, people from different backgrounds" and, in internal communications, it shows employees "that they belong" (Ragan, 2022). Among other strategies, Ragan (2022, para. 3) recommends the following:

- Allow specific social identity groups and individuals to indicate how they want to be identified when creating messages for PR, advertising, or other campaigns.
- Give opportunities to employees at organizations to self-identify if writing on behalf of an organization.
- Follow cultural leaders on social media.
- Co-create content with the social identity groups or individuals to ensure accurate depiction of their stories.
- Ensure that a person who represents the social identity or group approves or reviews your final written content.

In Chapter 2 you learned that there are multiple acronyms, abbreviations, and words used as descriptors for various identity groups (i.e., AAPI, BIPOC, Latinx, etc.). Before choosing an acronym, abbreviation, or word to describe an identity group in your writing, ask the person or group what their identity preferences are. Test your content appropriateness by using focus groups or employee resource groups within an organization. To avoid problematic issues, take a look at the tips contained in Boxes 3.1 and 3.2.

Box 3.1 Inclusive Writing Tips

- Remember that every social identity category may have other identity intersections. For example, there may be a person who identifies as gay, Latinx, Catholic, and a business executive, so avoid assuming anything about diverse individuals' politics, opinions, or expertise.
- Use physical descriptions only when they are relevant or central to the story or narrative. Don't use descriptors to refer to women that you would not use to describe men. If you are writing, for example, about a tennis player, avoid referring to beauty, body parts, or otherwise sexualizing their appearance.
- Use the preferred gender pronouns that a person indicates they identify with. She/her, they/them, he/him, etc.
- Use words such as "spouse," "partner," or "significant other" instead of husband, wife, boyfriend, or girlfriend when describing relationships.
- Use accurate terms such as undocumented immigrants or undocumented workers, but not "illegal aliens." Remember that people may not have legal documentation, but no human is illegal per se.
- Avoid age labels. If you are writing a story where your sources are older women or older men, avoid referring to them as "grandmas" or "grandpas," unless you are actually writing a story specifically about grandmothers or grandparents.
- If you are writing a story about investing in the stock market, are you only interviewing White males? Consider that there are experts from other genders, races, and social identity categories.
- If you are in a foreign country, writing a story to be consumed by readers in your home country, are you including diverse, local sources from that foreign country? For example, if you are a U.S. writer writing a story about a country such as Mexico, are you including diverse, local sources from Mexico and not just U.S. expats or U.S. experts providing their outsider perspective about Mexico?
- Whenever possible, ask people how they prefer to be identified, but also learn about the differences that exist between certain terms. A person might prefer to be identified as Latino, or Latina, or Chicano, or Chicana, or Latinx, or Hispanic, but differences exist

within each of those identifiers. For example, Latinx, Latino, or Latina refers to people who can trace back their ancestry to Latin America (where languages such as Spanish, Portuguese, French, and a large variety of Indigenous languages are spoken). Hispanic refers to people who can trace back their ancestry to places where Spanish is the main language. Both Mexicans and Brazilians are Latinos/Latinas/Latinx, but Brazilians are not Hispanic because their ancestry can be traced to a country where the main language is Portuguese, not Spanish. Also, there are intersections with ethnicity and race. For instance, there are Black Latinx, White Latinx, Asian Latinx, mixed-race Latinx, and more. Race and ethnicity are not interchangeable terms.

- Always check your own biases to avoid stereotyping and patronizing. Ask yourself, "Am I referring to this person in a way that respects their identity?"
- Create or refer to style guides and resources such as the AP Stylebook.

Box 3.2 Creating an Inclusive Style Guide

An *inclusive style guide* is *a document that defines and demonstrates how to consistently and accurately use acronyms, words, phrases, and descriptors related to diverse audiences, employees, consumers, and publics.* Many agencies and corporations create brand style guides for designers and media outlets to ensure a consistent look and feel when using logos, fonts, colors, and images. An inclusive style guide places greater emphasis on language and copywriting tips to use for diverse identities. The content can also be included within the organization's brand style guide. The motive for creating an inclusive style guide is to encourage accuracy, shared language, and ongoing learning within an organization. Creating an inclusive style guide assists copywriters and other communicators in consistency across organizational messages. During the creative process, it can help inspire conversations, generate questions, and inform decisions about whether certain phrases, words, terminologies, or images should be used in internal or external communications that refer to diverse individuals and communities. See Table 3.1 for the five key steps necessary to create an inclusive style guide.

Table 3.1 Creating an Inclusive Style Guide. Copyright Karen Lindsey, Ph.D.

Step 1	Step 2	Step 3	Step 4	Step 5
Define the purpose and reason for creating the guide. Outline and highlight the organizational need for an inclusive style guide.	Research identity categories, biased terminology, and social issues. Use the research to create lists of preferred words and terminology.	Offer clear, concise examples, tips on specific use of unbiased language, and preferred ways to use the guide for copywriting.	Test the accuracy of the content in the guide with community representatives, focus groups, and employee resource groups.	Regularly update the guide as acronyms, words, and terminology frequently change.

Using Generative Artificial Intelligence (AI) in Inclusive Writing

Artificial intelligence tools (such as ChatGPT, Gemini, Capcut, or Stable Diffusion, etc.) that compile and organize content gathered from large databases on the internet can help strategic writers in the writing process. However, there are concerning downsides of using generative AI related to diverse audiences.

For example, a Bloomberg analysis found that Stable Diffusion images underrepresent women and people of color in high-paying jobs and over-represent people of color as criminals – by quite a lot in comparison to actual U.S. statistics:

The world according to Stable Diffusion is run by White male CEOs. Women are rarely doctors, lawyers, or judges. Men with dark skin commit crimes, while women with dark skin flip burgers. Stable Diffusion generates images using artificial intelligence, in response to written prompts. Like many AI models, what it creates may seem plausible on its face but is actually a distortion of reality. An analysis of more than 5,000 images created with Stable Diffusion found that it takes racial and gender disparities to extremes — worse than those found in the real world.

(Nicoletti & Bass, 2023, paras. 1 and 2)

The content compiled by generative AI software is based on algorithms or mathematical formulas that search the internet. Within these formulas and databases there may be biased information. Therefore, output may be biased and inaccurate. Generative AI tools can be a good starting point to do initial research and to develop possible drafts of your strategic messages, but using these AI tools should not be the ending point.

To avoid biased or inaccurate writing: Fact-check. Cite. Copy-edit. Check for stereotypes and biased information. Conduct a thorough content review, get rid of the possible presence of stereotypes and biases in the generated content, and be respectful of intellectual property rights (including copyright and trademark laws). More importantly, use your research to consider the specific characteristics of the communities you want to reach. Adapt and personalize the information you will disseminate, and make sure that the final version of your writing demonstrates respect, sensitivity, and accuracy.

You can use generative AI tools to brainstorm, to gather initial information, to organize content, to structure drafts, to fill in some gaps. However, you still need to check your sources, cite them appropriately, avoid plagiarism, and add the essential "human touch" to everything you write.

Bibliography

Alexander, M. (2012). *The new Jim Crow: Mass incarceration in the age of colorblindness*. The New Press.

Bajaj, S., & Stanford, F. (2021). Beyond Tuskegee—vaccine distrust and everyday racism. *New England Journal of Medicine, 384*(5), e12.

Bush, L., & Bravo, V. (2022). Systematically applying DEI accreditation standards to a strategic communications curriculum. *Journal of Public Relations Education, 8*(4), 128–160.

Cadava, G. L. (2022, March). There's no such thing as 'the Latino vote.' Why can't America see that? *The Atlantic.* www.theatlantic.com/magazine/archive/2022/03/latino-voting-history-america/621302/

ChatGPT 3.5 (2023, September 20). https://chat.openai.com

Cho, S., Crenshaw, K., & McCall, L. (2013). Toward a field of intersectionality studies: Theory, applications, and praxis. *Signs: Journal of Women in Culture and Society, 38*(4), 785–810.

Clarke, C. (2023). *BIPOC abbreviation*. Merriam-Webster Dictionary. www.merriam-webster.com/dictionary/BIPOC

Coastworth, J. (2005, May 15). U.S. interventions. What for? *ReVista: Harvard Review of Latin America.* https://revista.drclas.harvard.edu/united-states-interventions/

Crenshaw, K. (2017). *On intersectionality: Essential writings*. The New Press.

De Moya, M., & Bravo, V. (2021). The new Cuban diaspora. In V. Bravo & M. De Moya (Eds.), *Latin American diasporas in public diplomacy* (pp. 123–158). Palgrave Macmillan.

DuVernay, A. (2016, October 7). *13th* [Documentary]. Available on Netflix or at www.youtube.com/watch?v=krfcq5pF8u8

Farwell, T., Waters, R., & Chen, Z. (2022). Revising SMART+ IE: A classroom activity for increasing diversity, equity, and inclusion in communication campaigns. *Advertising & Society Quarterly, 23*(1). https://muse.jhu.edu/article/853005

Froke, P., Bratton, A., McMillan, J., Sarkar, P., Schwartz, J., & Vadarevu, R. (Eds.). (2020). *The Associated Press Stylebook 2020–2022*. Associated Press.

Gamble, V. (1997). Under the shadow of Tuskegee: African Americans and health care. *American Journal of Public Health, 87*(11), 1773–1778.

Getty Center. (2021, April 27). *Where did writing come from?* www.getty.edu/news/where-did-writing-come-from/

Gonzalez, J. (2022). *Harvest of empire: A history of Latinos in America: Second revised and updated edition.* Penguin.

Goodman, D. (2020). Cultural competence for equity and inclusion. *Understanding and Dismantling Privilege, 10*(1), 41–60. www.wpcjournal.com/article/view/20246

Indeed Editorial Team. (2023, February 4). *What is snowball sampling? Definition, methods and example.* Indeed.com. www.indeed.com/career-advice/career-development/what-is-snowball-sampling-in-research

Jones, H. N. (2019, August 14). The 1619 Project. *The New York Times.* www.nytimes.com/interactive/2019/08/14/magazine/1619-america-slavery.html

Luccioni, A. S., Akiki, C., Mitchell, M., & Jernite, Y. (2023). Stable bias: Analyzing societal representations in diffusion models. *arXiv preprint. arXiv*: 2303.11408.

Maynard Institute. (2023). *Diversity training.* https://mije.org/diversity-training/

Meir, N. (2022, April 4). *Inclusive storytelling chapter added to AP Stylebook.* https://blog.ap.org/products-and-services/inclusive-storytelling-chapter-added-to-ap-stylebook

The Micropedia. (2021). *The Micropedia.* www.themicropedia.org/

MindManager. (2023). *Idea maps: A guide to visualizing your ideas.* www.mindmanager.com/en/features/idea-map/

MindTools. (2023). *Brainstorming.* www.mindtools.com/acv0de1/brainstorming

Nicoletti, L., & Bass, D. (2023). *Humans are biased. Generative AI is even worse.* Bloomberg.com. www.bloomberg.com/graphics/2023-generative-ai-bias/

Oxford Bibliographies. (2018, July 25). *Strategic communication – by Kjerstin Thorson.* https://doi.org/10.1093/obo/9780199756841-0007

Pew Research Center. (2023). *Research topics.* www.pewresearch.org/topics/

PRSA (Public Relations Society of America). (2023). *About public relations.* www.prsa.org/about/all-about-pr

Ragan. (2022). *Inclusive writing strategies that foster belonging.* https://ragantraining.com/inclusive-writing-strategies-that-foster-belonging/

U.S. Census Bureau. (2020a). *Hispanic origin.* www.census.gov/topics/population/hispanic-origin.html

U.S. Census Bureau. (2020b). *Foreign born data.* www.census.gov/topics/population/foreign-born/data.html

Unstereotype Alliance. (2024a). *#Unstereotype Alliance.* www.unstereotypealliance.org/en

Unstereotype Alliance. (2024b). *About the Unstereotype Alliance.* www.unstereotypealliance.org/en/about

WAC Clearinghouse. (2023). *What is writing in the disciplines?* https://wac.colostate.edu/repository/resources/teaching/intro/wid/

4 Visual Storytelling

Reframing Diversity and Inclusion

K. Michele Lashley

In a cave nestled within the landscape of the Indonesian island of Sulawesi (Calloway, 2019), a story unfolds. It's one whose characters include wild pigs, anoa buffalo, and a group of small half-human, half-animal beings. Is it the story of a hunting expedition that took place? Or of a dream? Or of a sacred ceremony? The answer is anyone's guess. But the significance of its existence is clear. This 43,900-year-old tale is considered by many to be the oldest story that's ever been recorded by human beings (Smith, 2019). And it's told solely through images.

As human beings, we're hardwired for stories. They teach us. They move us. They connect us. And, while stories that are read or spoken are commanding in their own right, those told through visuals are uniquely powerful. But why? One of the main reasons is that the human brain processes images 60,000 times faster than written content (Rulf, n.d.). That means visuals can trigger our emotions, tap into our memories, and convey meaning much faster than words alone can do.

Within the context of diversity, equity, and inclusion (DEI), the use of visuals to drive storytelling in strategic communications can be instructive – as well as destructive. When images accurately reflect the reality of social identity groups (i.e., race, gender, LGBTQ+, religion, disability, etc.), they can serve as essential tools in fostering belonging and understanding the variety of identities in our society. But, when inaccurate and/or misleading imagery is used, stereotypes persist and misunderstanding flourishes.

So, how can we – as strategic communicators – change the way imagery is chosen and used by brands[1] for both their internal and external communications? We'll do it step by step, image by image.

In this chapter, we'll focus on the following:

- Defining visual storytelling as a practice in strategic communications
- Exploring the importance of including accurate representations of social identity groups in visual communications

DOI: 10.4324/9781003411796-5

- Understanding the need for inclusiveness in creative and strategic decision-making
- Implementing guidelines to help create, choose, and use inclusive visual imagery
- Avoiding tokenism
- Identifying sources of inclusive imagery
- Making visual stories accessible to everyone

Visuals + Storytelling = Visual Storytelling

Before looking at ways to become more inclusive visual storytellers, we first need to understand what visual storytelling is – as well as what it isn't.

Let's start with what it isn't. It's not simply a picture. The idiom "a picture is worth a thousand words" might be true in some cases. But if those metaphorical thousand words aren't telling a story, then the picture is just a picture. It's not a story.

So, what *is* visual storytelling? In a presentation about the topic given during Content Marketing World 2019, Eric Goodstadt and Sacha Reeb of Manifest – an award-winning content marketing agency – provided an excellent definition: "*Visual storytelling involves the use of graphics, images, pictures and videos to engage with viewers in an effort to drive emotions, engage intercommunication, and motivate an audience to action*" (Content Marketing Institute, 2020).

In other words, visuals are used purposefully, strategically, thoughtfully, and creatively to tell a story that will lead an audience to *feel* something and to *do* something. This doesn't mean that words aren't also used. But it *does* mean that visuals play an integral role in the storytelling process from start to finish.

Now that we understand what visual storytelling is, let's look at ways we can create stories that are more inclusive, more authentic, and more representative.

"You Don't Know Me"

When you watch a show, shop online, or see a post on social media from a brand you follow, do you see people who look like you? Environments that feel familiar? Situations that resonate with your own experience?

If your answer is "rarely" or an outright "NO!" you're not alone. For example, 72% of men and women globally feel that advertising doesn't mirror their world and 63% "don't see themselves represented in most advertising" (Lacey, 2018). That's a *lot* of people who feel left out and unseen by the media. And that translates into a *lot* of missed connections between brands and those they claim to serve.

There's a popular business principle, attributed to author and speaker Bob Burg, that says, "All things being equal, people will do business with and refer business to, those people they know, like and trust" (Burg, n.d.). The phrase "will do business with and refer business to" can easily be switched to "will buy from," "will vote for," "will donate to," "will advocate for," and so on. It's a simple, yet powerful, idea.

With this principle in mind, here's a question: If there's nothing and no one in a brand's imagery that looks familiar, do you feel like you know the brand or – more importantly – that the brand knows *you*? And if you don't know the brand, you probably won't like it. And if you don't like it, you won't trust it. And if you don't trust it, it's highly unlikely you'll ever purchase from it, donate to it, vote for it, advocate for it, or engage with it in any way.

One of the most important – and *easiest* – things any brand can do to create that bond of know–like–trust with its audiences is to be diligent and consistent in ensuring ALL the communities within those audiences are accurately and consistently represented visually in their marketing.

Know That You Don't Know

Travel bans against individuals from select Muslim-majority countries. A push to build a wall along the U.S./Mexico border. The Women's March on Washington. NFL players kneeling during the national anthem in quiet protest of racial inequities and police brutality. These are just a few of the events that defined 2017 (History.com, 2018). And many brands were eager to join the collective culture-focused conversation – particularly around social justice issues. In some cases, though, it can be argued that such eagerness overshadowed the need for careful consideration about messaging and audiences.

For example, in 2017 a new Pepsi® commercial dropped, opening with a close-up of a can of Pepsi being opened. The next shot is one of a musician sitting in a chair on a rooftop, playing a cello as he looks out over the city's skyline. (Apparently, he gets caught in the rain a few frames later. But perhaps I'm misreading that.) Then, we see a young woman in a hijab poring over contact sheets of images she's captured with her camera – but she apparently isn't happy with *any* of them. Eventually, we see Kendall Jenner posing during a photoshoot as she watches a huge group of protestors making their way down the street in front of her. Although the generic signs being carried by the protestors are those with peace symbols, hearts, "LOVE," and "Join the Conversation," it appears to be a reference to the Black Lives Matter movement.

Let's skip ahead to the end of the commercial since we all know how it ends. Kendall leaves the photoshoot, rips off her blonde wig, wipes off her lipstick, changes into her street clothes, joins the protestors, and heroically hands a police officer a can of Pepsi. BOOM. Racial injustice and inequity are solved! Who knew that a simple can of soda was the answer?

The point of citing this example of visual storytelling gone bad isn't to assign blame. Instead, its purpose is to serve as a cautionary tale. If Pepsi, one of the world's most beloved and youth-oriented brands, can make this kind of mistake, we should all take a moment to figure out how we can avoid repeating it.

So, how *did* this happen? The details remain unclear. What we *do* know is this:

- The spot was created by an in-house team at Pepsi – not an external agency.
- PepsiCo initially went on the defensive, issuing a statement in response to the backlash. According to a report by CNBC, a Pepsi spokesperson emailed a statement that said: "This is a global ad that reflects people from different walks of life coming together in a spirit of harmony, and we think that's an important message to convey" (Handley, 2017).
- Pepsi pulled the spot the day after it dropped, saying "Pepsi was trying to project a global message of unity, peace and understanding. Clearly, we missed the mark, and we apologize" (Smith, 2017).

We can only speculate about the events and decisions that led to this spot being created and released. But the reactions shared by members of the public were very clear. Images included in the Pepsi spot were viewed by many as performative. Pepsi was viewed as yet another brand trying to jump on the Black Lives Matter bandwagon. And the choice of a White, wealthy supermodel to be the savior was highly questionable, to say the least. The visual story didn't just fall flat – it exploded in Pepsi's face. Which leads us to ask two simple questions:

1. Before the spot was produced – and certainly before it aired – did the Pepsi team ask for input from individuals who were actually *participating* in protests going on throughout the country?
2. Were activists on the frontline of the various movements consulted about the spot's concept and how it would be visualized?

There's also a third question which needs to be asked: Who was represented on the Pepsi team that came up with the spot and who *wasn't*? A tweet posted by @Travon shortly after the spot aired specifically addresses this, saying: "The Kendall Jenner Pepsi fiasco is a perfect example of what happens when there's no black people in the room when decisions are being made" (Travon, 2017).

In strategic communications, ensuring that everyone has a voice in the strategic and creative process should be obvious. Never assume that you know or understand how a community you don't belong to would react to a specific message or image. If you do, you'll likely get it painfully wrong.

Developing a true understanding of your audience takes a lot of focused effort. It doesn't involve simply going with your gut or making assumptions based on what you've seen in the media or have experienced in your own interactions with members of a particular audience. Instead, get to know the audience you're talking to by:

- **Asking questions**. Using a representative sample of your audience, ask participants how they feel about issues; what their needs, wants, aspirations, and challenges are; and how they describe their own experiences and those of their community. Ask them questions that go below the surface and get to know your audience as human beings rather than demographics.
- **Expanding your circle**. DEI isn't just a "work thing." It's an *us* thing. Far too often, we surround ourselves with others who look like us, think like us, believe like us, and live like us. And, to justify this, we'll explain to others that we have a Jewish friend or a Black friend or an LGBTQ+ friend. Instead, consider expanding your circle of friends, colleagues, and experiences to become more representative of our society. Not only will you grow as a person and as a strategic communications professional, but the conversations you have will be a LOT more interesting!

Also, brands should make sure their own house is in order first. Before incorporating DEI messaging and visuals externally, brands need to look internally. How representative is the leadership team? Is there diversity among employees? Other than talking about valuing DEI, how is the brand *living* that value? The bottom line: Brands shouldn't be hypocritical by telling their customers what *they* should be doing if the brand isn't doing it *itself*.

To be fair, Pepsi certainly isn't the only brand to have gotten visual storytelling wrong when it comes to inclusivity. Other brands have had their own fails. So, how can we prevent our brand from becoming one of those?

Reframing with the 3Ps

It can be easy to make missteps when it comes to creating and implementing inclusive visuals. However, the Unstereotype Alliance – an industry partnership initiative organized by UN Women to eliminate stereotypes in communications – has developed a tool to help visual storytellers avoid such missteps. It's called the 3Ps framework (Unstereotype Alliance, 2021).

Here's a quick summary of each P:

Presence

This refers to who's being featured in the images you're using in your communications. Ask questions such as these:

- **If there's a group, is it one that's diverse?** Or does it include a group of White co-workers with one Black person? Or Hispanic person? Or a woman wearing a hijab?
- **Does the scene look posed?** For example, does it feature a group of non-disabled individuals sitting at a table in a restaurant smiling at the one individual at the table who uses a wheelchair?
- **Are the subjects presented in a positive way?** From clothes to names to occupation to the copy being used in a communication, stay away from stereotypes. For example, not all members of the LGBTQ+ community dress or act like the gay character who's in your favorite show.

Perspective

When it comes to telling stories, you're either the one who's *telling* the story or the one the story is being told *about*. It's all about perspective, which is why it's important to understand whose perspective you're representing in any visual narrative. Questions to ask include:

- **Is the main character's personal experience and perspective being shared?** For example, if the main character is a person of Hispanic heritage, does the visual story being told accurately represent how they interact with the world around them?
- **Are there any scenes that overtly or covertly include stereotypes, objectification, or sexualization?** To find out, it's important to request input from those who are most qualified to make that determination. For example, if a person with a physical disability is portrayed in a commercial, a non-disabled individual isn't the one who should be deciding if the portrayal is stereotypical. Instead, multiple individuals who have a physical disability should be asked for input. *(Sidenote: It's important for us to remember that a single person in any group or community doesn't represent everyone. All of us – even if we're in the same community – live very different experiences. So, getting feedback about imagery should include reaching out to multiple members of the community being portrayed.)*
- **Is the character being shown in a positive light throughout the entirety of the visual story?** Whether deciding on the name of the character or the environment they're framed in or the work they're doing or the

clothes they're wearing, or the words being spoken, be sure to check stereotypes at the door. Context is key when it comes to authentically and accurately communicating inclusivity through visual storytelling. Just be sure you're representing characters positively rather than patronizingly.

Personality

An audience can tell when a character in a visual story is being represented superficially. This will cause your story to fall flat – just as flat as the 2D character you've created. Why? Because you're not giving the audience anyone or anything they can relate to. If they don't see themselves in the characters portrayed in your ad or video or social media campaign, they won't pay attention. When evaluating the personality of your characters – which is what allows them to become three-dimensional in the eyes of the audience – consider the following:

- **Are the characters the ones in control of their own lives?** Characters should be the ones in the driver's seat of their lives. At no point should they be acted *upon*.
- **Is each character's personality obvious?** Just showing people laughing as they gather around a laptop in an office doesn't reveal anything about the characters' personalities. Everyone's personality is different. So, find ways to express that visually.
- **What beauty standards are being promoted?** Is every female character tall, slender, blonde, and White? Does every male character look like they spend at least half of their day in the gym? If external beauty isn't the point of the story, then don't let it drive the visuals.

Tokenism: The Fallacy of Checking the Box

"We need to make sure we include a Black female in the shot. How else will they know we support Black Lives Matter?"

"Can we find a stock photo that has a person in a wheelchair participating in a meeting? That'll show people that we're ADA compliant."

"Does anyone have a lesbian friend we can bring in for this video shoot? We just need one. And ask her to wear cargo shorts."

All these scenarios – exaggerated as they may or may not be – are instances of tokenism. According to Hahn et al. (2017), *tokenism* is *the practice of making only a perfunctory or symbolic effort to be inclusive, especially by recruiting a small number of people from underrepresented groups in order to give the appearance of equality*. It's a superficial way of checking the DEI box in visual storytelling. It's the "let's-make-sure-we-have-one-from-each-category-to-show-we-believe-in-diversity" approach. Typically, it represents either extreme laziness or extreme misunderstanding on the part of the brand. And it also perpetuates stereotypes, exclusion, and misunderstanding.

How can you avoid tokenism in visual storytelling? Normalize social identity groups by showing them doing things *everyone* does – such as enjoying dinner with their family, going to a movie with friends, taking a walk, etc. Here are a few key strategies to help guide us (Sonko, 2022):

1. If you're using stock images or stock video to promote an organization, be sure they accurately reflect the makeup of the organization's workforce. Likewise, if the imagery is meant to represent the audience your organization serves, be sure it's an accurate one.
2. If you have the budget for a photoshoot, you can control the visual story being told. For example, if the photos will be used to communicate the origin story of your brand, your models might be current employees who accurately represent the brand's internal demographics.
3. Understand the intentions of why each individual is included in a photo, illustration, or video. If it's only to check a particular DEI box, step back and start over.

Practicing Visual Intersectionality

There are multiple ways that intersectionality is defined. Many of those are discussed in other chapters of this book. In this chapter, we'll look at how it relates to visual storytelling.

We've explored how authenticity in visual storytelling doesn't happen by accident. Instead, we know we need to closely examine how and why we're using specific imagery to represent specific social identity groups. Acknowledging intersectionality and representing it accurately is an essential part of this decision-making process.

For example, let's say you're shooting a commercial that includes scenes from a neighborhood picnic. You've done a good job ensuring that the casting was inclusive. At least you *think* you have. The cast includes people of all ages, body types, races, genders, etc. But have you thought about presenting any of the cast members in ways that will help the viewer see them as more than just superficial representations? If you haven't, the story you're telling isn't nearly as rich or as inclusive as you hoped it would be.

What if you included two Black men who are clearly a loving couple and have adopted a child? Or a trans woman who is holding hands with another woman? Or an elderly Latinx couple enjoying a game of bocce? These are *real* stories because they reflect *real* life.

These visuals of intersectional identities tell a more complete story of the characters in your commercial because they bring to light the complexities of identity, power, and oppression. The two Black men don't just have to face racial inequity. They also have to deal with the discrimination directed toward those in the LGBTQ+ community. And the fact that they parent a child? Well, that just adds another layer.

The Latinx couple doesn't just have to face discrimination based on their race and ethnicity. Because they're considered "old" in our society, ageism would also be a form of discrimination they have to navigate.

None of us have a single identity. We're far more complex than that. Normalize various social identities in situations that reflect a variety of social, economic, and cultural perspectives and reflect this in your visual storytelling.

Finding Inclusive Imagery

Budgets for visual storytelling projects run the spectrum – from next to nothing to millions of dollars. Ideally, it would be great to hire a professional photographer or videographer to shoot original imagery. Not only does this allow you to get the exact imagery you want, but it also means that others – including competing brands – won't have access to your assets for their own projects.

However, all is not lost if you *don't* have the budget for a professional photo or video shoot. There's an alternative: stock imagery. Many online sites offer inclusive stock photography, illustrations and video – some free and some paid. Examples include the following:

Free (However, some have licensing restrictions. So, be sure to do your due diligence.)

- The Gender Spectrum Collection by VICE: A library of LGBTQ+ stock photos featuring non-stereotypical images.
- Nappy: Provides high-resolution stock photos of Black and Brown people.
- Women of Color in Tech (#WOCINTECH): Features stock photos that showcase women of color working in the tech industry.
- Disabled and Here: Describes itself as "a disability-led effort to provide free & inclusive stock images from our own perspective, with photos and illustrations celebrating disabled Black, Indigenous, people of color (BIPOC)."

- The Jopwell Collection: Features stock photos of Black, Latinx, and Native American individuals in the workplace.

Paid

- Stocksy: Provides a collection of progressive stock imagery that includes "fresh interpretations of contemporary concepts and correcting for under-represented voices."
- TONL: A comprehensive collection of imagery that features authentically diverse narratives.
- Diversity Photos: Features inclusive photos and illustrations of individuals in a variety of settings and situations.
- CreateHER Stock: A platform that serves as a resource for stock imagery of women of color.
- Black Illustrations: A service that provides "beautiful illustrations of Black people for your next digital project."
- Getty Images DEI Imagery Search Guide: Detailed instructions that help users conduct searches for inclusive images and videos on the Getty Images website.

Additional stock imagery providers – both free and paid – include:

- Adobe Stock
- Shutterstock
- iStock
- Unsplash
- Pexels
- Pixabay
- Creative Commons

When choosing stock images, video, or illustrations, be diligent in evaluating each of them. Are they authentically inclusive? Do they accurately portray the visual story being told? Are marginalized communities represented positively? You can create amazing visual stories with stock imagery. Just be intentional during the selection process and include diverse perspectives from creative conceptualization to production.

Making Visual Stories Accessible

You've created an amazing piece of visual storytelling for your brand. It's one that everyone in your audience can benefit from and enjoy. Or is it?

According to the World Health Organization (WHO) (2023), "an estimated 1.3 billion people experience significant disability. This represents

16% of the world's population, or 1 in 6 of us." Knowing this, we have to ask ourselves if the visual stories we're creating are accessible to those with visual, auditory, or cognitive challenges.

Visual accessibility is the practice of designing visual content so that anyone – including those with disabilities, such as visual impairment – can easily, understand and use the content. The Nielsen Norman Group is a leader in user experience research. It offers several general guidelines for creating visually accessible content (Gordon, 2022). They include the following:

- **Use color contrast**. It can be challenging for those with visual impairments to see text on backgrounds that lack contrast. For example, it would be extremely difficult to read white text on a light-yellow background. There are many online tools for evaluating color contrast. To find them, just do a Google search for color contrast evaluation tools. WebAxe provides a comprehensive list of tools for you to explore.
- **Include alternative text (alt text) for images**. Some individuals with vision impairment use screen readers when accessing information online. To provide them with a more inclusive and immersive experience, use alt text. This involves providing a clear, concise description of images and other graphical elements. (Alt text should NOT be used for imagery that's only inserted for decorative purposes.) Don't use an image's caption as its alt text. Instead, actually describe the image itself. For example, for an image of a dog running on the beach, the alt text might be something like, "A black Labrador Retriever running along the edge of the water as the sun sets in the background." You wouldn't just say, "A dog running on the beach."
- **Test your visual story with end users**. Just as you would do quality assurance testing with a website before it's launched, you should also test the accessibility of your visual content with end users. They'll be able to tell you what's working and what needs to be improved.

Audio description can also be used for visual content. This involves a verbal narration of what's appearing on screen in nonspeaking sections of the video (Gordon, 2022).

Other resources that provide helpful guidance for making visual content more accessible include:

- Apple's Human Interface Guidelines
- W3C's Web Accessibility Initiative
- Google's Material Design

For those who have challenges with hearing, there are multiple ways you can make audio elements of your visual story more accessible. Two of the most popular approaches include:

- Using closed or open captions that provide on-screen text of the audio content.
- Providing transcripts of audio elements.

As the capabilities of AI continue to improve and expand, AI-powered tools for making video content accessible are also improving and expanding. The best way to determine which tools work for your audience is to experiment with them and re-evaluate them regularly. With AI and technology advancing at warp speed, this is something you should constantly be doing.

A Quick Recap: Qualities of Truly Inclusive Visual Storytelling

It's impossible to provide a complete list of every single element that defines inclusive visual storytelling. One reason is that there are simply too many. The other reason is that any such list will evolve over the years. What defines inclusivity today isn't what defined inclusivity a decade ago and it might not be what defines it in the future. Also, *how* we address inclusivity has and will continue to evolve over time.

What we *can* do is consistently check ourselves and our colleagues to make sure we're not unintentionally defaulting to the use of tropes and stereotypes in visual storytelling. Unfortunately, these can often be used as shortcuts for communicating messaging about DEI.

As we've discussed, no matter what social identity group you're portraying, avoid stereotypes, tokenism, and patronization. A Getty Images report (2021), titled "Inclusive Visual Storytelling: Best Practices for More Diverse Marketing," provides some excellent guidelines to help us with this. Some are included below, along with many the author uses in her own visual storytelling work:

Race & Ethnicity

- People of color aren't all the same *shade* of color. Some are darker and some are lighter.
- People of color don't share the same physical features. Just like their White counterparts, each individual is unique.
- People of color aren't always employees. They're also supervisors, business owners, and CEOs.

Gender

- There are women who drive 18-wheelers and men who are stay-at-home dads. Little girls who play baseball and little boys who play with dolls. Gender is fluid.
- Gender is expressed in more ways than simply a binary choice between masculine or feminine. There are individuals who don't fit into this traditional gender framework.

Sexual Orientation

- The LGBTQ+ community doesn't only include young people. It also includes those who are older.
- Many members of this community prefer the local holiday parade over the yearly Pride parade or going to a quiet dinner with friends over going to a drag show.
- Not every LGBTQ+ relationship is a romantic one. LGBTQ+ friendships are just as common as friendships between those who identify as heterosexual.
- Members of the LGBTQ+ community can be found in every profession and economic class.

Faith

- If a person's faith isn't part of the story or campaign, don't make it the focus.
- When you represent a faith-based ceremony or celebration, do your research so that you can portray it accurately.
- Determine if it's actually necessary to include symbols of a particular faith or if it's being done as a form of shorthand for bringing unwarranted attention to the faith.

Age

- Women over 40 still lead very active and fulfilling lives.
- Grandparents know how to text, email, FaceTime, and use emojis.
- Not everyone 65+ chooses retirement. An increasing number of older adults are starting second careers or launching their own businesses at or beyond the traditional retirement age.
- Older people aren't just friends with other older people.

Abilities

• Many individuals with physical disabilities live independently.
• Individuals with physical disabilities have non-disabled friends.
• An individual can have a physical disability and also be an athlete.
• Just because someone has a physical disability doesn't mean they require full-time or even part-time care.

Body Type

• Bodies come in all shapes and sizes, any of which can be incredibly fashionable.
• Be conscious of how you position shorter individuals in relationship to taller individuals.
• Portraying realistic body types doing a variety of activities tells a more authentic story.

What Stories Will You Tell?

Visual storytelling is the oldest and one of the most powerful communication tools we have. While we might not be telling stories of buffalo hunts today, we continue to tell stories of the human experience. And that requires us to have a strong sense of responsibility, empathy, and understanding.

There's no final destination when it comes to learning how to become more inclusive visual storytellers. It's an ongoing journey during which we'll experience tremendous learning and growth. It's also one during which we'll make mistakes. And that's okay – as long as we acknowledge them, take responsibility for them, and use them as points of learning so we can do better the next time.

It's the storytellers who always have and always will change our world. As a visual storyteller, you have an unequaled opportunity to help tear down harmful stereotypes, reframe DEI as something to be welcomed rather than shunned, and to make this world one in which *everyone* is viewed through the lens of belonging, dignity, and respect. It all depends on the visuals you select, the stories you decide to tell, and how you bring them to life.

Note

1 *For this chapter, "brand" is used as a universal term to refer to for-profit businesses, nonprofit organizations, political candidates, and causes.*

Bibliography

Burg, B. (n.d.). *All things being equal…* https://burg.com/2010/04/all-things-being-equal/

Calloway, E. (2019, December 11). Is this cave painting humanity's oldest story? *Nature.* www.nature.com/articles/d41586-019-03826-4

Content Marketing Institute (2020, March 20). *#CM World 2019 – Visual storytelling at its best – Eric Goodstadt & Sacha Reeb* [Video]. YouTube. https://youtu.be/j83s KBN8pLk?si=3pUS76RpiQh3Dflv

Getty Images (2021). *Inclusive visual storytelling: Best practices for more diverse marketing.* www.isba.org.uk/system/files/media/documents/2021-04/Getty%20Images%20 Imagery_%20Best%20practices%20for%20more%20diverse%20marketing.pdf

Gordon, K. (2022, October 30). *5 visual treatments that improve accessibility.* Nielsen Norman Group. www.nngroup.com/articles/visual-treatments-accessibility/

Hahn, D. L., Hoffmann, A. E., Felzien, M., LeMaster, J. W., Xu, J., & Fagnan, L. J. (2017). Tokenism in patient engagement. *Family Practice, 34*(3), 290–295. https://doi.org/10.1093/fampra/cmw097

Handley, L. (2017, April 5). *Kendall Jenner's Pepsi ad pulled after Twitter backlash.* CNBC. www.cnbc.com/2017/04/05/kendall-jenners-pepsi-ad-causes-twitter-storm-labeled-disrespectful.html

History.com (2018, August 21). *2017 events.* www.history.com/topics/21st-century/2017-events

Lacey, N. (2018, October 2). *Advertising is out of sync with world's consumers.* Ipsos. www.ipsos.com/en-us/news-polls/Advertising-out-of-sync-with-consumers

Rulf, D. (n.d.). *This is why our brain loves pictures.* IFVP. https://ifvp.org/content/why-our-brain-loves-pictures

Smith, A. (2017, April 5). *Pepsi pulls controversial Kendall Jenner ad after outcry.* NBCNews. www.nbcnews.com/news/nbcblk/pepsi-ad-kendall-jenner-echoes-black-lives-matter-sparks-anger-n742811

Smith, K. N. (2019, December 15). *A 43,900-year-old cave painting is the oldest story ever recorded.* Ars Technica. https://arstechnica.com/science/2019/12/a-43900-year-old-cave-painting-is-the-oldest-story-ever-recorded/

Sonko, T. (2022, September 22). *Understanding and identifying tokenism (Plus, 5 ways to avoid it!).* Affirmity. www.affirmity.com/blog/understanding-identifying-tokenism-5-ways-to-avoid/

Travon. (2017, April 4). The Kendall Jenner Pepsi fiasco is a perfect example of what happens when there's no black people in the room when decisions are being made [Tweet]. Twitter. https://twitter.com/Travon/status/849409230754983936

Unstereotype Alliance. (2021, February 4). *3Ps unstereotype marketing communications framework.* Unstereotype Alliance. www.unstereotypealliance.org/en/resources/research-and-tools/3ps-unstereotype-marketing-communications-playbook

World Health Organization. (2023, March 7). Disability. *WHO.* www.who.int/news-room/fact-sheets/detail/disability-and-health

5   Inclusive Digital and Social Media Strategies

Qian Xu

As of January 2024, the number of global internet users reached 5.35 billion, constituting 66.2% of the world's population. Out of them, 5.04 billion were active on social media, accounting for 62.3% of the world's population (Petrosyan, 2024). On average, internet users spend 143 minutes per day on social media and messaging apps (Dixon, 2024). However, there are differences in how people use the internet and social media across different countries and cultural backgrounds. For example, although many leading social media platforms are rooted in the United States with English as the predominant language, native Chinese social platforms like WeChat, Douyin, Kuaishou, and QQ have flourished among Chinese-speaking communities, owing to their ability to provide local context and content (Dixon, 2024).

Even within the same country, disparities emerge between different demographic and community groups in terms of frequency and purpose of social media use. For instance, Instagram, TikTok, and Snapchat are much more popular among American adults under 30, whereas the age gaps in X (formally known as Twitter) and Facebook are considerably narrower (Auxier & Anderson, 2021). Another example is Nextdoor, which garners greater usage among urban and suburban dwellers compared to those in rural areas (Auxier & Anderson, 2021).

As detailed in a report from We Are Social (2023), the days of universal online conversations revolving around widely shared popular culture are now behind us. Instead, online discourses are increasingly shaped by specialized online communities, alongside the presence of intricate and fluid personal identities. Hence, it's imperative to factor in these distinctions when crafting communication strategies for digital and social media. Ignoring inclusivity in your strategic plan could carry the risk of excluding people, alienating your audience, or limiting the reach of your content. In

DOI: 10.4324/9781003411796-6

this chapter, we will discuss inclusive digital communication strategies from the following perspectives:

- Gaining insights into diverse audiences through social listening and user testing
- Applying inclusive design to ensure digital accessibility
- Prioritizing representation and diverse voices in content strategy
- Sustaining brand safety without compromising inclusion
- Evaluating the effectiveness of inclusive digital communication strategies

Gaining Insights into Diverse Audiences Through Social Listening and User Testing

A successful inclusive digital strategy rests on the understanding of diverse audiences. When it comes to web and social media, let's discuss two unique research approaches that can help us gain nuanced insights into audiences: social listening and user testing.

Social Listening and Inclusive Audience Planning

Social media has heightened the transparency of consumer conversations surrounding brands and organizations, whether they involve critiques or endorsements, more than ever. We can employ social listening to extract valuable insights from these discussions, which can then be used to inform the creation of marketing strategies and important decision-making processes. **Social listening** refers to *the practice of monitoring and analyzing social media conversations about sentiment, opinions, trends about a brand, competitors, and industry at large* (Newberry & Macready, 2022).

Social listening can shed light on the path to inclusive audience planning in multiple ways. First, it helps us identify underrepresented groups and better understand their lived experiences. For example, after listening to Facebook fans' sharing of parenting journeys with children with disabilities, Hallmark recognized that not all motherhood looks the same. They then created the viral video "Dear Mom" for Mother's Day, featuring a mother whose daughter has Down syndrome. This allowed Hallmark to cultivate connections with a unique community and integrate their life story into its brand narrative.

Second, through social listening, we can gather feedback from underrepresented communities about their specific needs and preferences. Black Girl Sunscreen, a sunscreen brand focusing on women of color, a group frequently overlooked in discussions about sun protection, came across the following tweet: "For all my black ppl do y'all wear sunscreen?" They shared this tweet to their profile and responded with "We sure do!" Through this act of attentive listening, they not only uncovered a potential lead but also seamlessly incorporated the promotion of their offering into their social media strategy.

Furthermore, observing and analyzing consumer conversations on social media provides insights into the preferred languages and tones within different communities. This enables you to maintain inclusive and respectful communication in your digital content, preventing inadvertent offense or alienation of any community.

User Testing for Assessing Diverse Needs

Digital communication strategies encompass both content creation and the selection of platforms for content delivery. When your campaign or marketing plan involves designing or launching a website, a mobile application, or any other interactive interface, you need to incorporate user testing from the very beginning and throughout the process to understand audiences' diverse needs. *User testing* (or *usability testing*) is *a specific type of user research that evaluates the user's interaction with a digital interface to detect usability issues* (Usability.gov, n.d.).

User testing serves a primary goal of pinpointing barriers that impede individuals with varying abilities from accessing a digital interface. Engaging participants with disabilities in user testing helps identify shortcomings of the interface, which enables you to offer more equitable and inclusive access. For example, through user testing, we can determine whether the color contrast strategy adopted by a news website is effective for older people with impaired vision.

User testing could also reveal challenges people face, concerning language, cultural norms, and context of use, assisting in the development of a more culturally sensitive interface. For instance, user testing can determine if individuals from cultures that strongly favor minimal uncertainty would perceive a website's navigation system with many choices as overwhelming and less user-friendly.

Applying Inclusive Design to Ensure Digital Accessibility

Importance of Accessibility to Digital Communication

Our interactions with digital technology heavily rely on our abilities to see, hear, say, touch, learn, and remember. Nevertheless, approximately 16% of the world's population – an estimated 1.3 billion people – have reported experiencing a disability (World Health Organization, 2023). In the United States, up to one in four (27%) of adults live with some type of disability

(Centers for Disease Control and Prevention, 2023). If their needs are not taken into consideration when developing digital communication plans, you risk losing a significant portion of your audience or failing to engage with them effectively. Therefore, *accessibility* must not be an afterthought. It is an essential component of any inclusive digital communication plan.

Accessibility is required by law. The ***Americans with Disabilities Act*** (ADA), *the world's first comprehensive civil rights law for people with disabilities, prohibits discrimination against anyone with disabilities in everyday life* (ADA National Network, n.d.). Similar legislation exists in various countries and regions globally, including the Equality Act 2010 in the United Kingdom, the European Accessibility Act, the Accessible Canada Act, the Act on Welfare of Persons with Disabilities in South Korea, and the Equal Rights of Persons with Disabilities Act in Israel, among others (Bureau of Internet Accessibility, 2022).

Digital communication pertains to a particular facet of accessibility known as ***digital accessibility***. It is defined as *the design and creation of digital products, including both the interface and the content (e.g., website, social media, mobile application, electronic document, online campaign, etc.), to be available, approachable, or usable by people with disabilities and other special needs or functional limitations* (Kulkarni, 2019).

Web Content Accessibility Guidelines

The ***Web Content Accessibility Guidelines*** (WCAG), *a set of guidelines on how to make web content more accessible to people with disabilities published by the Web Accessibility Initiative of the World Wide Web Consortium* (W3C), stand out as the most widely adopted standards around the world (W3C Web Accessibility Initiative, n.d.-a). Although the word "web" is used in the title, the four core principles of WCAG can be applied to almost all digital content.

Being *perceivable* requires the presented content to be visible and detectable to all individuals. For instance, although the majority of people can engage with your social media campaign through visual means, those who are blind or visually impaired rely on screen readers. Consequently, it's essential to include descriptive *alt text* for images to convey content effectively. ***Alt text*** *refers to a written description that appears in place of an image when the image cannot be loaded or recognized.*

Being *operable* means that the interface should facilitate interaction for individuals through methods that are commonly adopted, even if these methods are not used by the majority. For instance, your campaign website should guarantee that all functions can be accessed using keyboards, thus eliminating the necessity for a mouse to operate specific interactive features.

This is important because tasks that require fine motor control with a mouse can pose challenges for users with motion impairments.

Being *understandable* requires a digital interface and its content to avoid unnecessary complexity, making it easy for all people to grasp. For example, choosing a cohesive color scheme for an online marketing brochure would simplify information processing and reduce cognitive load for neurodivergent individuals.

Being *robust* emphasizes prioritizing compatibility. Digital content should function reliably across a wide variety of technologies and platforms, such as different browsers, devices, and assistive tools. For example, an interactive advertisement should offer a consistent user experience regardless of whether it is viewed on a desktop, laptop, or any mobile device (e.g., smartphone or tablet) with varying screen dimensions.

Inclusive Design Tips for Web and Social Media Strategies

To successfully implement the guidelines of digital accessibility, you can embrace inclusive design practices. *Inclusive design* is *an approach born out of digital environments that aims to design and create products that understand and enable people of all abilities* (Gilbert, 2019). It empathizes with diverse abilities, needs, and experiences to generate inclusive design patterns for full participation and engagement (Joyce, 2022). In Chapter 4, you have already learned about using alt text for images, captions for videos, accessible text and visual elements, and inclusive language. These practices are also applicable to content for web and social media. Therefore, we will not reiterate those concepts in this chapter. Instead, we will introduce several common inclusive design practices that are particularly applicable to web and social media.

Moderate Use of Emojis. Emojis can infuse emotion and visual appeal into your online text. However, they may not be always friendly for everyone. Visually impaired or blind people who depend on screen readers may find emojis hard to interpret, given that screen readers can only verbalize the description of an emoji but not the intended meaning(s). For example, when a screen reader encounters a yellow heart emoji at the end of a social media post, it identifies this emoji as "yellow heart" rather than conveying the message of "great friendship" it represents.

To make emojis more accessible, it is essential to refrain from substituting them for text, as their nuanced meanings are challenging to convey through screen readers. Second, it is helpful to place emojis at the end rather than in the middle of a sentence to ensure a smoother reading experience for assistive technology. Third, emojis should be used sparingly. A birthday celebration Instagram post with six cake emojis is read as "cake cake cake cake cake

cake" by a screen reader, which could frustrate people. Finally, emoticons, the punctuation marks, letters, and numbers used to illustrate an emotion, should be avoided. Screen reader users may simply hear "semicolon parentheses" when encountering a smiley face emoticon like:).

User-Friendly Hashtags. To make hashtags accessible, the first step is to adopt Camel Case or Pascal Case formatting for words within a hashtag. *Camel case formats a compound word or phrase by starting the first word with either an uppercase or a lowercase letter and then capitalizing the first letter of all the other words* (e.g., #noFilter or #NoFilter). *Pascal case* is similar but *always capitalizes the first letter of each word* (e.g., #MyBodyMyChoice). This mix of lowercase and uppercase letters assists screen readers in recognizing individual words and correctly pronouncing the hashtag. It also benefits individuals who may struggle with identifying word patterns and relationships, including those with dyslexia or cognitive disabilities. For instance, #InclusiveDigitalStrategies is much easier to read than #inclusivedigitalstrategies. Just like with emojis, it is also helpful to avoid inserting hashtags in the middle of a sentence or the caption of a post.

Keyboard Accessibility. Your entire campaign or marketing website should be designed to allow audiences to navigate and interact with it solely through a keyboard. While most audiences may opt for a mouse, trackpad, or touch-screen, people with motor disabilities and visual impairments typically rely on keyboards for navigation. This means your website should support tab-based navigation for links and form filling to eliminate the need for a mouse.

Effective Heading Markups. Bold headings and headings in different sizes help visual audiences quickly grasp the organizational structure of your website content. For those who rely on screen readers, it is essential to add proper heading markups to your campaign and marketing websites. *Heading markups* are *the HTML and XHTML tags indicating heading levels* (e.g., <h1> main heading </h1>, <h3> sub-sub-heading </h3>). The embedded heading tag enables a screen reader to announce the text as a heading at a specific level, making it easier for people to skip or locate content.

Properly Formatted Hyperlinks. Here are several things you can do to make hyperlinks accessible. First, choose meaningful anchor text for your links. For example, "guidelines for digital accessibility" is more user-friendly than the vague phrase "click here." Second, you should avoid using all capital letters in a link, as this can pose challenges for people with reading disabilities. Additionally, it is better to display links as plain, readable text (e.g., "Internship Program in School of Communications") rather than a URL (e.g., www.elon.edu/u/academics/communications/academics/internship-program/).

Consistent Navigation. Regardless of the specific goals of your digital strategy, every page on your website should adhere to the same or very similar design, layout, content hierarchy, and control features. This consistency assists audiences in anticipating where to locate content with ease, which is particularly valuable for people with visual impairments, cognitive limitations, and intellectual disabilities.

Prioritizing Representation and Diverse Voices in Content Strategy

According to Meta (2021), the majority of consumers (71%) anticipate brands to actively feature inclusive content in their online ads and social media campaigns. Furthermore, Meta's studies also revealed that online campaigns with diverse representations tend to be more memorable than those featuring a single traditional representation. However, the actual representation in current online campaigns falls short of consumers' expectation. More than half (54%) of the surveyed consumers have felt that their own culture is not fully represented in online campaigns (Meta, 2021). To foster greater inclusivity in digital content strategies, it is crucial to prioritize diverse representation and amplify the voices of underrepresented groups.

Ensuring Representation

Ensuring diverse representation starts with a close examination of your core audience's demographics to identify which group is currently absent in your social media feeds and website content. Then, you should continuously monitor and enhance diverse, intersectional representations in your visual and written content. A successful case in point is Aerie's ongoing #AerieREAL campaign, which aims to promote body positivity and diversity. Across different social media platforms, this campaign features brand ambassadors from diverse careers and identity groups, with different body types and abilities in unedited images.

When emphasizing representation, it is important to exercise caution and avoid appropriating elements of marginalized cultures. For example, the trend of non-Black people popularizing words from African American Vernacular English on TikTok can be disconcerting and offensive to Black people who have faced discrimination and public criticism for using these words. You can never be too cautious in reviewing your digital content for any insensitive language with racist origins or negative connotations.

Amplifying Diverse Voices

Genuine inclusion in digital content goes beyond mere representation. It should also offer people meaningful opportunities to contribute and to be heard. This implies the need for you to pass the mic from time to time. Nickelodeon, the winner of the Multicultural Community Engagement Category at the 2023 Shorty Awards, initiated the social media campaign #28DaysofBlackCosplay. This campaign aims to uplift Black cosplayers and raise awareness of bullying, racism, and mental health issues in the Black community. Nickelodeon not only interviewed and featured the original creator of this hashtag but also encouraged fans to share their own content on social media to support this cause.

To amply diverse voices, here are several actionable items for you to consider. First, you can increase the visibility of your underrepresented followers by intentionally sharing content generated by them. Second, when sourcing new content, you can prioritize reaching out to creators from underrepresented groups and credit them properly through your digital platforms. Omnicom Media Group's Diverse Content Creators Network could be a valuable resource as it focuses on minority-owned, diverse publishers and content creators. Third, you can host social media live events featuring diverse guests. Finally, it is worthwhile to share content from other brands that address timely diversity, equity, and inclusion topics.

Collaborating with Diverse Influencers

Collaborating with diverse influencers offers brands another effective approach to craft an inclusive digital strategy. Influencers from underrepresented groups not only possess a deeper understanding of consumer interests and sentiments but are often at the forefront of social change and advocacy. Partnering with them to co-create content addressing the challenges faced by marginalized communities can demonstrate your brand's commitment to social justice and extend an authentic invitation for more profound conversations with consumers. A compelling example of this approach is Good Humor's response toward a viral video exposing the racist origins of a popular ice cream truck jingle "Turkey in the Straw." As the inventor of America's first ice cream truck, Good Humor launched the "New Jingle for a New Era" campaign, demonstrating solidarity with the Black community. In this campaign, they collaborated with RZA, the rapper and founder of Wu-Tang Clan, to compose a track blending the signature tones of an ice cream truck and RZA's Wu-Tang style. Edelman then transformed the music into a music video and shared it on almost all social media platforms, leading to the campaign trending on Twitter (now X) and making it to the front page of Reddit.

When partnering with diverse influencers, it is critical to ensure that both your brand and the influencer not only share the same vision and objectives but also genuinely commit to diversity and inclusion in action. While it may be tempting to collaborate with well-known influencers due to their extensive reach and large following, these influencers may not always accurately represent your target consumers. Therefore, you need to be conscious in identifying influencers who can bring authenticity and credibility to the campaign. To shed light on workplace inequities faced by the Asian American and Pacific

Islander (AAPI) community, Digitas created "The Other Side" campaign, inviting 20 AAPI professionals to share their personal "Other Side" stories on LinkedIn. Instead of collaborating with high-profile influencers, this campaign adopted a strategy involving micro-influencers (i.e., influencers with less than 100K followers), successfully drawing public attention to the issue.

Incorporating Inclusive Hashtags

Hashtag use is also a valuable tool in building inclusive digital content. First, you can draw insights from existing hashtag activism campaigns to better understand critical social issues that resonate with various communities. This knowledge serves as the foundation for more effective digital content planning. Moreover, your brand can actively participate in conversations surrounding diversity and inclusion by engaging with the relevant hashtags and trending topics on social media. This not only underscores your commitment to these impactful matters but also extends your reach to a broader and more diverse audience. Furthermore, the judicious use of inclusive hashtags transcends platform boundaries, facilitating cross-platform promotion and creating a sense of community among your followers.

Sustaining Brand Safety without Compromising Inclusion

Brand safety refers to *the consideration and the practice of ensuring that an ad does not appear alongside inappropriate content that might be offensive, controversial, illegal, or unethical* (World Federation of Advertisers, 2022a), such as hate speech, disinformation, or crime. The primary concern of brand safety stems from the idea that consumers may link the placement of advertisements with endorsement of the surrounding content. When this content is negative or controversial, it can harm the reputation of the advertised brand. Many widely used web and social platforms like Facebook, Instagram, X (formerly Twitter), YouTube, TikTok, Google, Amazon, and more provide features that enable brands to exert some level of control over the timing and placement of the ads, regardless of the different algorithms adopted by them.

Impact of Keyword Blocking on Diversity and Inclusion

No matter which digital platform you employ, one common practice for ensuring brand safety is the adoption of a *keyword blocklist*. This list, *also known as a keyword exclusion list, is comprised of words or phrases that a brand desires to avoid having its advertisements displayed alongside due to safety concerns* (Brand Safety Institute, n.d.). In addition to keyword blocking, brands may also employ URL blocklists to disassociate themselves from specific websites. However, the misuse of these blocklists can pose significant hurdles to achieving diverse, equitable, and inclusive advertising and harm digital media owned by or featuring underrepresented groups.

For example, consider a brand that adds "Black Lives Matter" to its blocklist to steer clear of divisive political news stories online. Unfortunately, this broad brand safety automation can inadvertently result in the exclusion of virtually all Black-owned and Black-centered online media. In this scenario, not only does it lead to the under-monetization of Black publishers and their content, but it also hinders the brand from connecting with a culturally influential community.

The primary issue with keyword-driven exclusion is its failure to consider context. A single word can possess diverse meanings and interpretations contingent upon its context of use. Excessive keyword blocking can, therefore, erroneously flag valuable content concerning race, gender, social justice, and other sensitive issues as unsafe. A recent analysis of the brand safety practices of a top 40 brand by Integral Ad Science revealed that this brand had blocked over 1,600 URLs containing LGBTQ+ keywords, despite 94% of them being entirely brand safe (Jowett, 2023).

Integrating Inclusion into Brand Safety Practices

To mitigate the potential adverse impact of keyword blocking on diversity and inclusion, it is essential to begin by carefully evaluating what genuinely constitutes unsafe content. The "Addressing D&I in Brand Safety Guide" published by the European Association of Communications Agencies (2021) encourages agencies and advertisers to remove words from the blocklist that objectively represent a community and do not have an inherent negative connotation, such as gay, lesbian, LGBTQ+, Black, Arab, Indian, Muslim, senior, dementia, and more.

Furthermore, this guide recommends a more refined approach to handling blocklists. Rather than blocking content targeting or discussing various communities, focus on blocking only negative narratives. Instead of an exact keyword match, using a combination of keywords can avoid a sweeping, one-size-fits-all strategy. When dealing with URLs and mobile applications flagged by blocklists, it is always helpful to consult people from diverse groups for confirmation before automatically excluding them.

In addition to refining blocking, you may protect your brand through the lens of *brand suitability*. Unlike brand safety, which focuses on avoidance, brand suitability centers around *applying the unique criteria determined by a brand's own values to decide ad placement*. Leveraging contextual intelligence and factoring in brand personality, brand suitability enables a more customized approach to protect brands without sacrificing diversity and inclusion.

To identify inclusion criteria tailored to your brand, you can implement the Brand Safety Floor and Suitability Framework developed by the Global Alliance for Responsible Media (World Federation of Advertisers, 2022b)

Evaluating the Effectiveness of Inclusive Digital Communication Strategies

Once you put inclusive digital strategies into action, it is paramount to conduct a thorough assessment of their effectiveness to ensure they yield the intended outcomes. The insights gained from this assessment are invaluable in guiding decisions about enhancing and optimizing your digital inclusive initiatives for sustained success.

Setting Clear Goals and Objectives

First, you need to establish clear goals and objectives to provide a framework for the evaluation. These goals and objectives should follow the SMART criteria to be Specific, Measurable, Achievable, Relevant, and Time-bound (Note: You can also incorporate the SMART+IE process discussed in Chapter 7). Your measurement plan should align with these goals and define the outcomes that you would like to achieve. For example, are you aiming to increase the diversity of Instagram followers? Are you trying to identify and collaborate with more YouTube influencers from underrepresented backgrounds? Are you seeking to reduce color contrast errors on your campaign website?

Measures and Key Performance Indicators (KPIs) for Inclusive Digital Strategies

Different goals and objectives determine how you measure success and effectiveness. Here are several diversity- and inclusion-related measures and KPIs for you to consider.

Reach, Impression, and Followers by Audience Segments. To obtain a general overview of the diversity within your digital audience, you can assess the audience composition through the following measures related to your digital content: *reach* (number of people who view your content), *impressions* (number of times your content is displayed regardless of whether it is clicked or not), and *followers* (people who subscribe or follow your accounts on social media). Dissecting these data by demographics, psychographics, and/or geographics, you can tell whether you are attracting a broad range of people, including those from marginalized or underrepresented backgrounds. You can also monitor how these measures change before and after implementing inclusive strategies.

Engagement by Audience Segments. You can adopt number of *shares*, *comments*, *likes*, and *reposts* to gauge how well social media content resonates with different segments of your audience and whether a broader range of people with different backgrounds actively participate in your inclusive initiatives. For websites and mobile applications, you can examine web/app *traffic* by audience segments to see if your inclusive strategy drives more diverse visitors to your digital platform. In addition, comparing user experience metrics, such as *numbers of visitors* and *unique visitors, page views, time on site/app, bounce rate*, and *interaction patterns* by audience segments, helps assess whether the platform provides an equitable experience for diverse users.

Accessibility. The adherence to WCAG principles – *perceivable, operable, understandable*, and *robust* – and the detailed corresponding success criteria, such as color contrast, alt text, readability, keyboard accessibility, consistent navigation, and more (W3C Web Accessibility Initiative, n.d.-b), are the primary measures for digital accessibility. Webpage *load time* (how long it takes for a webpage to fully load on screen) and website *responsiveness* (the flexibility of a website to fit with different screen sizes and devices) are also common measures for accessibility.

Impact. The success of your inclusive digital and social media strategies can also be measured through their business impact on underrepresented groups and contribution to societal change, representation, and inclusivity beyond immediate business objectives. For example, does the newly launched campaign website lead to a higher conversion rate among traditionally marginalized groups? Does your Facebook marketing plan involve more diverse influencers contributing to more diversified content? Does your marketing initiative positively influence brand perception and reputation within the underrepresented communities? And does your social media advertisement raise awareness of the challenges faced by a marginalized group?

Methods and Tools for Evaluation

Earlier in this chapter, we introduced using ***social listening*** and ***user testing*** to better understand diverse audiences. Both methods can also be used to collect data for measuring your digital inclusivity efforts. For social listening, you can either use native analytics features embedded in social media platforms, such as Facebook Insights, Instagram Insights, and X (formerly Twitter) Analytics, or third-party applications, such as Brandwatch, Sprout Social, Talkwalker, Meltwater, and more, to track reach, impression, followers, and engagement by audience segments.

For website and mobile applications, you can conduct user testing with people representing different abilities and cultural backgrounds to gauge whether the interface is perceived as inclusive and affords accessibility. There are also web and mobile accessibility evaluation tools and browser extensions, such as WAVE, A11Y Color Contrast Accessibility Validator, accessScan, AChecker, Google PageSpeed Insights, and GTmetrix. In addition to using self-evaluation tools and measures, you can assess your inclusive strategy by conducting competitor analysis and benchmark research to gauge how your performance works against your competitor and whether it aligns with industry standards. It is important to recognize that the journey of an inclusive digital strategy does not conclude with the measurement of performance. Upon obtaining assessment results, the next step is to adapt your existing strategy to ensure that you continuously broaden your reach, consistently provide inclusive content, and continually enhance accessibility in the long term.

Bibliography

ADA National Network. (n.d.). *What is the Americans with Disabilities Act (ADA)?* https://adata.org/learn-about-ada

Auxier, B., & Anderson, M. (2021). *Social media use in 2021*. Pew Research Center. www.pewresearch.org/internet/2021/04/07/social-media-use-in-2021/

Brand Safety Institute. (n.d.). *Brand safety glossary*. www.brandsafetyinstitute.com/resources/glossary

Bureau of Internet Accessibility. (2022). *International web accessibility laws: An overview*. www.boia.org/blog/international-web-accessibility-laws-an-overview

Centers for Disease Control and Prevention. (2023, May). *Disability impacts all of us*. www.cdc.gov/ncbddd/disabilityandhealth/infographic-disability-impacts-all.html

Dixon, S. J. (2024, February). *Global social networks ranked by number of users 2024*. www.statista.com/statistics/272014/global-social-networks-ranked-by-number-of-users/

European Association of Communications Agencies. (2021). *Addressing D&I in brand safety*. https://eaca.eu/di-brand-safety-guide/

Gilbert, R. M. (2019). *Inclusive design for a digital world: Designing with accessibility in mind*. Apress. https://doi.org/10.1007/978-1-4842-5016-7

Jowett, E. (2023). *Why blunt brand safety tools halt the progress of diversity*. AdvertisingWeek. https://advertisingweek.com/why-blunt-brand-safety-tools-halt-the-progress-of-diversity/

Joyce, A. (2022, January 30). *Inclusive design*. Nielsen Norman Group. www.nngroup.com/articles/inclusive-design/

Kulkarni, M. (2019). Digital accessibility: Challenges and opportunities. *IIMB Management Review, 31*(1), 91–98. https://doi.org/10.1016/j.iimb.2018.05.009

Meta. (2021). *The difference diversity makes in online advertising*. www.facebook.com/business/news/insights/the-difference-diversity-makes-in-online-advertising

Newberry, C., & Macready, H. (2022, December). *What is social listening, why it matters + 14 tools to help*. Hootsuite. https://blog.hootsuite.com/social-listening-business/

Petrosyan, A. (2024, January). *Number of internet and social media users worldwide as of January 2024*. Statista. www.statista.com/statistics/617136/digital-population-worldwide/

Usability.gov. (n.d.). *Usability testing*. www.usability.gov/how-to-and-tools/methods/usability-testing.html

W3C Web Accessibility Initiative. (n.d.-a). *WCAG 2 overview*. www.w3.org/WAI/standards-guidelines/wcag/

W3C Web Accessibility Initiative. (n.d.-b). *How to meet WCAG (quick reference)*. www.w3.org/WAI/WCAG21/quickref/

We Are Social. (2023). *Think forward 2023*. https://thinkforward.wearesocial.com

World Federation of Advertisers. (2022a). *Diversity & representation guide*. https://wfanet.org/knowledge/diversity-and-inclusion/dei-in-media-guide/about

World Federation of Advertisers. (2022b). *GARM brand safety floor + suitability framework*. https://wfanet.org/knowledge/item/2022/06/17/GARM-Brand-Safety-Floor--Suitability-Framework-3

World Health Organization. (2023, March). *Disability*. www.who.int/news-room/fact-sheets/detail/disability-and-health

6 Designing Culturally Sensitive Research

Lee Bush

One of the ways we better understand our audiences is by conducting primary research. This might involve conducting quantitative research like surveys or qualitative research like focus groups and interviews.

Designing culturally sensitive research means putting diversity, equity, and inclusion (DEI) first in primary research projects. That is, from the inception of your research and throughout the process, culture and its potential impact on attitudes, values, and behaviors is considered at the forefront of your research (Baugh & Guion, 2006). When we assume that all participants have the same experiences or perceptions, we miss the mark of truly understanding how diverse audiences think, feel, and behave.

Furthermore, as researchers, we bring our own identities, perspectives, and worldviews to the research process, and can often make assumptions about communications situations based on our own experiences. These assumptions can lead to narrow and inadequate research design and bias in interpreting results. By taking a DEI-first approach, we expand our understanding of communications situations and can apply that knowledge to our campaigns and programs.

This chapter will focus on ***applied communications research***. That is, *primary research that can be applied to a specific client or organizational communications situation or challenge*. We will discuss how to take a DEI-first approach to applied research by:

- Understanding how geo-cultural contexts pertain to research ethics
- Considering DEI at every step of the research process by taking an inclusive research approach
- Exploring research methods that challenge traditional processes

DOI: 10.4324/9781003411796-7

Research Ethics and Geo-Cultural Contexts

To understand how to conduct ethical research, you may have learned (or will soon learn) the principles outlined in the ***Belmont Report***, *the set of ethical principles and guidelines developed in the United States to protect human subjects of biomedical and behavioral research.* The Belmont Report (n.d.) includes three underlying tenets:

- Respect for persons (treating people as autonomous individuals, which includes voluntary participation and informed consent).
- Beneficence (weighing the risks and benefits of research; maximizing the potential benefits while minimizing the potential harms).
- Justice (distributing the benefits and burdens of research equally).

While these three principles form the basis of most international research guidelines, ethical principles are impacted by geo-cultural contexts. Ethical research practices applied in one cultural context may not apply in another (Dahal, 2020, p. 18). To become culturally sensitive researchers, we must understand the socioeconomic, political, religious, and cultural contexts of the regions in which we conduct our research.

Regional Ethics Considerations

The principles outlined in the Belmont Report can have different meanings or be more complex to apply in regions where values of family, kinship, and community can conflict with Western notions of individualism (Czymoniewicz-Klippel et al., 2010, p. 334). In some regions of China, for example, the word "autonomy" is influenced by Confucian ethics and can have two dimensions: the autonomous person and the relational person (Pratt et al., 2014, p. 57). Thus, in areas where family coherence provides an important social system, "the well-being of the whole family must be recognized and considered" (Cheng-Tek Tai, 2013, p. 64). This concept is similar to the feminist theory of "ethics of care," which recognizes people as interdependent, relational beings (Gilligan, 1983). Likewise, in Egypt and other Arab regions, "clan obligations unite extended families – grandparents, aunts, uncles, and cousins" and thus clan elders play an important role in decision-making (Abdel-Messih et al., 2008, p. 35).

Ethical values of Indigenous peoples (like in parts of Africa, Latin America, South Asia, the Oceania region, and elsewhere) add the principles of trust and reciprocity to the ethics mix (Dahal, 2020; Lovo et al., 2021). When conducting research with Indigenous communities, relationship building is paramount. This involves respecting and understanding the cultures of Indigenous communities and taking time to build trust with community leaders and members. Reciprocity means that the knowledge gained from the research should be shared with and benefit the community as much as the researcher. Research processes influenced by Indigenous ethics often push back against traditional Western methodologies in favor of more collaborative models, which we discuss later in this chapter.

Understanding these cultural contexts can impact how we gain informed consent in different geographic areas. Whereas informed consent in the United States is individualistic, a more communitarian approach may be necessary in other regions: first gaining the trust and consent of community leaders or elders for the study to proceed, then involving clans or extended families, and finally gaining consent of the individual participant (which is always necessary) (Lovo et al., 2021).

Likewise, in a study on global research ethics, Weinbaum et al. (2019) point out that weighing the principles of beneficence and justice might not be as straightforward in lower-income regions where communities rely on clinical trials and other forms of research for both economic and medical benefits. These situations can sometimes lead to what the authors call "ethics dumping," where researchers from countries with strict ethical guidelines exploit or take advantage of the needs of poorer communities. The authors conclude that: "Contrasting circumstances in different parts of the world affect the cost-benefit analysis that undergird some research ethics in practice" (p. 50).

These are just a few of the geo-cultural nuances that could impact research efforts. If you find yourself working on a research project for an organization that operates globally, it's important to study the cultural, political, religious, and socioeconomic contexts of each area and apply the Belmont principles in a culturally sensitive way. In addition, regional cultures come together in pluralistic societies such as the United States and European Union member states, and in interactions through the internet and social media. Understanding geo-cultural ethics can help researchers better approach research projects with these diverse communities.

Emerging Global Ethics Frameworks

Another reason it's important to consider the differences and potential intersections of regional ethics is because global challenges require global solutions (Hongladarom, 2019). We saw this with the COVID-19 pandemic where the wellbeing of the individual and wellbeing of the community were intertwined. Global situations such as the advent of artificial intelligence, the global impact of climate change, and the growing refugee crisis require that we research problems with an intercultural lens to develop solutions that will work for all.

Box 6.1 The Intersection of Regional Ethics Principles

An example of a research approach that intersects regional ethics is the "Research Manifesto for Ethical Research in the Downtown Eastside" (Neufeld et al., 2019). In an area of Vancouver, Canada hit hard by economic and social inequality, the community was inundated by researchers. People living in the area felt exploited by those conducting research for their own benefit rather than the benefit of the community. Thus, academics, nonprofit organizations, and individuals came together to create a research manifesto that outlined how researchers could take a community-based approach to research: considering the values of both the researcher *and* the community; researching *with* rather than *on* members of the community; and adhering to the concept of reciprocity, using research to benefit the community as a whole and not just the researcher.

We can see in this example the respect for individuals anchored in philosophies from the West, the concept of unity and being part of the greater whole from some regions in the East, and the models of mutual respect and reciprocity grounded in African and Indigenous philosophies.

In addition, digital technologies have made it increasingly easier to collaborate on and conduct research remotely, as well as to access "big data" from countries all over the world. Newer technologies such as AI are driving consideration of ethics globally. Weinbaum et al. (2019) assert that efforts by international professional societies, like the Global Initiative on Ethics of Autonomous and Intelligent Systems, will increasingly play a role in developing global ethics frameworks (p. 52). Because younger people are entering the workforce at the advent of these technologies, your generation may be at the forefront of creating these evolving intercultural frameworks.

An Inclusive Approach to Strategic Research

For the purposes of this book, we define ***inclusive research*** as *seeking out, understanding, and considering the full spectrum of lived experiences of our audiences.* In the past, many market researchers took a mass market approach to developing audience insights, gathering data on majority opinions and then generalizing results to all identity groups (Shaw, n.d.). The problem with this approach is it assumes that all people experience our brands, products, policies, or programs in the same way.

According to Corinne Moy, council member for the European Society for Opinion and Market Research, inclusive research ensures that "everyone's voice is heard and that their opinions are respected and taken on board" (Moy, 2022). This requires that researchers take difference into account throughout the research process – from conducting background research and developing research questions, to research design and sampling, to data analysis and interpretation. From a public relations standpoint, the results of inclusive research should not only be applied to external communications; they should also inform the development of organizational policies and practices.

Culturally sensitive research should address cultural factors such as shared orientation, historical and political factors, language, worldviews, and specific behaviors that determine cultural distinctiveness (Tillman, 2002). In addition, inclusive research is accessible to all participants, with an understanding of the needs and accommodations of differing physical, sensory, and cognitive abilities.

The remainder of this section will discuss how to take an inclusive research approach in every phase of the strategic research process.

Conducting Preliminary Research and Developing Research Questions

Applied research projects often start with conducting background research on the topic or issue and developing a research objective and research questions for your study. Your background research should investigate the different cultural contexts that could impact the perspectives of your audiences and your study should include research questions that address these contexts. As discussed in Chapter 1, we often don't know what we don't know. Thus, it's important to review a variety of online or academic sources to uncover cultural nuances you may not be aware of.

For example, a student group in a communications research course wanted to investigate the impact of the TikTok "That Girl" trend (women documenting their daily health and beauty routines) on the cosmetic purchasing habits of college-aged women. In preliminary online research, they found that women of color often don't feel well represented on the TikTok app (see, for example, Brown, 2023). This led students to develop research questions addressing representation as it relates to the trend and subsequent survey questions asking participants to rate how represented they felt in skin tone, skin texture, hair type, and body shape. The results of their survey confirmed that Black and Asian participants did not feel represented in the "That Girl" trend in terms of skin tone and hair type.

The above example shows how unearthing cultural contexts at the preliminary research phase can impact each part of your study. When students began to consider culture as an explanatory variable, it led to changes in their research questions, instrument design, interpretation of the data, and implications for the client. In addition, the students were cognizant of recruiting a diversity of college women for their survey to have enough data to adequately answer their research questions.

Research Instruments: Language and Terminology

In developing culturally sensitive research, pay careful attention to the language and terminology used in your recruitment and research instruments. Language can both invoke and obscure meaning, but it also can reveal biases or lack of knowledge from the researcher, causing participants to lose confidence in the research or leave the study altogether.

Language and terminology should first be considered in how you refer to research participants. A good rule of thumb is to let participants self-identify wherever possible. In their investigation of best practices for researching race and ethnicity, Burlew et al. (2019) report that Latinx and Asian American participants prefer to be identified by country of origin, Indigenous populations by tribal affiliation, and multiracial participants prefer multiple-selection items (p. 357). Providing multiple-selection demographic items considers the intersectionality of participants.

When asking about sex, gender, or sexuality, first know the difference between the three. Second, be inclusive of the diversity of LGBTQ+ identities and let participants self-select in their own words whenever possible (see Vanderbilt University, n.d.). To create inclusive surveys, Penn Libraries (n.d.) also recommends including a "prefer not to say" option, a "none of these" option, and to randomize how the identities are displayed to avoid bias of one identity over another. Also avoid using "other" boxes as this can signal to participants that their identities are outside the "norm."

In developing research instruments, use inclusive language, take historical or cultural contexts into consideration, and avoid terms that invoke stereotypes or bias. For example, asking parents in a survey if they follow any "mom bloggers" isn't inclusive of the many fathers who blog on parenting. When researching social identities that you are unfamiliar with, use background research to better understand participants' use of terminology within social identity groups.

Another reason to pay attention to language is that terms can mean different things to different people. For example, the term "out of pocket" to an American can mean someone is not available; in the UK it can mean out of money. And, to some African Americans, it can mean out of line or acting inappropriately. From this example, we can see that phrases have different meanings depending on geography and culture.

Recruiting Participants and Conducting Your Research

Many strategic communications students are required to take a research class where they conduct primary research projects with their peers as participants. When reaching out to peers, students often find that participants end up mirroring their own identities (the same class year, gender, race, etc.). But this phenomenon is not limited to the classroom. In 2010, behavioral scientists Henrich et al. found that most participants in psychological research studies were Western, Educated, Industrialized, Rich, and Democratic – or WEIRD as an acronym. Yet, scientists were making broad-based assumptions about human psychology based on this narrow group.

Whether in the classroom or the professional world, avoiding a narrow research sample requires being intentional in your recruitment efforts and developing a strategy to effectively include diverse participants (Burlew et al., 2019). This can be done in several ways, including reaching out to community partners (as described below), hiring research professionals like the Inclusive Market Research group who are experienced in reaching diverse audiences, or including quotas in quantitative samples for key groups of interest (Moy, 2022). Explore different ways to recruit participants based on group preference. For example, marginalized communities may feel more comfortable participating in research with community groups they already know and trust.

When conducting focus groups or interviews, consider the comfort level of participants with the interviewer or moderator. Burlew et al. (2019) found that the race or ethnicity of the interviewer can impact participants' responses. Also consider the topic of your interview or focus group and whether it requires engaging separate focus groups. When researching a sensitive topic like sexual relationships, for example, participants may feel more comfortable in a focus group with others of their same identity group.

Consulting with Community Experts

The optimal way to conduct inclusive research is with an inclusive research team. If your research team lacks diversity, it's best to consult with someone from the community when designing and recruiting for your study. This could include consulting with academic experts, local or national nonprofit organizations, or others who are trusted in the community.

For example, during the COVID-19 pandemic, the Ad Council in the United States embarked on a vaccine education initiative in partnership with the COVID Collaborative. By bringing in experts who were adept at understanding and reaching different cultural communities, they found that people have different reasons for vaccine hesitancy based on race, nationality, and religion (Ad Council, n.d.). Without this understanding, they would have taken a one-size-fits-all approach to the campaign rather than developing content that addressed the unique needs of each community.

You may also consider partnering with local organizations or experts to conduct your research. We discuss this type of collaborative research later in the chapter.

Representing People with Disabilities

Disability should be treated like any other aspect of diversity and inclusion, including the understanding that people with disabilities come from all walks of life and thus have intersectional identities.

To represent people with disabilities in your research, it's important to first understand the diversity of people's experiences. People with disabilities include those with physical disabilities such as mobility issues; sensory disabilities such as vision or hearing loss; mental illness, cognitive or neurological disabilities; or those with long-term illnesses (United Nations, 2006). In addition, disability is often not visible and can change over time (Benness, 2019). Thus, answers to questions about disabilities may differ depending on when participants are surveyed or interviewed.

Diversity of experiences also relates to how people talk about their disability. Some people prefer people-first language (person with a disability), while others may have a different preference. As with other diverse communities, it's helpful to ask research participants to self-identity in surveys or ask how they would like you to refer to their disability in interviews or focus groups (Hermans, 2023). Terminology in this community changes frequently and preference is determined on an individual basis. Consider using resources like the Disability Language Style Guide (2021) to help frame questions that are language sensitive as well as inquiring about preferences during the research process.

When recruiting research participants, ask what accommodations participants might need – like screen readers, sign language interpreters, or accessible access to research facilities – and adapt consent forms to each participant's unique needs. As with all consent, participants may not feel comfortable disclosing their disability or answering certain questions. Be cognizant of participants' privacy – never force participants to disclose information – and make questions optional (Inclusive Research, 2021). In creating research materials, develop a habit of making materials compliant with the Americans with Disabilities Act (or the legal framework from your region).

People with disabilities may need flexible timelines to participate in or complete your research. For example, a participant may rely on a caretaker or transportation service to get them to a research facility, or someone with a chronic illness may not feel well enough to participate on a certain day and need to reschedule. Develop the timeframe for your research accordingly.

Analyzing and Reporting Research Results

In quantitative research, we often include demographic questions in our research only to compare how identity groups differ from the dominant group. In doing so, we center the dominant group as the "norm" while further marginalizing already marginalized communities. By comparing results *only* on demographic differences or combining all demographics and only looking for the mode (most frequently occurring variables), we often ignore the cultural contexts that could explain those differences.

One way to avoid this is to disaggregate data. *Disaggregating* data means *to break data down into distinctive categories, often by social identity groups such as race, gender, or income.* This data can then be further disaggregated by within-group differences. For example, when researching voting patterns, we often see polls report on demographic differences of race, lumping everyone from the same race together. This doesn't help us understand voting patterns of, say, Latinx voters. By disaggregating data by country of origin, we can further understand that Cuban Americans vote very differently than Mexican Americans and begin to explain the cultural nuances that underly those voting patterns. Disaggregating data should be discussed *before* designing your research project so you can design your research in the most effective way to develop meaningful analysis.

Another way to analyze cultural differences is to move back and forth between quantitative and qualitative data (Martin Rogers, 2018). While quantitative data can show you the "what" of overall patterns, qualitative data is much more helpful in investigating the "why" of those patterns. For example, if Apple had had in-depth conversations with women before it launched the AirTag, women would likely have raised a red flag about the tags' potential to enable stalking, which is exactly what happened (see, for example, Pritchard, 2022).

When reporting on cultural differences in your results, don't just report that there *are* differences, determine the cultural mechanisms that may account for those differences (Awad et al., 2016). These contexts should then be used to determine the implications of your research for your communications.

Avoiding Harm

When researching diverse communities, researchers need to pay particular attention to avoiding harm. In addition to the vulnerable subjects outlined in the Belmont Report, marginalized communities can experience additional harms based on their social identity. This includes harms from discussing sensitive topics like racism, homophobia, or socioeconomic status.

For example, be aware of stereotype threat when researching diverse groups. *Stereotype threat is the pressure to avoid being judged by negative group stereotypes.* Stereotype threat can impede information processing and prevent participants from speaking honestly with researchers (Burlew et al., 2019). For example, Black women may avoid showing emotions in focus groups to avoid the stereotype of the "angry Black woman."

When researching LGBTQ+ identity groups, the LGBT Foundation (n.d.) in the UK has developed an ethics guide that outlines best practices and approaches. Researchers can avoid harms by using LGBTQ+ inclusive language, familiarizing themselves with the full spectrum of gender identity, identifying support services that may be needed when discussing sensitive topics, and ensuring that research will be used for the benefit of the community rather than exploiting them. In addition, pay special care to anonymity and confidentiality to avoid unintentionally outing someone during the research process.

Nontraditional, Collaborative Research Methods

Traditionally, Western research methods have taken a positivist approach to social science research. The positivist approach asserts that reality is objective, and the role of the researcher is to be a neutral observer who looks for patterns and then generalizes them to the larger population. While the Western view can shed light on cultural differences, it can often silence the very voices we wish to uplift, discounting the ability of communities to identify, understand, and analyze their own situations (Zavala, 2013).

In recent decades, more *collaborative research approaches* have emerged in which *researchers and participants share equal power as co-creators of knowledge. These approaches share the common principle of researching* with *rather than* on *vulnerable communities* (Gomez et al., 2019, p. 3). Collaborative research approaches go by many names, including decolonizing research, community-based research (CBR), communicative research, inclusive research, participatory action research (PAR), and community-based participatory research (CBPR). While each vary in underlying ideologies, they share some common principles, which are outlined below.

Focus on Community-Identified Needs

In traditional research studies, academic and professional researchers identify the topic and outline the research questions they want to address. This approach, however, often leaves out the issues that are important to the community participating in the research.

For example, in the field of public relations, where building mutually beneficial relationships is a key tenet, Aghazadeh and Aldoory (2023) point out that PR research has historically been used to reach organizational goals, but rarely used to identify and address community needs (p. 1). They state: "Without engaging publics fully and without a willingness to prioritize their interests, practitioners and researchers risk not truly addressing their needs in PR efforts, such as campaigns and social advocacy" (p. 2).

By putting community-identified needs first, strategic researchers can make the process truly mutually beneficial, building greater trust with the communities with which they are researching. In addition, when participants know their needs are being prioritized, they are much more likely to participate in the research.

Participants as Co-Creators of Knowledge

At the heart of collaborative research is the principle that both researchers and participants share equally in the co-creation of knowledge. This means engaging individuals, communities, and community organizations throughout the research process, from developing the research questions and design to analyzing and interpreting results. Treating participants as co-creators of knowledge transforms the research process, from one where the researcher holds all the power to one that acknowledges multiple means of knowledge construction and where the community sets the direction for the research (Zavala, 2013). In cultural contexts, these "ways of knowing" are often grounded in cultural experiences and ancestral histories, as well as in the relational and community contexts in which interactions occur (Datta, 2018; Gerlach, 2018).

Collaborative research approaches are less about which types of data-gathering methods are used and more about the process of collaborating (Zavala, 2013). For example, Gomez et al. (2019) describe strategies such as advisory committees, working groups, and plenary meetings as some ways to manage the collaboration process (pp. 4–5). Specific methodologies for gathering data should be based on the cultural and community contexts for the project and may include more intuitive methods like dialogic discussions and storytelling. While methodologies for collaborative research are often qualitative in nature, they can also be quantitative or a combination of the two.

Action-Based Impact

A third principle often shared by collaborative processes is that of effecting change. That is, along with identifying community-based needs, the research should lead to developing solutions that address those needs. Results and

---

Box 6.2 The LGBTQ Institute's Community-Based Research Approach

To examine the experiences of LGBTQ+ people in the American South, the LGBTQ Institute used a community-based participatory research model to conduct its inaugural Southern Survey (Wright et al., 2018). The Institute's advisory board (a collective of advocates and academics) established the areas of focus for the survey, and then, over the course of a year, "quarterly public meetings were held to obtain community input on key questions they would like to be asked" (p. 3). More than 150 people attended the meetings and provided input. To recruit participants, the Institute partnered with 146 non-profit and community organizations. Partners received recognition, participated in bi-weekly conference calls, and could use the data for their own policy development and advocacy needs (p. 4).

---

proposed solutions should be collaboratively shared with others in the community and with those who have the power to institute change. In addition, collaborative research can empower participants to enact change on their own (Institute of Development Studies, n.d.).

Several examples of action-based research can be found at the Youth Participatory Action Research Hub (YPAR). Housed at UC Berkeley, YPAR trains youth to "conduct systematic research that improves their lives, their communities, and the institutions intended to serve them" (UC Berkeley, n.d.). The process has been used by young people in Guatemala to research issues impacting their health and wellbeing and propose solutions to political decision makers; by students in San Francisco to address gender bias in the school dress code; and by youth in Salinas, California to investigate and propose solutions to environmental chemical exposures in the area.

Collaborative Research in Strategic Communications

Aghazadeh and Aldoory (2023) urge the PR field to explore the use of community-based participatory research models to fulfill the PR principle of building mutually exclusive relationships, improve community welfare, foster cultural understanding, and enact social change (pp. 1–2). However, they caution that collaborative research approaches are not suitable for every research project and require considerations such as researcher expertise, time, flexibility, and resources (pp. 5–6).

Collaborative approaches can work best in situations where the goals for the research and the goals of the community align. They are particularly useful in social justice work and community development and have been used extensively in health interventions, education, and by nongovernmental organizations. Vaughn and Jacquez, (2020) also report that "researchers across disciplines have increasingly engaged all types of stakeholders, including consumers, end-users, patients, youth, and individuals from marginalized communities" in participatory research approaches.

In some industries, collaborative research is considered on a continuum, with varying levels of community involvement (Vaughn & Jacquez, 2020). In strategic communications research, this continuum could extend from being consultant-driven on one end of the spectrum, where researchers consult with community members on their research design, to community-driven on the other end, where an extensive collaborative research model with shared decision-making is employed. Regardless of which level you employ, practitioners should conduct extensive research on the principles and processes of collaborative research before engaging in such a project.

Bibliography

Abdel-Messih, I. A., El-Setouhy, M., Crouch, M. M., & Earhart, K. C. (2008). Developing cultural competence and overcoming ethical challenges in the informed consent process: An experience from Egypt. *The Journal of Research Administration*, *39*(2), 33–40.

Ad Council. (n.d.). *The history of our COVID-19 vaccine education initiative*. www. adcouncil.org/our-impact/covid-vaccine/our-covid-19-vaccine-retrospective

Aghazadeh, S., & Aldoory, L. (2023). Community based participatory research for public relations: Realizing potential for researcher–participant relationships. *PR Review*, *49*(1), 102290. https://doi.org/10.1016/j.pubrev.2023.102290

Awad, G. H., Patall, E. A., Rackley, K. R., & Reilly, E. D. (2016). Recommendations for culturally sensitive research methods. *Journal of Educational and Psychological Consultation*, *26*(3), 283–303. https://doi.org/10.1080/10474412.2015.1046600

Baugh, E., & Guion, L. (2006). Using culturally sensitive methodologies when researching diverse cultures. *Journal of Multidisciplinary Evaluation*, *4*(1), 1–12.

The Belmont Report. (n.d.). U.S. Department of Health and Human Services. www. hhs.gov/ohrp/regulations-and-policy/belmont-report/index.html

Benness, B. (2019, December 8). *My disability is dynamic*. Medium. https://medium. com/age-of-awareness/my-disability-is-dynamic-bc2a619fcc1

Brown, M. (2023, January 18). #BlackGirlFollowTrain creates a network for Black female content creators to support one another. NBC News. www.nbcnews.com/ news/nbcblk/blackgirlfollowtrain-provides-community-black-women-tiktok-rcna65551

Burlew, K. A., Peteet, B. J., McCuistian, C., & Miller-Roenigk, B. D. (2019). Best practices for researching diverse groups. *American Journal of Orthopsychiatry*, *89*(3), 354–368. https://doi.org/10.1037/ort0000350

Cheng-Tek Tai, M. (2013). Western or Eastern ethics in globalized bioethics? An Asian perspective. *Tzu Chi Medical Journal, 25*(1), 64–67. https://doi.org/10.1016/j.tcmj.2012.05.004

Czymoniewicz-Klippel, M. T., Brijnath, B., & Crockett, B. (2010). Ethics and the promotion of inclusiveness within qualitative research: Case examples from Asia and the Pacific. *Qualitative Inquiry, 16*(5), 332–341. https://doi.org/10.1177/1077800409358872

Dahal, B. (2020). Research ethics: A perspective of South Asian context. *Edukacja, 1*(152), 9–20. https://ibe.edu.pl/images/EDUKACJA/NUMERY/2020-01/PDF/1._Research_Ethics_A_Perspective_of_South_Asian_Context.pdf

Datta, R. (2018). Decolonizing both researcher and research and its effectiveness in Indigenous research. *Research Ethics, 14*(2), 1–24. https://doi.org/10.1177/1747016117733296

Disability Language Style Guide. (2021). National Center on Disability and Journalism, Arizona State University. https://ncdj.org/style-guide/

Gerlach, A. (2018). Thinking and researching relationally: Enacting decolonizing methodologies within an Indigenous early childhood program in Canada. *International Journal of Qualitative Methods, 17*, 1–8. https://doi.org/10.1177/1609406918776075

Gilligan, C. (1983). Do the social sciences have an adequate theory of moral development? In N. Haan, R. N. Bellah, P. Rabinow, & W. M. Sullivan (Eds.), *Social science as moral inquiry* (pp. 33–51). Columbia University Press.

Gomez, A., Padros, M., Rios, O., Mara, L-C., & Pukepuke, T. (2019). Reaching social impact through communicative methodology. Researching with rather than on vulnerable populations: The Roma case. *Frontiers in Education, 4*(9). https://doi.org/10.3389/feduc.2019.00009

Henrich, J., Heine, S. J., & Norenzayan, A. (2010). The weirdest people in the world? *Behavioral and Brain Sciences, 33*(2–3), 61–83. https://doi.org/10.1017/S0140525X0999152X

Hermans, A. (2023, January 3). *How can research better represent people with disabilities?* Urban Institute. www.urban.org/urban-wire/how-can-research-better-represent-people-disabilities

Hongladarom, S. (2019, May 21). *The case for uniting East and West to build ethical AI.* Quartz. https://qz.com/1620028/we-need-to-unite-eastern-and-western-philosophies-to-build-ethical-ai/

Inclusive Research. (2021, May 18). *Introduction: A practical guide to inclusive research.* Medium. https://medium.com/inclusive-research/introduction-a-practical-guide-to-inclusive-research-8a3c87375b0e

Institute of Development Studies. (n.d.). *Participatory action research.* www.participatorymethods.org/glossary/participatory-action-research

LGBT Foundation. (n.d.). *Ethical research: Good practice guide to researching LGBT communities and issues.* https://lgbt.foundation/wp-content/uploads/2023/08/Ethics20Guide.pdf

Lovo, E., Woodward, L., Larkins, S., Preston, R., & Nabobo Baba, U. (2021). Indigenous knowledge around the ethics of human research from the Oceania region: A scoping literature review. *Philosophy, Ethics, and Humanities in Medicine, 16*(12). https://doi.org/10.1186/s13010-021-00108-8

Martin Rogers, N. (2018, April 4). *Race data disaggregation: What does it mean? Why does it matter?* Minnesota Compass. www.mncompass.org/data-insights/articles/race-data-disaggregation-what-does-it-mean-why-does-it-matter

Moy, C. (2022, November 29). *Consumer insights need an inclusive approach too.* World Federation of Advertisers. https://wfanet.org/knowledge/item/2022/11/29/Consumer-Insights-needs-an-inclusive-approach-too

Neufeld, S. D., Chapman, J., Crier, N., Marsh, S., McLeod, J., & Deane, L. A. (2019). Research 101: A process for developing local guidelines for ethical research in heavily researched communities. *Harm Reduction Journal, 16*(1), 1–11. https://doi.org/10.1186/s12954-019-0315-5

Penn Libraries. (n.d.). *Creating inclusive surveys.* https://guides.library.upenn.edu/inclusive-surveys/demographics

Pratt, B., Van, C., Cong, Y., Rashid, H., Kumar, N., Ahmad, A., Upshur, R., & Loff, B. (2014). Perspectives from South and East Asia on clinical and research ethics: A literature review. *Journal of Empirical Research on Human Research Ethics, 9*(2), 52–67. https://doi.org/10.1525/jer.2014.9.2.52

Pritchard, T. (2022, April 7). *Apple AirTag stalking is worse than anyone realized – what you can do.* Tom's Guide. www.tomsguide.com/news/apple-airtag-stalking-is-worse-than-anyone-realized-what-you-can-do

Shaw, J. (n.d.). *A practical guide to inclusive market research.* Kadence International. https://kadence.com/a-practical-guide-to-inclusive-market-research/

Tillman, L. C. (2002). Culturally sensitive research approaches: An African-American perspective. *Educational Researcher, 31*(9), 3–12.

UC Berkeley. (n.d.). *Youth Participatory Action Research Hub.* https://yparhub.berkeley.edu/why-ypar

United Nations. (2006). *Convention on the Rights of Persons with Disabilities.* Adopted 12 December 2006. www.ohchr.org/en/instruments-mechanisms/instruments/convention-rights-persons-disabilities

Vanderbilt University. (n.d.). *How to ask about sexuality/gender.* www.vanderbilt.edu/lgbtqi/resources/how-to-ask-about-sexuality-gender

Vaughn, L. M. & Jacquez, F. (2020). Participatory research methods: Choice points in the research process. *Journal of Participatory Research Methods, 1*(1). https://doi.org/10.35844/001c.13244

Weinbaum, C., Landree, E., Blumenthal, M., Piquado, T., & Gutierrez, C. I. (2019). *Ethics in scientific research: An examination of ethical principles and emerging topics.* RAND Corporation. www.rand.org/pubs/research_reports/RR2912.html

Wright, E., Roemerman, R., & Higbee, M. (2018). *LGBTQ Institute Southern Survey: Design and methodological overview.* The LGBTQ Institute at the National Center for Civil and Human Rights.

Zavala, M. (2013). What do we mean by decolonizing research strategies? Lessons from decolonizing, indigenous research projects in New Zealand and Latin America. *Decolonization: Indigeneity, Education & Society, 2*(1), 55–71. https://digitalcommons.chapman.edu/education_articles/index.3.html

7 Integrating DEI into the Campaigns Planning Process

Lee Bush

When we understand the importance of diversity, equity, and inclusion (DEI) in strategic communications, we begin to understand our role as communicators in stewarding inclusive campaigns. Whether we work for an agency, a corporation, or a nonprofit or government entity, our role as culturally proficient campaign planners is three pronged: developing campaigns that are representative and inclusive of our audiences, building a more equitable ecosystem in which the industry operates, and working toward fostering a more inclusive and equitable society. This means bringing diverse audiences into the planning process and acting on their concerns; expanding visibility and support for diverse media outlets; diversifying our supplier base and paying them equitably; and exploring where our organizational goals align with social justice issues.

In earlier chapters, you learned how to put DEI first in every aspect of strategic communications. Here, we put it all together to develop inclusive and equitable campaigns by:

- Discussing the alignment of the business and moral case for DEI
- Learning how to approach preliminary research with intentionality
- Exploring tools for integrating DEI into campaign goals and objectives
- Taking a cultural approach to audience selection and strategy development
- Revisiting lessons learned in earlier chapters for developing creative content
- Discussing industry practices for supporting diverse media outlets
- Exploring emerging questions in campaign measurement and evaluation

Why Inclusive Campaigns Matter

In Chapter 1, we discussed two rationales for practicing DEI in strategic communications: the business case and the moral case.

DOI: 10.4324/9781003411796-8

In describing the business case, organizations often point to the purchasing power of diverse audiences. For example, in the United States, the buying power of African Americans, Native Americans, and Asian Americans combined rose from $458 billion in 1990 to $3.2 trillion in 2021, making up 17.4% of America's total $18.5 trillion buying power (Melancon, 2023). Likewise, the buying power of Hispanic households during this timeframe rose from $213 billion to $2.1 trillion, or 11.3% of the total U.S. buying power (Melancon, 2023). In addition, the buying power of the U.S. LGBTQ+ community was $1.4 trillion in 2022 and $4.7 trillion globally (LGBT Capital, 2022). These statistics will continue to increase over the coming decade.

While these numbers help us see the total market for inclusive campaigns, strategic communications is about more than persuading an audience to purchase a brand or product. It's about building mutually beneficial relationships with stakeholders and developing campaigns that are relevant to and connect with our audiences. In this realm, the industry is moving toward linking the business and moral case for DEI, with an understanding that the two are intrinsically intertwined. Matterkind (2022), a media marketing company under Interpublic Group's Kinesso brand, calls this "conscious marketing": "marketing that is relevant and respectful to people while still delivering for brands" (p. 5).

For example, a Microsoft Advertising study (2020) determined that inclusive advertising drives trust, builds loyalty, and leads to purchase intent for Gen Z consumers. Microsoft found that authentic representation drove trust with all Gen Z identity groups and produced feelings of joy, acceptance, safety, confidence, celebration, relief, and relaxation (p. 5). Conversely, 49% have stopped purchasing from brands that don't represent their values (p. 4).

In relation to the moral case for DEI, the theory of corporate responsibility to race (Logan, 2021) discussed in Chapter 1 outlines the responsibility organizations have in achieving a more equitable society because of past racial harms perpetuated by corporations. Dentsu, one of the world's largest communications conglomerates, recognizes this responsibility and takes a bold stance in its DEI report to "build a fair and more equal society where everyone is equipped to thrive" (Dentsu, 2022, p. 4). A few of its initiatives include partnering with the World Economic Forum's Racial Justice in Business Initiative, instituting a Cultural Fluency methodology in its strategic planning and creative processes, and taking steps to mitigate bias in its AI (artificial intelligence) tools.

In the process of building more inclusive campaigns, the industry is realizing that the ecosystem in which we operate is itself not equitable. Industry systems and practices often exclude content creators and influencers with diverse identities, don't include diverse media outlets in media planning models, and lack equitable practices in hiring and paying diverse suppliers.

Building inclusive campaigns also means making progress on these issues as we work through our planning processes.

In the remainder of this chapter, we go through a few key components of the planning process and discuss how you can take a more inclusive and equitable approach in each.

Preliminary Research

Regardless of which planning model you use, almost all start with research – both formal and informal. It's important to note, however, that research happens at all phases of the planning process, not just at the beginning. While Chapter 6 addresses in detail how to conduct inclusive primary research, here we will focus on conducting informal, or secondary, research with intentionality.

The Client Briefing

One of the first ways we gather information is through the client briefing. Whether your client is internal or external, a client briefing gives planners the opportunity to better understand the client's challenge and ask deeper questions about the client's goals and desires. Embedding DEI into your campaign should start here, by interrogating how DEI can and should be incorporated into the campaign.

A few questions you might want to ask include:

- What are the organization's values when it comes to DEI? Does the organization have a DEI statement? Is it published? In what ways do they fulfill their DEI commitment?
- What is the organization doing to make their workplace more inclusive and equitable? Do they have internal goals and strategies in place? If so, how can their external campaign align with these internal strategies?
- What is the organization's history and reputation with diverse audiences? Is the organization known for being inclusive in its external communications? Have their past campaigns been inclusive of diverse audiences and cultures? If so, in what ways?
- Are there any specific DEI areas that need to be addressed in the campaign? What mistakes has the organization made that need to be rectified? Conversely, are there opportunities to elevate the organization's DEI initiatives and impacts?

Acknowledging that organizations are at different places in their DEI maturity – with some fully committed and others unaware of or just beginning to address it – bringing these issues to the forefront is a good place to start. It helps planners know where and how an inclusive campaign might align with the organization's values; or, conversely, where an inclusive campaign might be seen as empty rhetoric.

Be prepared to answer client questions about why inclusive campaigns are important. Here you can cite both the moral and business case, and how the two are intertwined.

Background/Secondary Research

When embarking on a strategic campaign plan, we often start by conducting background research and developing a research brief. A research brief might include background on the client or issue, the market, current trends in the category, competitors, target audiences, media coverage, previous or similar campaigns, or critical social or political issues that could impact the campaign.

When conducting background research, our natural tendency is to view this research from our own perspective and experiences. However, this can mean we miss key pieces of information or misinterpret data by not considering other contexts. The key is to develop an ***inclusive research brief, one that looks at the problem or challenge through different cultural lenses and approaches DEI with intentionality***.

What does it mean to approach DEI with intentionality in a research brief? Let's look at an example. Let's say you have been asked to develop a communications campaign for a streaming TV client. If you conduct a general Google search on the market for streaming, you'll find information on the size of the market, the key players, how the market is segmented (by channel, component, region, etc.), and trends in the streaming market. You might stop there, but you would miss key information that could impact your campaign. For example, searching with intentionality by intersecting the streaming market and African Americans, you would find that Black viewers use free ad-supported streaming services more than other viewers, are more likely to have 5G internet subscriptions, and that, while 60% believe showcasing diverse content is critical to choosing a streaming platform, only 32% believe portrayals of the Black community are accurate (Media Culture, 2023).

Searching further with intentionality, you would find that 80% of people with disabilities in the UK have experienced accessibility issues with streaming, including issues like no or poor captions, bad navigation, no audio descriptions, or flashing images (Scope, 2020). Further, you would find that a new streaming service was launched in July 2023 with content by and about people with disabilities (Heasley, 2023).

This information gives you a broader and deeper perspective on the client challenge and unlocks opportunities to connect more authentically with existing or emerging audiences. You can then identify where there are gaps in secondary research that need to be further explored in primary research for your campaign.

Defining the Challenge and Setting Goals and Objectives

After preliminary research and analysis, the next step in the planning process is to clearly define the challenge or opportunity and develop goals and objectives for the campaign. Goals are the broad, general outcomes desired, while objectives focus on specific, measurable impacts for the campaign. If you think of your campaign as a roadmap, goals can be considered your final destination – where you want to arrive – while objectives are the milestones you want to reach along the way. Below are two tools to use in this process.

Conduct a SWOT-DEI Analysis

After conducting preliminary research, campaign planners often apply that research to a SWOT analysis to identify and evaluate the Strengths, Weaknesses, Opportunities, and Threats for an organization or campaign. In recent years, the process has been used to analyze DEI initiatives in the workplace (Crevecoeurve West, 2023) and in economic development and public health initiatives. For example, the Public Health Foundation in Washington, D.C. has recently introduced a SWOT-IE process to examine how health departments are addressing issues of equity and inclusion in their communities (PHF, 2023).

While the SWOT analysis process is beneficial to external campaign planning, rarely do we think to incorporate DEI into this analysis. There are two ways you can do so. First, you could conduct a traditional SWOT analysis for your campaign, and then add elements to the analysis addressing equity and inclusion. However, this treats DEI as a separate issue rather than an integral part of the planning process. Instead, we recommend conducting your SWOT with an intersectional DEI mindset from the start.

Let's take the above discussion of a streaming platform brand as an example. A strength for your campaign might be that you have a strong brand identity with the general market. However, applying a DEI mindset would mean taking this a step further to ask, "With *whom* do we have a strong brand identity? Is our brand identity positive for all our audiences?" For example, you know from your secondary research that people with disabilities have experienced accessibility issues with streaming platforms. And, looking at your research through the lens of intersectionality would tell you that Black streaming users with disabilities may feel underrepresented in both race *and* accessibility. Thus, while you may have a strong brand identity with *some* audiences, you may have weaknesses with others that could be specifically addressed in your campaign.

Applying a DEI mindset to the SWOT analysis is particularly helpful in identifying missed opportunities to expand your market, weaknesses in addressing the needs of diverse audiences, or identifying threats that may not be on your radar. For example, while TikTok's growth has skyrocketed since its launch in 2016, Black content creators have questioned whether they are equally seen and supported on the platform (Brown, 2023). TikTok executives have acknowledged this criticism and laid out action steps to foster a more inclusive community, including establishing a creator diversity council and engaging experts in reviewing its products and policies (Pappas & Chikumbu, 2020). If left unaddressed, this issue could threaten TikTok's community principles of preventing harm and championing inclusion, and its mission "to inspire creativity and bring joy" (TikTok, 2023).

SMART+IE Objectives

Long used by communications professionals in campaign planning, the SMART acronym stands for developing objectives that are Specific, Measurable, Audience-Focused (as well as attainable, achievable), Realistic, and Time-bound. Similar to incorporating DEI into the SWOT analysis process, Waters et al. (2022) advocate for integrating an inclusion and equity (+IE) mindset into the SMART objective-setting process.

Before embarking on a SMART+IE mindset, the authors recommend first examining the organization's mission and commitment to DEI, and how this commitment is being carried out in the organization. Only when DEI is woven into the culture can an inclusion and equity mindset be extended systemically to external campaigns. In developing SMART+IE objectives, the authors propose four questions to be considered by campaign planners (pp. 144–145):

1. How does the campaign lift up marginalized communities?
2. Is clear, engaging language used to include traditionally excluded audiences?
3. Are metrics in place to assess the +IE components?
4. How does the campaign align with the DEI perspectives of the organization?

The authors advocate involving diverse voices in the campaign planning process to avoid tokensim and elevate marginalized voices, to consider what harm might come from either intentionally or unintentionally excluding different stakeholders, and to ask what systemic changes are impacted by the work. They state: "By incorporating inclusion and equity into every objective written to guide campaigns, they (practitioners) are showing a true commitment to social justice and holding themselves accountable to their organizations and clients as well as broader society" (p. 146).

Waters and Farwell (2022, pp. 194–195) give an example of turning a SMART objective into a SMART+IE objective in an employee recruitment campaign.

> SMART Objective: "Recruit a team of 50 new entry-level employees from the Dallas-Fort Worth Metroplex for Project XYZ by August 31, 2022."

> SMART+IE Objective: "Recruit a team of 50 new entry-level employees from the Dallas-Fort Worth Metroplex for Project XYZ using feedback from internal BIPOC and LGBTQ employee resource groups by August 31, 2022."

The revised objective leads to recruiting a more inclusive team of employees by bringing the knowledge and experiences of traditionally marginalized voices into the recruiting process.

Taking a Cultural Approach to Audience Selection and Strategy Development

The above integration of DEI into the SWOT and SMART campaign planning processes helps communicators develop relevant goals and objectives for the campaign and drives the next phase of campaign planning: audience selection and strategy development. In this area of campaign planning, the industry is seeing a paradigm shift.

In the past, campaign planners often targeted the "general market," a broad, amorphous notion of a mostly homogenous audience, often segmented by demographics or psychographics. However, this approach can lead to leaving out marginalized communities, minimize intersectionality, and ignore important historical and sociopolitical contexts that influence our identities. In essence, when you target everyone "in general," you end up targeting no one. As content marketing strategist Andrew Chen (2022) states: "Brands must learn to redefine the general market … The antiquated notion of a 'general market' target that is nondiverse is quickly being replaced by tailored brand strategies that take into account the unique consumer mindsets of various groups."

Taking a ***cultural approach to audience segmentation*** *where the unique needs, experiences, cultures, and intersectional identities of audiences are considered in campaign planning* can be more effective in developing campaigns that are authentic, relevant, and more meaningful for our audiences. From various industry resources (AXInsights, 2022; Blair Loeb, 2021; Conscious Ad Network, n.d.; Daykin and Smith, n.d.-a), here are key questions to consider when developing your audience.

- Who does your audience leave out? This question may be even more important than who your audience includes. You might be surprised to find that identities excluded from your organization's leadership and management – as well as your campaign team – are the same identities excluded from target audiences.
- Does your audience reflect where the market or issue is headed? Or are there audiences you've ignored in the past that could help grow your brand, organization, or sphere of influence and advocacy?
- Is your audience understanding steeped in genuine cultural insights into diverse perspectives? Or are your research insights homogenous generalizations about the "general market"?
- How do diverse audiences perceive your brand or organization? Are perceptions similar? Or do certain identity groups view your brand differently?
- What are the experiences, needs, and values of your audience as they relate to your brand, service, or issue? Are they similar? Or are there differences that could impact how communities connect with your brand or issue?

The answer to these questions can help you begin to identify target audiences, conduct additional research where there are gaps in your knowledge, and create strategies that will resonate with each segment. In many cases, these strategies may converge; in others, they may diverge and require nuanced content and messaging for different audience segments. For instance, in the streaming TV example above, you may want to create messaging that addresses the accessibility frustration of people with disabilities. To do so, you'd first want to connect with the disability community to determine where your streaming product could address these frustrations and get their input on the best strategies for communicating to people with disabilities.

Taking a cultural approach to audience segmentation can reveal new strategies that more traditional segmentation might not consider. These include establishing and building previously unidentified community relationships; partnering with organizations that are engaged with underrepresented communities; advocating for causes that are important to your audience; and creating added value for consumers through new products or services that address their specific needs.

Representation and Creative Development

Our responsibility in developing messaging and creative content is twofold: to eliminate biases and harmful stereotypes and to develop content that authentically reflects the diverse cultures that make up our audiences. Chapter 4 provides extensive guidance on creative development. We reiterate some of this guidance below and provide additional considerations.

Eliminate Stereotypes

At the very base level, we need to ensure that our content doesn't create or perpetuate harmful stereotypes. Let's revisit, from Chapter 1, what a ***stereotype*** is: *applying uneducated judgements or generalizations to everyone in a group*. For example, we may make assumptions that everyone who is homeless doesn't have a job, when in fact more than half of unhoused people in the United States do. Or that all Asian people are good at math. Or that all Latinos are immigrants. Or that all women are "nurturing," while all men are "unemotional." When it comes to creative storytelling, these stereotypes can often be turned into harmful tropes or devices we fall back on to tell a story.

Not only are these stereotypes and tropes inaccurate, but they are also harmful to the people being stereotyped and can shape the way society understands and categorizes people (Wang Yuen, 2019). For example, a study by the Campaign Against Living Miserably (CALM, 2021), a suicide prevention movement in the UK, found that stereotypes of men as being unemotional, lazy, or "sex obsessed" can do real psychological damage and prevent men from seeking mental health resources when they need them. These stereotypes are compounded for men of color and gay or nonbinary men.

As both storytellers and members of society, we are exposed to these stereotypes too. So, knowing we have our own unconscious biases, how do we achieve a more inclusive creative process?

Start with Your Creative Brief

The World Federation of Advertisers' "Guide to potential areas for bias in the creative process" is a helpful resource in this area (Daykin & Smith, n.d.-a). In developing the creative comms brief, they start with the question: "Are you bringing representative inspiration and deep insight to the brief?" (p. 6). If representation and culture are important to your campaign (and they should be), you need to spell that out in your brief and make it top of mind in the development process. Likewise, the Geena Davis Institute on Gender and Media says to "get specific" about social identity in your campaigns, briefs, and casting documents using an intersectional lens; sexualize women less; write and cast for a wider range of social identities; and "establish tangible measurements to evaluate your creative briefs before moving into production" (Alcantara, n.d.). Many agencies have instituted creative review boards to check creative work for stereotypes and authentic storytelling.

As outlined in Chapter 4, authentic representation doesn't mean just plopping a few diverse images in your social media ad or PR campaign. Authentic representation means your characters "go beyond being a 'mannequin' for the product" and that your content gives voice, agency, and authority to the people whose stories are being told (Unstereotype Alliance, 2021). Your creative will be more effective when you provide an authentic and comprehensive picture of your audiences and what your brand can do for them.

Bring in Different Perspectives

It's worth emphasizing, as we have throughout this text, that diverse teams create more inclusive campaigns. If this diversity is absent in your teams, you could fall prey to **cultural reductionism**, *unable to view situations from a perspective other than your own* (Krownapple, 2016, p. 131), as discussed in Chapter 1. Bringing in individuals, experts, or organizations that are steeped in diverse cultures and making them partners in the creative process can ensure your content is genuine rather than performative.

You can access several helpful resources to diversify your creative perspectives. For example, the Advertising Association (n.d.) of the UK provides actionable advice to improve Black Representation in Marketing (BRiM). The National LGBT Media Association in the United States provides a best practice guide for LGBTQ+ campaigns (NLMA, 2022). UNICEF (2021), the UN agency that provides humanitarian and developmental aid to children, has published a playbook on promoting diversity and inclusion in advertising surrounding children and families. When you approach your creative with intentionality, you'll find many resources for developing content that is both inclusive and equitable.

Diversify Your Supplier Talent

Many agencies and companies are adopting supplier diversity programs, increasing their business with "women-owned, ethnic/minority-owned, veteran-owned, LGBTQ-owned, disability-owned, and small businesses" (ANA, n.d.). When developing creative, think about who is behind the camera as well as in front of the camera. This includes your production crews, photographers, freelancers, and directors. For example, the People of Colour Collective (POCC) is global network of more than 1,000 creative professionals across the United States and Europe who bring inclusive content to campaigns (POCC, n.d.). Hiring and partnering with more diverse talent can ensure you are being inclusive throughout the entire creative process, making your campaigns more effective.

Cross-Cultural Media Planning

Not only do audiences want to see more authentic representation in communications content, but they also want brands to go beyond mainstream media and be more inclusive in where that content appears. One study in the

UK showed that 92% of multicultural consumers want brands to advertise in diverse media channels (Daykin & Smith, n.d.-b, p. 9). ***Diverse media channels*** are channels *that are owned by and/or primarily serve underrepresented communities.*

While multicultural audiences do, of course, consume mainstream media, diverse media outlets create spaces for communities to come together, discuss their unique concerns, celebrate their shared traditions and cultures, and be seen in their full humanity rather than being under- or misrepresented as they often are in mainstream media. For example, during the COVID-19 pandemic, in which Asian Americans were particularly vulnerable, AAPI news outlets covered stories on the communities' frontline workers, combatted misinformation, provided resources for accessing healthcare and vaccines, and helped the community process and respond to the spate of Asian hate crimes that accompanied the pandemic (Rajagopalan, 2021).

While the industry has made strides in taking a cross-cultural approach to media planning (see Box 7.1), it is still falling short of its goals. In the United States, while multicultural consumers make up more than 40% of the consumer market, only a fraction of advertising spending goes toward these audiences (AXIOS, 2021; DDH, 2023, p. 3). Advertisers have previously shied away from using diverse outlets because of their lower audience numbers. However, not only are diverse audiences growing, but today's programmatic media technologies can curate diverse media suppliers together to help advertisers achieve scale (McEleny, 2021). Research shows that focusing on diverse media outlets is not only more effective in reaching diverse audiences, but it's also seen by audiences as showing genuine support for their communities (DDH, 2023, p. 11).

In addition to the inclusive digital strategies outlined in Chapter 5, below are several broad recommendations for developing a cross-cultural media plan.

Box 7.1 Working Toward a More Diverse Media Landscape

In the past few years, many large agencies made pledges to support minority-owned and diverse media channels (Roca, 2022). While this started an important conversation, the action to make this a reality is often lagging. Here is what some in the industry are doing to move the conversation forward.

Nielsen: For diverse-owned media companies to compete in the media landscape, they need three things: visibility, minority-owned business certification, and metrics to show their ROI. Nielsen is working with ANA's Alliance for Inclusive and Multicultural Marketing and MAVEN Media Framework to identify and provide media metrics for diverse media brands; adjusting its pricing and policies for diverse media suppliers; and, in partnership with Procter & Gamble, developing funds to help outlets secure certification as a Minority Business Enterprise (Nielsen, 2022).

GroupM: WPP's Group M launched a Media Inclusion Initiative (MII) in 2021 to create opportunities and investment for diverse media companies and content creators. In 2023 they expanded the initiative to include a pledge for allocating 5% of clients' media spend across Black, Hispanic, AAPI, and LGBTQ+ focused media. In the first 18 months, MII saw triple-digit growth in client investments in Black-owned media (GroupM, 2023).

TelevisaUnivision & OMG: In 2022, TelevisaUnivision, the world's leading Spanish-language media company, launched its Hispanic household data graph. Using account logins, IP addresses, and purchase data, the graph provides advertisers with accurate data of the Hispanic market that third-party estimates often get wrong. Omnicom Media Group (OMG) was the first to integrate the data graph with its own identity-based solution, Omni ID, making it easier and more effective for clients to engage with Hispanic communities (Boyle, 2022; TelevisaUnivision, 2022).

Research Diverse Media Outlets

Do your research to go beyond "mainstream" outlets. There are hundreds of media outlets – both for-profit and nonprofit – as well as media conglomerates that reach underrepresented groups. Just to name a few: Urban One is the largest distributor of Black cultural content, reaching 80% of Black Americans through radio, television, digital, podcasts, and more; there are more than 600 Latino media outlets in the United States and Puerto Rico and 400 Indigenous outlets in North America; and publications like Out Magazine and LGBTQ Nation cover news, politics, fashion, travel, and culture for the LGBTQ+ community. Don't neglect local outlets. With the myriad of local newspapers folding in the United States, AXIOS reports that ethnic news outlets are sprouting up in "news deserts" across the country to fill the void (AXIOS, 2021).

In the PR field, spend time building relationships with journalists and content creators from these outlets. Invite them to your news briefings and events. Ask what stories their users are interested in and how your organization can help. And don't forget newswires like Hispanic PR Wire, U.S. Asian Wire News, and Black PR Wire when it comes to distributing your news and content.

Tailor Communications to the Media Outlet

Diverse communities can spot inauthentic content from a mile away. Make sure your content is tailored to the specific needs and values of the community you wish to reach, and that you uphold inclusive values and actions within your organization. Targeted outlets are steeped in the cultures, aspirations, languages, and concerns of their communities and thus understand how best to reach them. Spend time engaging with these outlets to better understand how your content aligns with their needs. This might include participating in sponsorships, partnerships, or digital events such as live Q&As (The Communications Network, n.d.). Keep intersectionality in mind. The LGBTQ+ community, for example, also celebrates Hispanic Heritage Month.

In the PR field, tailor your outreach to journalists and content creators. For example, use statistics, stories, languages, and visuals that directly relate to each community.

Diversify Influencers, Sources, and Spokespeople

As discussed in previous chapters, make sure the people who are telling and delivering your content reflect the diversity of your audiences. For example, in the influencer marketing space, influencers are predominantly straight, White, privileged, and non-disabled (Shearer, 2019). Black content creators also point out that brands often use White influencers when speaking to mainstream audiences, as if "mainstream" equated with White, and that influencers of color are paid less than their White peers (Geyser, 2022; Marcelle, n.d.). When choosing influencers, make sure you are using a diversity of voices, experiences, abilities, and – especially in fashion and beauty – skin tones and body types, and pay them equitably.

Likewise, examine your list of sources and spokespeople. Do they reflect the makeup of your audiences? If not, research and develop a more inclusive list of sources who are credible and resonate with your audiences. A word of caution: Be careful not to exploit sources and spokespeople. Instead, bring them into the planning process early to get their input about what is important to them and the communities they speak with and how your proposition aligns with those interests.

Measuring for Equity and Inclusion

Note: See Chapter 5 for DEI measurement considerations and tools for digital and social media.

While there are several tools for measuring DEI internally, frameworks for measuring DEI in external campaigns are just recently emerging. As the World Federation of Advertisers states, "We are all just starting this journey and need to create a learning culture" (Daykin & Smith, n.d.-a, p. 15).

Typically, communicators develop KPIs (key performance indicators) for measuring campaign success based on two factors: outputs (also called outtakes) and outcomes. Outputs relate to the short-term impacts of the campaign, such as the reach of ads and articles, website visitors, number of contest entries, and social media engagement. Outcomes relate to longer-term impacts, like increases in sales, membership, or donations; changes in attitudes and perceptions; or changes in behavior (like the number of people who get vaccinated or stop texting when driving). The details of your SMART+IE process will define these KPIs in relation to DEI. An important consideration will involve asking with *whom* you have made an impact.

Here are a few additional considerations:

- Did your campaign eliminate stereotypes from your organization's content? For example, SeeHer (n.d.), a coalition of marketers, agencies, and media companies, has developed a data-driven methodology called GEM® (Gender Equality Measurement) to identify gender bias in content. Likewise, Creative Equals (n.d.) is a consultancy that helps clients and agencies conduct DEI audits across their businesses, supply chains, and workforce to determine their progress organization-wide.
- Did you build new relationships with partners, organizations, or suppliers? Were these partnerships mutually beneficial? Interview your partners to determine their perspectives, what works well, and where the relationship could be improved.
- Did the campaign further audience insights that can be used in future campaigns? Conduct a post-campaign evaluation to determine key learnings.
- Did you reach underrepresented people or communities that were previously missing from your campaigns? What was their feedback? The ability to disaggregate large data sets (discussed in Chapter 6) and/or supplement quantitative data with qualitative measures will be key in measuring audience impact.
- Did you diversify your media sources? What were the outputs and outcomes of doing so?
- Did you make an impact on a community or social justice issue? How can you qualify or quantify this impact? For example, did you raise awareness of a social justice issue? Change attitudes? Increase donations to the cause? Increase signatures on a petition? What change did your campaign create?

Bibliography

Advertising Association. (n.d.). *Black Representation in Marketing (BRiM)*. https://adassoc.org.uk/brim/

Alcantara, F. (n.d.). *Underrepresentation and misrepresentation have no place in advertising today – insights from the Geena Davis Institute's CEO*. Adweek. www.adweek.com/partner-articles/underrepresentation-and-misrepresentation-have-no-place-in-advertising-today-insights-from-the-geena-davis-institutes-ceo/

Association of National Advertisers (ANA). (n.d.). *Supplier diversity resources*. www.ana.net/content/show/id/supplierdiversity

AXInsights (2022, June 17). *How to create a multicultural marketing strategy*. https://audiencex.com/insights/how-to-create-a-multicultural-marketing-strategy/

AXIOS. (2021, November 13). *Race and media in America*. www.axios.com/2021/11/13/race-and-media-in-america

Blair Loeb, J. (2021). *Audience development as DEI initiative: A beneficial loop*. Jaemi Blair Loeb Consulting. https://jaemiloeb.com/audience-development-as-dei-initiative-a-beneficial-loop/

Boyle, A. (2022, November 22). *How TelevisaUnivision's household graph helps reach Hispanic audiences*. Adweek. www.adexchanger.com/data-exchanges/how-televisaunivisions-household-graph-helps-reach-hispanic-audiences/

Brown, M. (2023, January 18). #BlackGirlFollowTrain creates a network for Black female content creators to support one another. *NBC News*. www.nbcnews.com/news/nbcblk/blackgirlfollowtrain-provides-community-black-women-tiktok-rcna65551

Campaign Against Living Miserably (CALM). (2021, April 6). *The Mandate: What it means to be a man today*. www.thecalmzone.net/what-it-means-to-be-a-man-today

Chen, A. (2022, March 2). *5 key takeaways from brands that got their diversity, equity, and inclusion influencer marketing strategy right*. Influencer Marketing Hub. https://influencermarketinghub.com/diversity-equity-inclusion-influencer-marketing-strategy/

Conscious Ad Network. (n.d.). *Diversity, equality, & inclusion*. www.consciousadnetwork.com/the-manifestos/diversity/

Creative Equals. (n.d.). www.creativeequals.org/

Crevecoeurve West, B. (2023, April 26). *The power of SWOT analysis in advancing diversity, equity, and inclusion initiatives in the workplace*. LinkedIn. www.linkedin.com/pulse/power-swot-analysis-advancing-diversity-equity-berthine/

Daykin, J., & Smith, B. (n.d.-a). *Diversity & representation: Guide to potential areas for bias in the creative process*. World Federation of Advertisers. https://wfanet.org/knowledge/diversity-and-inclusion/wfa-guide-to-potential-areas-for-bias-in-the-creative-process

Daykin, J., & Smith, B. (n.d.-b). *Diversity & representation: Focus on media planning & buying*. https://wfanet.org/knowledge/diversity-and-inclusion/dei-in-media-guide/about

Dentsu. (2022). *Diversity, equity & inclusion report 2022*. www.dentsu.com/diversity-equity-and-inclusion-report-2022

Direct Digital Holdings (DDH). (2023). *Dollars & DEI: Multicultural consumers' insights on brands' media buying and marketing practices*. https://directdigitalholdings.com/whitepaper

Geyser, W. (2022, October 14). *Diversity, equity, & inclusion (DEI) in influencer marketing: Racial and gender inequalities report*. Influencer Marketing Hub. https://influencermarketinghub.com/dei-influencer-marketing-report/

GroupM. (2023, March 9). *Media Inclusion Initiative: Creating opportunities for diverse media companies and content creators*. www.groupm.com/newsroom/groupm-expands-media-inclusion-initiative-to-include-five-percent-pledge-for-black-hispanic-aapi-lgbtq-communities/

Heasley, S. (2023, July 11). *New streaming service to focus on disabilities*. Disability Scoop. www.disabilityscoop.com/2023/07/11/new-streaming-service-to-focus-on-disabilities/30450/

Krownapple, J. (2016). *Guiding teams to excellence with equity: Culturally proficient facilitation*. Corwin Press.

LGBT Capital. (2022). LGBT market statistics. www.lgbt-capital.com/index.php?menu_id=2

Logan, N. (2021). A theory of corporate responsibility to race (CRR): Communication and racial justice in public relations. *Journal of Public Relations Research, 33*(1), 6–22. https://doi.org/10.1080/1062726X.2021.1881898

Marcelle, C. (n.d.). *An analysis of diversity in influencer & social media marketing*. Chantelle Marcelle.com. https://chantellemarcelle.com/influencer-marketing-reflects-social-media-diversity-issue/

Matterkind. (2022, June). *Diversity, equity, and inclusion: A holistic approach*. www.businesswire.com/news/home/20220725005008/en/Matterkind-Releases-New-Report-Exploring-Diversity-Equity-and-Inclusion-Across-Advertising

McEleny, C. (2021, December 9). *A marketers guide to diverse media planning*. The Drum. www.thedrum.com/industryinsights/2021/12/09/marketers-guide-diverse-media-planning

Media Culture (2023, September 1). *The streaming revolution and its profound impact on African American media consumption*. www.mediaculture.com/insights/streaming-impact-on-african-american-media-consumption

Melancon, M. (2023, June 6). *America's economy continued to grow and diversify while recovering from COVID-19*. Terry College of Business, University of Georgia. www.terry.uga.edu/americas-economy-continued-grow-and-diversify-while-recovering-covid-19/

Microsoft Advertising. (2020). *The psychology of inclusion and the effects in advertising*. https://about.ads.microsoft.com/en-us/blog/post/july-2020/the-psychology-of-inclusion-and-the-effects-in-advertising

National LGBT Media Association (NLMA). (2022, September 15). *5 best practices for your LGBTQ+ marketing campaign*. https://nationallgbtmediaassociation.com/5-best-practices-for-your-lgbtq-marketing-campaign/

Nielsen. (2022, February). *Winning for the long term: Investing in diverse-owned media*. www.nielsen.com/insights/2022/winning-for-the-long-term-investing-in-diverse-owned-media/

Pappas, V., & Chikumbu, K. (2020, June 1). *A message to our Black community*. TikTok. https://newsroom.tiktok.com/en-us/a-message-to-our-black-community

People of Colour Collective (POCC). (n.d.). https://wearepocc.com/

Public Health Foundation (PHF). (2023). *Expand your SWOT analysis to include inclusion and equity: Make it a SWOTIE*. www.phf.org/resourcestools/Pages/

Expand_Your_SWOT_Analysis_to_Include_Inclusion_and_Equity_Make_it_a_ SWOTIE.aspx

Rajagopalan, K. (2021, May). *Asian media on the front lines: How community media have served Asian Americans during the pandemic*. Center for Community Media. https://asianmediafrontlines.journalism.cuny.edu/

Roca, M. (2022, February 23). *We need to disrupt the media supply chain*. Adweek. www.adweek.com/media/we-need-to-disrupt-the-media-supply-chain/

Scope. (2020). *Accessibility and video on-demand streaming services*. https://business.scope.org.uk/businesscase/streaming

SeeHer. (n.d.). *What is GEM®?* www.seeher.com/what-is-gem/

Shearer, A. (2019, November 5). *Diversity and representation in influencer marketing – the uncomfortable truth*. LinkedIn. www.linkedin.com/pulse/diversity-representation-influencer-marketing-truth-shearer/

TelevisaUnivision. (2022, November 17). TelevisaUnivision announces Omnicom Media Group as first agency integrating with its Hispanic Household Data Graph [Press release]. https://corporate.televisaunivision.com/press/2022/11/17/televisaunivision-announces-omnicom-media-group-as-first-hispanic-household-data-graph-agency-partner/

The Communications Network. (n.d.). *Outreach*. www.comnetworkdei.org/outreach

TikTok. (2023, March). *Community principles*. www.tiktok.com/community-guidelines/en/community-principles/

UNICEF. (2021). *Promoting diversity and inclusion in advertising: A UNICEF playbook*. www.unicef.org/documents/promoting-diversity-and-inclusion-advertising-unicef-playbook

Unstereotype Alliance. (2021, February 4). *3Ps Unstereotype marketing communications framework*. www.unstereotypealliance.org/en/resources/research-and-tools/3ps-unstereotype-marketing-communications-playbook

Wang Yuen, N. (2019, June 4). *How racial stereotypes in popular media affect people – and what Hollywood can do to become more inclusive*. Scholars Strategy Network. https://scholars.org/contribution/how-racial-stereotypes-popular-media-affect-people-and-what-hollywood-can-do-become

Waters, R. D., Chen, Z. F., & Gomez-Barris, L. (2022). Rethinking campaign management to include a "SMART + IE" mindset. In D. Pompper (Ed.), *Public relations for social responsibility: Affirming DEI commitment with action*. Kindle edition.

Waters, R. D., & Farwell, T. M. (2022). Shaping tomorrow's industry leaders by incorporating inclusivity into campaign planning curriculum: Student reactions to the SMART+IE mindset in strategic communication efforts. *Journal of Public Relations Education*, Winter 2020. https://journalofpreducation.com/2023/02/24/shaping-tomorrows-industry-leaders-by-incorporating-inclusivity-into-campaign-planning-curriculum-student-reactions-to-the-smartie-mindset-in-strategic-communication-efforts/

8 Working on Diverse Teams

Karen Lindsey

We've all been there. You've been placed on a team or in a group with people you don't know. You may even encounter people with different cultural or socioeconomic backgrounds. Whether working on group projects in a university classroom or on a global team in an advertising or public relations agency, it is likely that you will be on a team with someone who has a social identity different from your own. In today's global workplace, cross-cultural teams are a part of the modern working world. Often we focus on the challenges of working on a team with members who are different from ourselves, but the good news is that a Cloverpop study found that organizations with diverse teams deliver better results 60% of the time and make better decisions in 87% of cases (Larson, 2017; Stahl, 2021). Teams comprised of different identities may increase the complexity of communication and task completion. With self-awareness, thoughtful planning, and mutual respect, the value of being on a diverse team can be realized with outstanding results.

In Chapter 2, we outlined behavioral insights with a focus on various social identity categories. In this chapter, we offer insights on how identity and culture affects teamwork. Culture is often defined as system of shared understandings, values, and norms (DiMaggio, 1994, p. 27).

In this chapter, you will learn:

- The definition of optimal distinctiveness theory and its application to teamwork
- Ways to practice cultural awareness and self-awareness as a team member
- Tips to participate effectively on diverse teams

Optimal Distinctiveness Theory

In team situations, we want to both belong and retain our individuality. One theory that helps us understand these dynamics is *optimal distinctiveness theory*, which, simply put, suggests that *individuals have a desire to attain a*

DOI: 10.4324/9781003411796-9

balance of both inclusion and distinctiveness in social and team situations (Leonardelli et al., 2010). When we recognize that these two seemingly opposing needs can be highly activated when participating in diverse teams, it helps us to think about our own self-perception, biases, and role in creating productive team dynamics. Let's explore a few key elements connected to this theory to better understand how to work effectively on culturally and identity diverse teams.

Practice Self-awareness

Self-awareness is the best way to think about our role in a diverse team. When we consider team situations where we have wanted to both belong and remain true to our identity, self-awareness emerges as a solid first step. But what does it really mean? To be *self-aware* is to possess *conscious knowledge of one's own character, feelings, motives, opinions, and desires in various social and cultural situations.* Can you think of a situation where you have been part of a team and wanted to both belong and remain true to who you are? When working as a member of a culturally diverse team, it's important to think about the cultural context each person brings to the team's tasks. *Cultural context* refers to *learned societal behaviors, attitudes, and values of what is considered accepted or expected in given situations.* We each inherently define what we think is acceptable or appropriate based on our own lived experiences and other social identity characteristics. This way of thinking can create challenging team and group dynamics, especially if there is a majority of any one social identity represented.

Within optimal distinctiveness theory, we consider *in-groups*, *which refer to people belonging to a group or team who share identity characteristics and possibly similar behaviors and opinions,* and *out-groups* as *people who do not identify with the social identities and characteristics of the larger group or team in which they are participating.* For example, in some workplaces a leader may assume a good team-building activity would be to hold a golf outing without considering whether or not everyone can or would want to play golf. If there is someone on the team who has not learned to play golf, they may choose not to attend the golf outing, creating an out-group situation.

If a person is outnumbered by others with shared social identities they may not speak up. Their participation may decrease or they may appear defensive because they do not feel safe. When all team members can openly share their ideas and opinions, it increases the ability of the team to be creative and productive. Each team member must have *organizational psychological safety*, *the feeling of being able to speak up, take risks, and make mistakes without fear of negative consequences* (Edmondson & Lei, 2014).

Sometimes team members will ask culturally diverse team members to take on certain tasks because of their social identity. For example, assigning math-related tasks to an Asian team member because a common stereotype is that Asian people are good at math. Or a women might be asked to take notes. Making assumptions about a team member's skills and preferences for participation is demeaning. A better approach might be for each team member to share what role or skill they excel in. This approach creates greater psycholocial safety on the team.

Have you ever been the only person representing your social identity category on a team? If so, you quickly notice who is part of the in-group and how their ideas are accepted or listened to with greater ease. Although every team member can possess biases based on their own cultural context and social foundations, when as strategic communicators we are participating in a diverse team, we are most effective when we continually seek to be self-aware, understand our own biases, listen, and ask intelligent questions if we don't understand a person's way of communicating or meaning.

When we practice self-awareness, we recognize that we all have a desire to belong, be authentically ourselves, and feel psychologically safe enough to contribute. To establish psychological safety, team members must trust each other.

Learn about Other Cultures

When participating in a team with individuals of diverse identities, we often see participation, decision-making, and task completion through our own cultural, geographical, social, and political understanding. Let's consider two social-political ways to think about the many variations in communication styles, behavior, and decision-making that occur on teams.

The first is **individualism**, which *involves the belief that every person is self-reliant, self-motivated, and the focus is on achieving individual success.* A good example is in educational systems in the United States, where students learn early on that success is typically defined by an individual grade. With an individualist mindset, a student working on a group project for a class is primarily concerned with what grade they will get on the project and will exhibit behaviors that focus on excelling in their individual work without prioritizing the team's work. With this mindset, a good individual grade has more value because it demonstrates the individual's effort was greater. The individual grade is viewed as more important since grades are often used as an indicator of having demonstrated personal knowledge as measured in U.S. educational systems. Besides the United States, other places that score high on individualism are England, Australia, and Germany (Oyserman et al., 2002).

In many Eastern cultures, *the focus is more about actions that prioritize the greater good of society, a group, or family.* This is known as **collectivism**. In the classroom, students with a collectivist mindset prioritize group success rather than their own individual achievement. They may seek to maintain harmony while on a team by not speaking up. Using the example of a group project, a person with a collectivist mindset appears more concerned with collaboration rather than their individual grade. Examples of countries with a greater orientation toward collectivism include Argentina, Brazil, China, Ghana, Guatemala, Japan, and Indonesia (World Population Review, 2024).

When individualism and collectivist ways of thinking are added to the complexities of teamwork, it is highly possible that misunderstandings will occur in pursuit of accomplishing a task. Disagreement and misunderstandings within diverse teams often occur in two ways:

1. **Language-based misunderstanding** is an *unintentional error in comprehension by receivers due to the form of language employed by senders in communicating a message* (Fiset et al., 2023). On teams where there are individuals who have been born in or educated in a different country or culture, one person's understanding, experience, or even feelings associated with a word or expression can be very different. Language-based misunderstandings occur when words have different meaning than intended or when we use words that are not understood by other cultures. Let's look at a few examples.

   In the United States, we might use idioms such as "my bad," meaning "I've made a mistake" or "pass the buck," to indicate that someone else is responsible for the task. These are examples of phrases that might confuse someone for whom English is their second language. Can you think of other phrases commonly used in Western culture that might be confusing to someone who is from another culture or speaks another language?

   In Chapter 2, we learned how English words do not always directly translate for those who speak other languages. Likewise, when we listen to another person speak their speaking pace, volume, and word choice may be different from your own, leading to misunderstandings. Take time to listen carefully and politely ask questions if you don't understand the meaning or use of certain words and phrases. In some cultures, there are colloquialisms or slang that are commonly used and understood only among those who belong to that specific culture or identity group. It is especially important to be aware that if you do not belong to the culture, race, or identity group that uses a certain slang word or colloquialism, you should not use the words in an attempt to be clever or to try to fit in. One of your authors lived and worked in the deep southern part of the United States and often heard people say, "bless your heart." Being from the Midwest, she quickly learned never to try to use this phrase because it has multiple meanings. It can be used to express genuine sympathy if something goes wrong, but sometimes can convey condescension. If you are not from the South and try to use that phrase, it can be viewed as mocking, inauthentic, and insulting.

Colleagues in Germany might use the expression *"Abwarten und Tee trinken,"* which translates as "Wait and drink tea," meaning "Wait and see." This phrase might express both an inability to change a future outcome as well as acceptance of the outcome (Bohn, 2020).

The way we use words in conversation or other types of communication can hold a variety of meanings and cause misunderstandings based on geographic culture, translation, and language traits. It is critical for team success to be authentic in your style of communication and ask respectful questions if you honestly do not understand what is meant or how someone else is using words or phrases.

2. **Behavioral-based misunderstanding** occurs *when an individual acts in a way that is contradictory or considered socially impolite compared to what you believe is acceptable in a social or workplace situation.* Let's look at an example of how collectivism and individualism can unintentionally clash. A business executive tells the story of when her team was working with a Chinese delegation visiting the United States. The head of the Chinese delegation was greeted at a restaurant meeting by a member of the American team. The American team member told the senior-ranking Chinese executive to "sit where you like," assuming it was a welcoming offer. It was immediately viewed as an insult by the Chinese team. Why? Because the Chinese executive should have been escorted to a seat at the head of the table next to the highest-ranking executive of the American team. Broadly speaking, deep respect for rank and titles is typically ingrained in Chinese citizens, and is a key part of collectivism. Younger generations of Chinese citizens who frequently interact with and relate to the Western world through social media and entertainment may display and understand individualism more than older generations. While one example is not intended to classify billions of Chinese citizens, overall the dominant cultural behaviors may be classified as collectivist.

So how do you know what to do if you are part of a geographically diverse team? Beyond authentically and respectfully asking questions, you can conduct your own inquiry. There are many widely available online guides and resources designed to help understand general business protocols for different countries. The cross-cultural consulting firm Commisceo Global (n.d.) has cultural insights and business practice guides available on their website for more than 80 countries (www.commisceo-global.com/resources/country-guides).

Listen and Learn to Understand Team Member Differences

A simple yet important step to work cohesively on a diverse team (or any team) is to listen first. *Active listening includes observing and processing differences in communication styles and body language before assuming or responding.* For example, in the United States, many citizens are taught that it demonstrates confidence to look an authority figure in the eyes when speaking to them. In some Asian cultures, it is considered rude and disrespectful to look an authority figure in the eyes when speaking to them. Rather than assuming another person's behavior or way of speaking is intended to be offensive, consider culture and a combination of other elements that influence team communication and participation in group settings. Let's look at a few.

Personality

Have you ever taken a personality assessment? From Myers-Briggs to DISC to Enneagram, psychologists have developed a variety of ways to anticipate an individual's behavior and communication preferences. Each team member not only brings cultural practices and social identity characterisitics to a team, but they also bring an individual personality type. We often categorize personality types in three ways: introvert, extrovert, and ambivert.

Personality types are best explained by thinking about when and where people become animated, energetic, and involved. For example, many *extroverts* are *energized by verbally communicating or processing ideas out loud, working on teams, and meeting new people at an event.* *Introverts* *gain energy from solitude and become quickly drained when asked to constantly verbally communicate or interact without having time to think and process ideas.* A common myth is that introverts are shy. Many are not. Introverts may prefer to engage in a deeper conversation with one or two people in a social setting, while the extrovert might try to talk with and meet as many people as possible (Houston, 2019; Van Edwards, 2022).

Some people are *a combination of introvert and extrovert, and can switch between the two personality types depending on the situation.* This is referred to as an ***ambivert.*** The ambivert is able to quickly switch between introversion and extroversion based on the situational context (Houston, 2019; Van Edwards, 2022). There is great debate about whether or not ambivert is an accepted personality category even though the word was coined in 1927 by psychologist Kimball Young (Nickerson, 2023).

Researchers suggest it is possible for anyone to develop and practice ways of positively interacting beyond one personality type when necessary for team participation (Houston, 2019; Van Edwards, 2022). For example, a predominantly introverted person can learn how to manage and socialize in a group setting, while a predominantly extroverted person can learn how to work independently (Houston, 2019). The combination of personality type, social identity, and cultural practices greatly influences the way a person participates in a team, responds to questions, takes direction, or even accepts critiques.

Time

Another often misunderstood concept on teams is time and punctuality. As part of a global team, you may have to rephrase what you mean when you say you expect team members to "be on time." The concept of punctuality can be perceived differently depending a person's cultural background. For example, when doing business in Costa Rica and Kenya, small talk is important before getting down to business. Meetings may start later than the previously announced time, but guests are expected to be at the meeting at the original time that was communicated. In Germany there is a tendency to focus intently on time and the lack of punctuality may be perceived as rude or disrespectful. It is typical for German-based team members to be exact about meeting start and end times, project schedules, and project delivery deadlines (Commisceo Global, n.d.). In other countries, such as Brazil and France, the tendency is to perceive time as more flexible, so you must clearly discuss agreed-upon project delivery timeframes and meeting times (Commisceo Global, n.d.).

The intercultural and destination training firm IOR offers a few tips to ensure teams comprised of diverse members understand each other's outlook on time. First, create agendas and communicate meeting start and end times in advance of the meeting. If necessary, include time for pre-meeting socializing. During meetings, communicate clearly and provide context when asking open-ended questions. Check for understanding before moving on to another topic. Finally, build in regular progress updates for team member to ensure final deadlines are understood and met (IORWorld, n.d.).

Visualization

The preference for visual images is another consideration for diverse teams. People in certain professions and industries might prefer animations, bar charts, diagrams, graphs, or pie charts rather than words. For example, often people in technical or STEM fields may respond better to presentations and explanations that include flow charts and diagrams, while people in creative professions typically prefer colorful artwork or infographics to express an idea and share information.

In today's global workplace, visual storytelling is a compelling way for strategic communicators to share data and insights from their research. When conducting a presentation, it is helpful to think about how you might use images, charts, diagrams, graphs, and fewer words to assist in communicating across language differences, learning differences, or profession preferences.

Brainstorming

One technique many strategic communicators use in meetings is **brainstorming**, *a technique where people in a group or team are prompted to spontaneously, verbally share words, suggestions, or thoughts as a means of generating ideas or solutions.* The main purpose of brainstorming is to create a fast-paced, unstructured, free-flowing exchange of ideas.

For some cultures, brainstorming in a meeting can be off-putting. The standard approach of "everyone shout out ideas" is common for Western advertising and public relations professionals. When working as part of a team, especially an international team, avoid suddenly starting a brainstorming session. Try sending an agenda before the meeting that will include the general topics to be discussed. Those who prefer to have more time to generate ideas independently or by consulting others will feel better prepared to participate.

Work Collaboratively to Adapt to Differences

To work collaboratively, everyone on a team must be able to actively participate. Based on personality alone, every team member will have a preferred way to accomplish a task. Preferences may be rooted in cultural, generational, personality, or other social identity nuances.

At the start of any project, team members should get to know some basic things about each other without being invasive. It can be as simple as discussing what activities or interests you have in common or what unique interests or hobbies individual team members might have. If a fellow team member prefers not to reveal or engage in the discussion, do not assume anything negative about why. In the interest of the project, you can move on to the task-related inquiry. Ask who prefers writing, designing, or researching. Once you know a few basics, you can begin to discover the skills and talents each person brings along with their cultural perspectives.

Discuss and establish a short list of mutual agreements for meetings and interactions. Sometimes referred to as **working agreements**, they can be a *short, written list of up to five items that the team agrees is acceptable behavior to create respectful interactions.* For example, working agreements for a team might include:

- Allow others to finish sharing their ideas or thoughts, even if you disagree.
- If you disagree, respond with a focus on the idea, not the person.
- Don't dominate the conversation, and give everyone a chance to speak.
- We will communicate using the following platforms and technologies …
- Meetings will start and end at …

If you are the leader or member of a cross-cultural team and decide you want participation from everyone, consider approaches that allow different options for team participation. Based on ability, language, culture, and personality types, not everyone will talk for equal amounts of time. Provide a variety of ways for input to be offered. For example, those who come from a more collectivist culture may prefer to spend some time discussing ideas together before contributing ideas or solutions to the group. What are some other ways you can think of to accommodate different ways of sharing and participating in a project with shared goals?

Two types of differences that are often encountered and overlooked on teams include age and ability. Let's take a more in-depth look at these two types of differences:

Generational Differences

As of 2023, there are five generations in the workplace: Traditionalists, Baby Boomers, Millennials, Generation X, and Generation Z (Perry, 2023). Each generation brings a different perspective on how to accomplish tasks or provide team updates. For example, Gen Z may prefer to use Slack for group communication, while Boomers may prefer email. When teams are choosing collaborative technologies to communicate, consider what is most efficient for the entire team. Be willing to ask about and use different methods to ensure everyone can participate. In Chapter 2, we discussed guarding against ageism and the stereotypes that we may have due to someone being older or younger. Recognize your own biases and assumptions based on a person's age, whether younger or older.

Ability Differences

In Chapter 5, we discussed thoughtful considerations about accessibility and creating inclusive content for social media. When we explore working on inclusive teams in the workplace, we consider and adjust for team members' different abilities. On diverse teams, ensure that both physical and cognitive ability is accommodated.

A word that has grown in awareness and usage is **neurodiversity**, which describes the idea that *people experience and interact with the world around them in many different ways; there is no one "right" way of thinking, learning, and behaving, and differences are not viewed as deficits* (Baumer & Frueh, 2021). Judy Singer, an Australian psychologist, first wrote about neurodiversity in 1998 to describe what she referred to as a "political term" to advocate for "neurological minorities" (Baumer & Frueh, 2021; Harris, 2023). By 2023, the word became part of a movement seeking to increase inclusion and understanding of autism spectrum disorder (ASD), attention deficit hyperactivity disorder (ADHD), and other neurological conditions (Harris, 2023).

As with any difference in ability, it is important to ask what a person needs and prefers in a teamwork situation. Make simple adjustments related to sounds, space, and designate break times for longer meetings (Wood, 2023).

Remember the Value of Diverse Teams

Research conducted by Deloitte (Bourke, 2018) shows that teams comprised of diverse individuals enhances creativity and innovation by 20%. The different ways of thinking and experiencing the world enables diverse teams to spot risks in everything from messaging to reducing risks by up to 30%. More and more consumers and companies care about the diversity of the team making creative and communication decisions, which can have a positive impact on an organization's sales, revenue, and reputation (Indeed.com, 2023).

According to a LinkedIn study (2018) on global recruiting trends, 49% of companies believe it is important for diversity to be part of their organizational culture as it allows them to better understand and represent their customers. From age to race to gender to ability, every identity category brings a valuable perspective to creative decision-making.

Diverse team members may be aware of cultural nuances to how an audience might interpret a brand's version of what is humorous or beautiful. For example, in 2018 luxury brand Dolce & Gabbana ran a series of ads on their social media platforms meant to promote a fashion show in Shanghai. One of the ads depicted an attractive, elegantly dressed Chinese model appearing to giggle and look confused as she struggled to eat spaghetti and pizza with chopsticks. A voiceover mocks her for fumbling and jabbing at the food, offering to instruct her on the proper way to eat the food. Social media was immediately flooded with posts criticizing the brand and media coverage highlighted the insensitivity of the depiction. After Chinese citizens expressed outrage over the brand's cultural insensitivity, Chinese celebrities and models refused to attend the fashion show. The fashion show was later cancelled (NPR, 2018).

In assessing this situation, one might even ask if the brand had a local agency or anyone on the creative team who understood the Chinese culture and why the ads were demeaning. If the work environment was one of representation, collaboration, and safety, the creative approach might have been different and helped the brand avoid the embarrassment and insensitive use of humor.

Having cross-cultural representation on the team when making creative decisions can help to raise awareness of sensitive terminology, portrayals, and the realities of lived experiences. Even with diverse representation in the creative process, effective strategic communicators always recognize that no one person should be asked to constantly speak on behalf of an entire culture, community, or identity group's experiences, opinions, behaviors, or values. If a team member chooses to do so, it's important to listen and consider their perspective.

The many differences encountered as part of a diverse team can feel overwhelming at first. Being willing to listen, learn, be flexible, and empathetic can result in highly creative output and become an enriching experience for everyone on the team (Box 8.1).

Box 8.1 Teamwork Tips

1. Create psychological safety by getting to know your team members. At the start of a project, discuss and establish a mutual agreements list. Each team member should be given the opportunity to offer input on how the team will work together. This includes roles and responsibilities, task completion deadlines, and meeting times that consider everyone's schedule.
2. Accept that there may be differences of opinion. Listen and demonstrate respect for differences, especially those rooted in cultural, social, and societal experiences. Seek to resolve differences that impede completion of the task through authentic conversations.
3. Demonstrate care, concern, and understanding when in doubt about a person's response or motives in how they interact with the team. Try to determine if it is a language, cultural, ability, or personality misunderstanding.
4. Practice cultural intelligence. Avoid stereotyped notions or making assumptions about team member roles on the team based on social identity or surface-level observations (i.e., age, ability, race, gender, etc.).
5. Learn about other cultures and what may be influencing approaches to accomplishing tasks, including time, language, and participation. Review business protocol guides available online before embarking on a project in another country.
6. Remember that an individual's personality type may also influence their interactions on a team, along with cultural behaviors and specific geographic communication styles.

Bibliography

Baumer, N., & Frueh, J. (2021, November 23). *What is neurodiversity?* Harvard Health Publishing. www.health.harvard.edu/blog/what-is-neurodiversity-202111232645

Bohn, T. (2020, January 6). *10 useful German phrases that Germans actually use. Babbel Magazine.* www.babbel.com/en/magazine/the-ultimate-list-of-10-very-useful-german-phrases

Bourke, J. (2018, January 22). The diversity and inclusion revolution: Eight powerful truths. *Deloitte Review*, Issue 22. www2.deloitte.com/us/en/insights/deloitte-review/issue-22/diversity-and-inclusion-at-work-eight-powerful-truths.html

Commisceo Global. (n.d.). *Country and culture guides.* www.commisceo-global.com/resources/country-guides

DiMaggio, P. (1994). Culture and economy. In N. Smelser & R. Swedberg (Eds.), *The handbook of economic sociology* (pp. 27–57). Princeton University Press.

Edmondson, A. C., & Lei, Z. (2014). Psychological safety: The history, renaissance, and future of an interpersonal construct. *Annual Review of Organizational Psychology and Organizational Behavior, 1*(1), 23–43.

Fiset, J., Bhave, D. P., & Jha, N. (2023). The effects of language-related misunderstanding at work. *Journal of Management*, 01492063231181651

Harris, J. (2023, July 5). The mother of neurodiversity: How Judy Singer changed the world. *The Guardian.* www.theguardian.com/world/2023/jul/05/the-mother-of-neurodiversity-how-judy-singer-changed-the-world

Houston, E. (2019, April 9). *Introvert vs extrovert: A look at the spectrum and psychology.* PositivePsychology.com. https://positivepsychology.com/introversion-extroversion-spectrum/

Indeed.com. (2023, April 21). *The benefits of diverse teams in the workplace.* www.indeed.com/career-advice/career-development/diverse-team-benefits

IORWorld. (n.d.). *Managing time perceptions across the globe.* www.iorworld.com/resources/culture-on-the-go-time-perception-across-cultures/

Larson, E. (2017, September 21). New research: Diversity + inclusion = better decision making at work. *Forbes.* www.forbes.com/sites/eriklarson/2017/09/21/new-research-diversity-inclusion-better-decision-making-at-work/?sh=1839fbab4cbf

Leonardelli, G. J., Pickett, C. L., & Brewer, M. B. (2010). Optimal distinctiveness theory: A framework for social identity, social cognition, and intergroup relations. *Advances in Experimental Social Psychology, 43*, 63–113.

LinkedIn. (2018, January 10). *Global recruiting trends 2018: The 4 ideas changing how you hire.* https://news.linkedin.com/2018/1/global-recruiting-trends-2018

Livermore, D. (2016, May 27). Leading a brainstorming session with a cross-cultural team. *Harvard Business Review.* https://hbr.org/2016/05/leading-a-brainstorming-session-with-a-cross-cultural-team

Nickerson, C. (2023, September 22). *What is an ambivert? An in-depth definition and guide.* Simply Psychology. www.simplypsychology.org/ambivert.html

NPR (2018, December 1). Dolce & Gabbana ad with chopsticks provokes public outrage in China. *NPR.* www.npr.org/sections/goatsandsoda/2018/12/01/671891818/dolce-gabbana-ad-with-chopsticks-provokes-public-outrage-in-china

Oyserman, D., Coon, H. M., & Kemmelmeier, M. (2002). Rethinking individualism and collectivism: Evaluation of theoretical assumptions and meta-analyses. *Psychological Bulletin*, *128*(1), 3–72.

Perry, E. (2023, August, 3). Five generations in the workplace: How to manage them all. *BetterUp*. www.betterup.com/blog/generations-in-the-workplace

Stahl, A. (2021, December 17). 3 benefits of diversity in the workplace. *Forbes*. www.forbes.com/sites/ashleystahl/2021/12/17/3-benefits-of-diversity-in-the-workplace/?sh=58329c022ed2

Van Edwards, V. (2022). *What is an ambivert?* Science of People. www.scienceofpeople.com/ambivert/

Wood, C. (2023, March 17). *7 ways to help your neurodiverse team deliver its best work*. CIO.com. www.cio.com/article/464910/7-ways-to-help-your-neurodiverse-team-deliver-its-best-work.html

World Population Review. (2024). *Collectivist countries*. https://worldpopulationreview.com/country-rankings/collectivist-countries

9 Inclusive Leadership

Karen Lindsey

At the height of the social justice movement in the summer of 2020, leaders of large corporations and other organizations in the United States were called upon to communicate their stance on diversity, equity, and inclusion (DEI) in response to inequities uncovered by police brutality, a global pandemic, and an increasingly volatile political climate. As the United States began to grapple with racial unrest, political division, and collective uncertainty, leaders in charge of big brands were required to be more thoughtful in their verbal and written communications about DEI. Beyond showing diverse identities in advertising and donating to social causes, leaders and their communications teams began to take a closer look at both their internal and external messages to ensure their actions aligned with their espoused organizational and personal values.

Throughout this book, we have primarily focused on approaches for strategic communicators to help brands reach diverse audiences through advertising and public relations strategies. Alongside demonstrating the external brand commitment to DEI in advertising and public relations, executive or C-suite leaders often call upon strategic communicators or Chief Communications Officers (CCOs) to assist them in framing and delivering key messages to internal (i.e., employees) and external audiences (i.e., publics). From speeches to media interviews, today's leaders set the tone about the organizational commitment to DEI. Employees and various publics expect the words and actions to align. In this chapter we will:

- Define inclusive leadership
- Review inclusive communication behaviors for leaders
- Discuss the benefits of inclusive leadership for brands and organizations
- Offer tips to help the strategic communicator advise and create inclusive leadership communications

DOI: 10.4324/9781003411796-10

Defining Inclusive Leadership

Racial unrest. Climate change. Economic uncertainty. What does it have to do with leadership and strategic communications? Everything. Strategic communicators play an important role in helping leaders craft and frame messages about DEI for internal and external audiences. The Edelman Trust Barometer special report on business and racial justice (2022) found that 82% of those surveyed indicated they expect CEOs to do something in response to systemic racism and injustice. Further, 54% of survey respondents believed that their companies are not delivering on the promises made in 2020 to address racism (Edelman, 2022). This chapter focuses on both the C-suite executive's role and the strategic communicator's role in internal and external communications for DEI.

Inclusive leadership was first publicly described by Nembhard and Edmondson (2006), who simply defined it as a relationship style that accepts differences. While that definition is accurate, over the years other scholars built on this definition to emphasize that *inclusive leadership* more specifically *involves behaviors by leaders that exhibit openness, accessibility, and authenticity in their interactions with followers that acknowledge the diverse characteristics and identities of their teams* (Carmeli et al., 2010; Ospina & El Hadidy, 2011). For many C-suite leaders, actualizing the definition of inclusive leadership is daunting. When we talk about inclusive leadership, there is often an assumption that it solely focuses on placating various identity categories with advertising, events, employee resource groups (ERGs), and donations to nonprofits. Another way to consider inclusive leadership is as a manifestation of *relational leadership*, which highlights a leader's *social influence in organizing, listening to, and understanding the needs of followers within the context of relational dynamics* (Uhl-Bien, 2006). Inclusive leadership requires leaders to authentically listen, show empathy, value differing viewpoints, demonstrate a desire to build trust, find a common ground to reach organizational goals, apologize if they make a mistake, and authentically communicate through words, data, and actions.

Modeling inclusive leadership and inclusive communication is a way for many organizations to demonstrate to internal and external audiences that their brand is aligned with their stated organizational values and commitment to DEI. Organizational culture plays an important role in the leadership ecosystem. Scholars suggest that *organizational culture is assumptions, beliefs, habits, language, symbols, values, and accepted interactions that influence employee behavior in various workplace situations* (Ravasi & Schultz, 2006). Organizational culture is viewed as a collective phenomenon and creates an implied agreement of behaviors and communication styles among people who work together within an organization. When a person or group of people accept and adhere to the tenets of an organizational culture, it creates a sense of belonging in the workplace (Baumeister & Leary, 1995). Individuals who belong to historically marginalized identities (i.e., Black, LGBTQ+, Latinx, etc.) may closely scrutinize matters of fairness, consistency, and inclusion by organizational leaders. In other words, do the words match the actions?

Culture, Values, and DEI

While organizational culture greatly influences employee performance and belonging, Bourne and Jenkins (2013) suggest that organizational values can include future and present orientations and are both individual and collective. Inclusive leaders are expected to create environments where the organization's stated mission and values align. So, what does this mean for the inclusive strategic communicator?

If you search any major brand's website, you are likely to find a section describing the organization's values. *Organizational values are a set of core beliefs or words that govern a business, its philosophy, and how employees are expected to act.* Organizational values are typically communicated in three to five different words or short sentences. For example, Sodexo, a global food service management and catering company, lists their organizational values as loyalty, transparency, integrity, and respect for people (Sodexo. com, 2023). The company's website prominently features pages that show how their value of "respect for people" aligns with their support and investments in DEI and environmental justice activities.

DEI-savvy strategic communicators know that words and the alignment with actions matter to employees and other publics. Organizational values are typically believed to be fixed; however, with multiple generations and social identities in the workplace, organizations may change their values due to social-political issues, market conditions, and technology. The International Business Machines Corporation (IBM), the U.S.-based multinational technology corporation, is a good example of an organization that had to reimagine their values based on changes in technology, their workforce, and society. In the 1980s, the company focused on core values that included respect for the individual, the best customer service, and superior accomplishment of all tasks. The company now includes in their values diversity and inclusion, innovation, being yourself, and focusing on change (IBM, Business Strategy Hub, 2023).

To gain optimal employee engagement around DEI, organizational leaders are involved in continuous communication and building trust through consistent public and private actions, and learning from personal missteps when they occur.

At the core of inclusive leadership is trust, authenticity, and a long-term commitment to diversity, equity, inclusion, and belonging efforts. To instill greater trust and arrive at business results, the inclusive leader will need to communicate frequently with internal and external audiences. Strategic communicators play a critical role in advising, creating, and supporting a communications strategy for an organization's DEI initiatives.

The Role of the Strategic Communicator

The intersection of complex social and political issues has given rise to the importance of the strategic communicator or Chief Communications Officer (CCO). As workplaces continue to employ a growing number of individuals from different social identities, and as organizations seek to do business globally, the role of the strategic communicator in shaping DEI communications requires further examination.

In the *Future of Corporate Communications Study* (2023) conducted by Edelman, from corporations to nonprofits there is a growing need for communicators to not only develop communications but also to advise on strategy. For a glimpse into the changing role of future CCOs and strategic communicators, here are the four key insights from the Edelman (2023) study:

1. Communications leaders have cemented their place as critical strategic partners.
2. Communicators inform and guide enterprise decision-making from a central position as a connector.
3. The enterprise agenda is driven by a new multi-stakeholder dynamic, which CCOs and their functions manage from the inside out.
4. Communications leaders will be at the center of shaping the next phase of stakeholder capitalism.

Beyond solid writing and verbal communications skills, the future CCO will need to understand an array of business, social, and political issues. CCOs and inclusive, strategic communicators will have developed the ability to advise senior executives with knowledge, confidence, and courage.

Internal Audiences

The modern workforce is characterized by an intergenerational and culturally diverse workforce. Sixty percent of Chief Communications Officers (CCOs) or similarly titled communication leaders in the Edelman study emphasized the importance of employee engagement (Edelman, 2023). Researchers suggest that before communicating with internal or employee audiences, an important consideration for inclusive leaders is to think carefully about team members' differences and support their need for belonging to further each team member's contributions, rather than ignoring differences (Randel et al., 2016).

The strategic communicator is often called upon to assist C-suite leaders, managers of various departments, and others to communicate with employees of an organization. This support often comes in the form of developing online or website content, writing news releases or speeches, and providing overall communications support for messages about diversity, equity, inclusion, and belonging initiatives. Internal communication efforts often involve working cross-functionally with individuals or groups in other areas of an organization such as a DEI vice president, human resources, legal, marketing, or employee resource groups (ERGs). In addition to advising on strategy, communications professionals may help increase visibility of DEI efforts internally by planning events, writing about a diverse employee's contributions, or developing online content to showcase the organizational commitment to DEI.

While these approaches to showcasing DEI are part of communicator's role, it represents one step in communicating inclusivity. If employees observe that communications actions are not in alignment with how employees are treated, promoted, or retained, highlighting DEI may cause more harm than good. To instill greater trust and arrive at the business results diversity can bring, the inclusive leader will need to communicate frequently and act consistently with internal and external audiences about their commitment to DEI.

External Audiences

Immigration. Wars. Sustainability. Supreme Court decisions. These are just a few of the polarizing, politicized topics facing inclusive leaders and strategic communicators. The speed and size of geopolitical, social justice, and environmental issues affecting our world continues to grow. Multiple research studies show that both employees and external publics expect leaders to speak out on social and political issues (Edelman Trust Barometer, 2022, 2023; Ragan & HarrisX, 2022). For example, three in five CEOs and other communications leaders believe that organizations should take a stand on issues of public interest (Ragan & HarrisX, 2022). Similar proportions believe organizations should stand up for the rights of their employees, even when doing so harms revenue (Ragan & HarrisX, 2022).

Within a divisive society there are inherent risks in speaking out or aligning with a marginalized group. Answers about how, when, and what to do are constantly being debated among executives, employees, the general public, and communicators. Before crafting and releasing any external statements on

DEI and geopolitical issues of the day, strategic communicators and leaders will want to ask themselves these questions:

- Have I taken time to process the issue privately before making a statement publicly?
- What are my personal values and what are the organizational values that align with why we are speaking out on this issue?
- Does the issue have an immediate impact on employees, customers, and key stakeholders?
- What is the level of urgency?
- What positive or negative history does my organization have with the issue or topic?
- What current policies or practices in our organization might relate to this issue?
- What are the risks and benefits of speaking out?

Even after answering these questions, there can be critical or negative responses from both internal and external audiences. Many public relations firms are building services around CEO activism. In some instances, CEOs have also collectively taken a stance on issues. For example, in 2015, before the United Nations climate-change-agreement negotiations took place in Paris, the CEOs of 14 major food companies – Mars, General Mills, Coca-Cola, Unilever, Danone Dairy North America, Hershey, Ben & Jerry's, Kellogg, PepsiCo, Nestlé USA, New Belgium Brewing, Hain Celestial, Stonyfield Farm, and Clif Bar – signed an open letter calling on government leaders to create a strong accord that would "meaningfully address the reality of climate change" (Chatterji & Toffel, 2018).

Creating an Inclusive Leadership Communications Strategy

An inclusive leader must have urgency in communicating about DEI to be able to quickly point to visible changes in the organization. For example, inclusive leaders may direct their communications team to change the company logo on social media during Hispanic Heritage Month or any of the months celebrating various social identity groups to demonstrate their allyship. Sometimes leaders will pay for advertising in the program booklet at a cultural event to indicate they support a diverse community. While these approaches are a good start, if the organization does not have ongoing internal policies, hiring and promotion practices, or investments in diverse communities, these approaches can be viewed by both employees and external publics as *performative allyship*, which refers to *organizations and individuals who support marginalized groups on a surface level when it is convenient.*

To create an effective internal and external DEI communications plan, the strategic communicator may work with departments such as human resources, legal, marketing, employee resource groups (ERGs), Chief Diversity Officers, and other publics. Before activating a DEI communications plan, strategic communicators will want to ask themselves and their leaders the following questions:

- Why does this strategy matter to our organization and for our business? (include moral and business reasons)
- What data do we have or need on the beliefs and behaviors around DEI among our employees?
- What data do we have or need on the public perception of our commitment to DEI?
- What are the compelling facts and actions that demonstrate our commitment to DEI?
- How are our shared values demonstrated within the organization and across social identity intersections (both internally and externally)?
- Do our policies, practices, and organizational history align with our messaging?
- How can or do we amplify the authentic experiences of our diverse employees, external constituents, and consumers as they engage with the organization?
- If we take a stance on a social-political issue, what are the risks and benefits? Are we willing to accept those risks?
- What are my own personal biases and history with diversity, equity, inclusion, and belonging?

Inclusive Leadership and Communications

The communication style of the inclusive leader plays a critical role in the trust among internal and external publics. In a study examining the communication behaviors of leaders perceived to be inclusive, Zandan and Shalett (2020) utilized a diverse panel of 50 communication experts who specialize in speech, rhetoric, social influence, and organizational communications. The panel watched 30 senior executive speakers and evaluated whether they were communicating using an inclusive style. After observing the speakers, the panelists rated each on a one-to-seven Likert scale. They applied a combination of computational linguistics, vocal mapping, and facial micro-expression analysis to determine what makes a leader appear inclusive from an audience perspective. The communications panel evaluated and benchmarked senior leaders who also identified as inclusive leaders at Fortune 1000 firms. Their findings revealed three communication behaviors for inclusive leaders to practice.

1. **Use audience centered language**. According to the study, inclusive leaders personalized their language 36% more frequently than the average senior leader. The findings indicate that inclusive leaders are more relatable when they use examples and can authentically amplify the stories of various identity groups relating to organizational success. Further, inclusive leaders are careful to be self-aware and authentic in order to communicate in a natural style that considers their own personal values, organizational values, and audience concerns. Leaders who strive to be inclusive communicators recognize that their personal and workplace experiences may not be the same as those of their employees. Strategic communicators can help leaders by identifying powerful experiences of diverse groups and help leaders demonstrate that they understand others' perspectives.

2. **Demonstrate subject matter expertise**. Inclusive leadership communication can be incorrectly described as simply not using offensive language when delivering speeches or being interviewed by the media. However, diverse internal and external audiences want to see and hear inclusive leaders demonstrate that they understand and are knowledgeable in their espoused commitment to DEI. The study found that inclusive leaders demonstrated subject matter expertise 21% more frequently than the average senior leader. Leaders who are delivering business messages to internal and external audiences may accomplish this by using numerical examples with relevant stories or anecdotes related to their overall business to support their points about DEI.

3. **Demonstrate authenticity**. Inclusive leaders are perceived as 22% more authentic relative to the average leader Authenticity in inclusive communications allows a leader to be more engaging and comfortable when speaking to large audiences, especially on a subject like DEI. The study found that inclusive leaders speak with conviction and use natural nonverbal cues (i.e., hand gestures, eye contact, vocal inflection). For example, in this study PepsiCo's former CEO, Indra Nooyi, was rated high for using an authentic communication style When viewing or listening to her speeches, researchers observed that Nooyi's tone is relaxed and conversational. She does not appear to be rehearsed or speaking in a "stage or speech voice." Researchers observed that her gestures appear intentional and natural for the points she makes while speaking.

The three behaviors from the Zandan and Shalett study (2020) represent a starting point for strategic communicators who may be called upon to assist executive leaders in aligning their personal communication styles with internal and external messages about DEI. Delivering speeches is only one part of an inclusive leadership communications strategy. Let's look at personal traits that impact inclusive leadership.

Inclusive Leadership Traits

Korn Ferry, a global organizational consulting firm, conducted a study identifying five core enabling traits that inclusive leaders use in their disposition toward differences (Korn Ferry Institute, 2023; Tapia & Kirtzman, 2023): authenticity, emotional resilience, self-assurance, inquisitiveness, and flexibility (Korn Ferry Institute, 2023, p. 9). While these traits are important for any effective leader, the Korn Ferry study goes further in elaborating that these traits alone are not enough for inclusive leadership (Korn Ferry Institute, 2023, p. 10; Tapia & Kirtzman, 2023). In addition to the traits, the researchers offer five skills-based competencies for the inclusive leader:

• Builds interpersonal trust
• Integrates diverse perspectives
• Optimizes talent
• Applies an adaptive mindset
• Achieves transformation

These competencies require centering values and ethics alongside self-awareness, a willingness to learn, and patience. Many executive leaders want quick, visible results when addressing DEI. So, they often start by hiring DEI executives, also called Chief Diversity Officers (CDOs). A LinkedIn study (Anders, 2023) shows that between 2019 and 2022 the hiring of CDOs jumped 169%, making it the fastest-growing executive role in U.S. companies (Anders, 2023). By 2023, 18% of the CDOs were either leaving, had left, or were let go from companies including Nike, Disney, Netflix, and Warner Brothers Discovery (Mallick, 2023). Why? Many companies failed to address the root causes of organizational inequities, the role was poorly defined, and the role lacked decision-making power (Mallick, 2023; Starner, 2023). An inclusive leadership strategy requires a high degree of iterative learning, self-awareness, values-driven motivations, authentic communication, and an ongoing commitment to integrating DEI into every aspect of an organization's business operations and goals.

An inclusive communications strategy is like many other strategies necessary for business growth requiring investment, learning, and continuous improvement. Inclusive leaders will have powerful talking points and the ability to demonstrate genuine commitment as DEI initiatives are aligned with values, ethical practices, and care for people, linked to strategic plans, business processes, and organizational culture.

Many people refer to DEI as a journey, which implies simply traveling from one place to another, but DEI is a powerful business strategy, a moral imperative, and a complex, continually changing ecosystem that leaders can effectively address. Even when new acronyms appear and abbreviations change, with increased globalization, stakeholder expectations, and diverse population growth, the topics of DEI and inclusive leadership are here to stay.

Bibliography

Alfonseca, K., & Zahn, M. (2023, July 7). How corporate America is slashing DEI workers amid backlash to diversity programs. *ABC News.* https://abcnews.go.com/US/corporate-america-slashing-dei-workers-amid-backlash-diversity/story?id=100477952

Anders, G. (2023, February 1). *Who's vaulting into the C-suite? Trends changed fast in 2022.* LinkedIn. www.linkedin.com/pulse/whos-vaulting-c-suite-trends-changed-fast-2022-george-anders/

Atcheson, S. (2021, February 10). Performative allyship is in your workplace: Here's what to do about it. *Forbes.* www.forbes.com/sites/shereeatcheson/2021/02/10/performative-allyship-is-in-your-workplace-heres-what-to-do-about-it/?sh=1fdccf2a5ba9

Banaji, M. R., & Greenwald, A. G. (2016). *Blindspot: Hidden biases of good people.* Bantam.

Baumeister, R. F., & Leary, M. R. (1995). The need to belong: Desire for interpersonal attachments as a fundamental human motivation. *Psychological Bulletin, 117*(3), 497–529.

Bennis, W., & Thomas, R. (2007). *Leading for a lifetime: How defining moments shape the leaders of today and tomorrow.* Harvard Business Press.

Bourne, H., & Jenkins, M. (2013). Organizational values: A dynamic perspective. *Organization Studies, 34*(4), 495–514. https://doi.org/10.1177/0170840612467155

Brown, J. (2019). *How to be an inclusive leader: Your role in creating cultures of belonging where everyone can thrive.* Barrett-Koehler Publishers.

Carmeli, A., Reiter-Palmon, R., & Ziv, E. (2010). Inclusive leadership and employee involvement in creative tasks in the workplace: The mediating role of psychological safety. *Creativity Research Journal, 22*(3), 250–260. https://doi.org/10.1080/10400419.2010.504654

Chatterji, A., & Toffel, K. (2018). The new CEO activists: A playbook for polarized times. *Harvard Business Review.* https://hbr.org/2018/01/the-new-ceo-activists

Edelman. (2023). *Future of corporate communications study.* www.edelman.com/2023-future-of-corporate-comms

Edelman Trust Barometer. (2022). *Special report: Business and racial justice in America.* www.edelman.com/trust/2022-trust-barometer/special-report-business-and-racial-justice

Edelman Trust Barometer, (2023). *Social fabric weakens amid deepening divisions.* www.edelman.com/trust/2023/trust-barometer

Fuller, P., & Murphy, M. (2020). *The leader's guide to unconscious bias: How to reframe bias, cultivate connection, and create high-performing teams.* Simon & Schuster.

IBM, Business Strategy Hub. (2023). https://bstrategyhub.com/ibm-mission-statement-vision-core-values-analysis/

Korn Ferry Institute. (2023). *The 5 disciplines of inclusive leaders*. www.kornferry. com/insights/featured-topics/diversity-equity-inclusion/5-disciplines-of-inclusive-leaders

Kutlaca, M., & Radke, H. R. M. (2023). Towards an understanding of performative allyship: Definition, antecedents, and consequences. *Social and Personality Psychology Compass, 17*(2), e12724. https://doi.org/10.1111/spc3.12724

Mallick, M. (2023). October 16 *What's next for Chief Diversity Officers?* FastCompany. www.fastcompany.com/90967182/whats-next-for-chief-diversity-officers

McGhee, H. (2022). *The sum of us: What racism costs everyone and how we can prosper together*. One World.

Nembhard, I. M., & Edmondson, A. C. (2006). Making it safe: The effects of leader inclusiveness and professional status on psychological safety and improvement efforts in health care teams. *Journal of Organizational Behavior, 27*(7), 941–966.

Ospina, S., & El Hadidy, W. (2011). *Leadership, diversity and inclusion: Insights from scholarship*. National Urban Fellows Public Service Leadership Diversity Initiative.

Ragan & HarrisX. (2022). *HarrisX/Ragan CEO-Communicators perceptions survey: Findings reveal CEOs perceptions of the communications function*. www.ragan.com/white-papers/harrisx-ragan-ceo-communicators-perceptions-survey/

Randel, A. E., Dean, M. A., Ehrhart, K. H., Chung, B., & Shore, L. (2016). Leader inclusiveness, psychological diversity climate, and helping behaviors. *Journal of Managerial Psychology, 31*(1), 216–234.

Ravasi, D., & Schultz, M. (2006). Responding to organizational identity threats: Exploring the role of organizational culture. *Academy of Management Journal, 49*(3), 433–458.

Sodexo.com. (2023). https://us.sodexo.com/home.html

Starner, T. (2023, June 9). *DEI efforts are falling short and diverse leaders are leaving*. World at Work. https://worldatwork.org/resources/publications/workspan-daily/dei-efforts-are-falling-short-and-diverse-leaders-are-leaving

Tapia, A., & Kirtzman, F. (2023). *The 5 disciplines of inclusive organizations: How diverse and equitable enterprises will transform the world*. Berrett-Koehler.

Uhl-Bien, M. (2006). Relational leadership theory: Exploring the social processes of leadership and organizing. *The Leadership Quarterly, 17*(6), 654–676.

Workplace.com. (2023). *Organizational values: What are they and why are they important?* www.workplace.com/blog/organizational-values

Zandan, N., & Shalett, L. (2020, November 19). What inclusive leaders sound like. *Harvard Business Review*. https://hbr.org/2020/11/what-inclusive-leaders-sounds-like

10 Reputation Management and DEI

Karen Lindsey

The Edelman Trust Barometer study (2022) indicates that demonstrating societal leadership is now a core function of business. Companies and their leaders are now expected to be able to articulate and demonstrate their position on everything from environmental concerns to social justice actions. When a company communicates or does not communicate a stance on issues, it affects their credibility, trust, and ultimately their reputation among employees, the public, and other stakeholders. In this chapter, you will learn:

- What is reputation management?
- The role of strategic communicators
- What is political consumerism?
- Proactive and reactive ways to manage a reputation

What Is Reputation Management?

Diversity, equity, and inclusion (DEI) issues can emerge when an organization least expects it. With the growth of divisive politics and global crises, strategic communicators are often called upon to be both proactive and reactive in their work. This requires having a solid communications plan around an organization's values, its leaders, its business operations, and a defined way to address unplanned negative occurrences. *Reputation management* involves *creating and managing communication strategies designed to influence and build authentic relationships, and elevate positive actions, beliefs, and opinions about an individual or brand* (Davies & Miles, 1998; Sproutsocial. com, 2023).

The Role of Strategic Communicators

Reputation is a business and organizational asset. In a study conducted by Weber Shandwick of 2,227 executives across 22 markets worldwide, 63% of

DOI: 10.4324/9781003411796-11

the executives indicated that reputation has a noticeable impact on market value (Weber Shandwick, 2020). The reputational risks associated with failing to focus on DEI and aligning practices with actions can cause a failure to attract and retain employees, and can mean losing customers, missing out on new markets, and even causing harm to marginalized communities (Miller, 2021).

Reputation encompasses elements of a brand's image, its history, its leadership, employee loyalty, consumer confidence, and relationships with stakeholders. When it comes to DEI and diverse audiences, advising, creating, and delivering the narratives on behalf of an organization both internally and externally are part of the communicator's role. Some key aspects of the job might include:

- Advising executives and employees on internal and external communications
- Monitoring and tracking social and political issues
- Managing the lifecycle of a crisis including media relations
- Using employee, public, and other stakeholder storytelling
- Working with community organizations to create sponsored events

A key objective of reputation management for DEI is to ensure that an organization's image accurately reflects its beliefs and actions with internal and external publics. Building an authentic and credible reputation with diverse publics takes time, and managing a reputation is an ongoing process.

Managing a Reputation: Proactive and Reactive

Strategic communicators involved in advertising, DEI, public relations, and corporate social responsibility jobs play an essential role in advising, developing, monitoring, and maintaining a brand's reputation. We consider reputation management for inclusive strategic communicators in two ways: proactive and reactive.

Proactive

To build authentic relationships and trust among diverse audiences, strategic communicators employ a variety of digital tools and tactics to earn trust and establish a positive narrative among diverse audiences.

- **Inclusive content creation.** Creating and pushing content that authentically represents various diverse communities or is relevant to a specific social identity is especially important on social media platforms. One way to protect an organization from embarrassing missteps is by using a diverse team of creatives, utilizing diverse influencers, engaging with community members, and ensuring organizational storytelling aligns with internal realities. Content creation increases visibility, shapes a brand narrative, and establishes a trusted history of the organization's commitment to DEI in the event of a crisis.

- **Search Engine Optimization (SEO).** Employing SEO techniques includes researching and creating a list of keywords to use for on-page social media or website optimization and link building. Using SEO techniques ensures that content and information about an organization or individual ranks higher in search engine results. Partner with good web designers for the technical side of SEO.

- **Media monitoring and online listening.** This involves monitoring trends, hashtags, online comments, and reviews on platforms such as Instagram, TikTok, Threads, Yelp, TripAdvisor, or other organization-specific sites. As part of a proactive strategy, you set up alerts using keywords or phrases to track public opinion and public perception of a product, service, or issue. Using media monitoring tools such as Brandwatch or Cision can help. By effectively capturing themes, you learn about trends and issues important to diverse communities to stay ahead of conflicts that may be forming.

- **Online complaint engagement.** Timeliness in addressing small concerns or negative comments that appear online is a critical component of earning trust. Ensuring concerns are heard, mitigated, and addressed with two-way communication helps brands create pathways to prevent an individual online complaint from becoming amplified into a community's online protest.

- **Community advocate and media relationships**. Building and maintaining relationships with community advocates and activist organizations helps strategic communicators authentically learn, support, and understand concerns that affect diverse communities. Investments in community programs and advertising in minority-owned media outlets further demonstrate a commitment to DEI. Forming sincere relationships through employee volunteerism within diverse communities can clarify economic realities, power dynamics, and even identify areas of community mistrust. Earning these relationships takes time, investments, and sincerity. The relationships should not only be used to promote a brand's presence during diverse history celebratory months (i.e., Asian American and Pacific Islander Heritage Month, Black History Month, Pride Month, etc.).

To avoid appearing performative, inclusive communicators will create communications plans that involve multiple layers of alignment. This includes aligning leadership messaging to the business mission and organizational values. Sharing the measurable, organizational actions on DEI from a leadership and a diverse group's voice-centered perspective is also powerful. Communicators act as advisors, strategists, and tacticians to help leaders and organizations understand that allyship requires an ongoing commitment that involves developing sincere relationships, listening, speaking out on issues, participating in community service, measuring results, and investing in programs meaningful to diverse communities.

For example, the ice cream brand Ben & Jerry's has consistently woven into their internal organization and public image a stand on social justice issues. On their website, they noticeably list sections that include "Issues We Care About" and "Movements We Support" (Ben & Jerry's, 2023). The brand and its past and current CEOs have a long history of being active on social media in speaking out against racial injustices and other issues which they clearly align with their values and mission beyond making ice cream (Shi, 2021). Despite ongoing criticism, the brand created a foundation and publicly supports causes relating to everything from fair trade to LBTGQ+ rights (Ben & Jerry's, 2023). Since 1989, the company has also published its investments and results in its Social and Environmental Assessment report found at www.benjerry.com/about-us/sear-reports. This proactive, transparent approach demonstrates a clear alignment of the brand's values, organizational actions, public messaging, and evaluation of measurable results. Their consistent activist-like history and self-accountability earns them trust in diverse communities, with their employees, and with customers.

Reactive

From a natural disaster that disproportionality affects a marginalized, low-income community to an employee posting a derogatory message on social media, having authentic relationships and a credible reputation in diverse communities is helpful if a crisis erupts. A crisis can cause immediate and long-term damage to an organization's reputation among diverse publics and allies. Strategic communications professionals are often involved in managing a crisis.

Scholars have extensively studied and defined the steps to communicating during and after a crisis, leading to reputation repair and recovery (Coombs, 2015; Fink et al., 1971; Mitroff et al., 1987). For the purposes of this chapter, we define ***crisis management*** as using *proactive and more often reactive strategies to address untrue or negative occurrences, images, and messages that might threaten an organization's reputation and its relationship with its publics and stakeholders.* There are a variety of occurrences that can trigger a DEI-related crisis for an organization, including but not limited to:

- Social justice or consumer protests
- Discrimination lawsuits
- Employee activism

- Environmental issues
- Executive or employee social media statements
- Financial improprieties
- Sexual misconduct by employees or executives
- Natural disasters
- Mass shootings and workplace violence
- Product recalls or safety incidents

For example, employee activism and public protests played a role in 2020 when a crisis for Starbucks erupted on social media after an internal dress code memo was circulated. The memo prohibited employees from wearing Black Lives Matter apparel while doing their job. In response, Starbucks publicly admitted that their policy was divisive. Within days they reversed their policy, allowed workers to wear BLM pins, and even created their own shirt for employees to wear in support of BLM (Aratani, 2020; Segran, 2020).

Timeliness is an important element in addressing a crisis. Responding quickly and accurately activates trust in diverse publics but does not guarantee credibility. During a crisis, strategic communicators may become involved in responding to the media or assisting leaders in communicating known facts about the who, what, when, where, and why of the situation. Fact-checking, delivering accurate messages, ensuring the credibility of spokespersons, and assembling a crisis response team can help set the course for an authentic, truthful tone during a negative occurrence.

Political Consumerism

More than ever before in history, diverse consumers and their allies are holding organizations accountable by using their buying power to either admonish or show support of a brand. This is a type of political consumerism that has a long history of advancing societal change for marginalized people. *Political consumerism* refers to *the use of the market as an arena for politics to change institutional or market practices found to be ethically, environmentally, or politically objectionable and to reward companies for favorable practices* (Stolle & Micheletti, 2013). Strategic communicators are increasingly aware of the rise of political consumerism and the need to apply both proactive and reactive strategies. This involves an ongoing alignment of values, actions, and messages. Let's look at two forms of political consumerism: boycotts and buycotts.

Boycotts

Boycotts have been around since the 1800s and played a pivotal role in the late 1950s and 1960s Civil Rights Movement. A *boycott* is *an individual consumer's decision to respond to and participate in a collective call to refrain from purchasing from a specific company, brand, or engaging with a government entity for the explicit purpose of exerting pressure to achieve objectives related to social, environmental, or economic change* (Ettenson & Gabrielle Klein, 2005; Friedman, 2002; Hoffmann, 2011).

The word "boycott" has an interesting history. In the 1880s, Charles Cunningham Boycott oversaw the management of the land of a powerful Irish landowner in Ireland. Boycott's job was to collect rents from farmers who lived on and worked the land and evict those who could not pay their rent. He routinely exploited the tenant farmers by charging outrageous fines for petty transgressions, such as their livestock straying onto his land or if the farmers were late to work. The fines sometimes exceeded their wages. A widespread economic downturn caused a crisis in agriculture and famine was constant among the farmers. Many could not pay their rent. After a series of meetings failed to convince the landowner to lower rents, tenant farmers refused to pay when Boycott came to collect the rent. Mr. Boycott tried to serve eviction notices to those who refused. Newspapers covered the incidents and to support the protests, local businesses agreed not to work with Boycott unless he lowered the rents (O'Dowd, 2023). Eventually, the tenant farmers won out and Boycott's last name became the verb we use today to describe a protest tactic designed to force positive change.

In the United States, another historic example occurred in the late 1950s. The Montgomery Bus Boycott was sparked by the arrest of Rosa Parks, a seamstress in Montgomery, Alabama who was on her way home from work. Parks was known to have repeatedly disagreed with a segregation law that required Black passengers to give up their seats to White passengers when the bus became over-crowded, requiring Black passengers to stand. Parks was sitting in the "colored" section and when the bus became crowded, the bus driver ordered her to get up and give her seat to a White man. She refused and was arrested, convicted, and fined for the offense. Her individual act and its injustice led to a 381-day protest where Black citizens refused to ride the bus, causing a loss of between 30,000 and 40,000 bus fares (History.com, 2024). After the negative publicity and impact on their revenue, the bus company reluctantly stopped the practice. The boycott ultimately ended when the U.S. Supreme Court ruled that segregation on public buses is unconstitutional (Martin Luther King Jr. Institute, 2023; National Park Service, 2023).

Today, long-term boycotting of a specific organization is a frequent tactic used by the animal rights organization PETA. In 2012, PETA began a boycott of Air France. Air France was the only known major European airline still shipping monkeys to laboratories for experimentation (Carstens, 2022). PETA created a campaign that involved international demonstrations, on-flight protests, disruption of executives' speeches, and bold advertisements calling on the airline to stop its practices. Celebrities from Jane Goodall to Peter Gabriel got behind the campaign. For years, these actions were consistently covered by the media, casting a negative light on the airline's reputation. Ten years later, in 2022, Air France announced they would no longer ship monkeys to laboratories for research purposes (Carstens, 2022).

Buycotts

Conversely, when publics support a business's stance on social, ethical, or political issues, it can work to an organization's advantage. An emerging trend that focuses on spending money with brands that align with a social or political cause is to **buycott**, which refers to *an individual or collective call for consumers to intentionally spend their money in support of a brand or business with which they agree on social, moral, political, or environmental issues* (Kam & Deichert, 2020).

When faced with a global pandemic and civil unrest starting in 2020, activists and advocates across the United States encouraged the Black community to buy from Black businesses. Organic campaigns emerged on social media with the hashtag #Buyblack (Alcorn, 2021; TAG TEAM Marketing, 2023). Lists of Black-owned businesses were widely circulated, and many entrepreneurs saw growth in revenue. A majority (96%) of Black-owned businesses are sole proprietorships and that figure is only 80% for non-Black-owned businesses (Bank of America, 2022; Baboolall & Fitzhugh, 2021). The call to support Black-owned business had another astonishing effect: growth in Black-owned banks and an increase in new small businesses. By 2021, an estimated $150 million in equity capital had been invested in Black-owned banks. FDIC records in the United States show that a total of 142 minority-owned depository institutions grew their combined assets more than 15%, from about $248.6 billion at the end of 2019 to more than $287 billion at the end of 2020 (Alcorn, 2021; Bank of America, 2022). Minority-owned banks are a small component of the estimated $21 trillion U.S. banking system, but they play a large role in serving Black and Brown communities (Alcorn, 2021). Even though many Black-owned businesses had a tougher path to recovery after the pandemic and social justice efforts (Baboolall & Fitzhugh, 2021), the impact of the buying power of diverse groups was leveraged and elevated through buycotts. Authentically communicating actions that demonstrate a commitment to DEI can establish a trusted relationship with diverse publics. Let's look at how earning trust from diverse communities is an informed, ongoing business decision.

Trust: The Foundation of Reputation Management

Trust is the foundation of interaction with any of a brand's publics and is even more important within the span of diverse publics. Gone are the days when adding an image of a Chinese person or disabled person to advertising was sufficient to demonstrate that an organization cares about diversity. Executives who give speeches about their commitment to DEI but don't support it across hiring, promotion, personal interactions, and general business practices can do more harm than good to an organization's reputation. Diverse communities and identity groups are creating their own narratives about the authenticity of social, ethical, and political positions of brands and their leaders. Diverse publics closely observe the alignment of a brand's espoused values with actions. These publics are using their buying power to hold brands and their leaders accountable. The well-equipped strategic communicator is constantly seeking ways to align values to messages, and to communicate authentically and ethically to earn public and employee trust.

Marketing executive Susan Beerman (2021) offers proactive tips for strategic communicators and inclusive leaders seeking to earn trust, maintain trust, and add a history of caring about DEI to proactively manage a brand's reputation. She states that brands should:

- Identify potential reputational risk [and their] impacts, e.g., supplier [issues], workplace harassment issues, regulatory noncompliance, and others. Consider the likelihood and severity of any reputational risks you uncover.
- Look at customer service satisfaction scores and comments. Ask to see hotline (or online) reports to understand what customers and employees are saying. This information can provide an excellent barometer for how the brand's culture is doing.
- Be an internal champion for closing the gaps on issues that present reputational risk. Have a proactive plan in place for the times when you may need to react. Brands today need to live up to their own stated values or be called out on it.
- Establish relationships with peers in compliance, legal, HR, and environmental, social and governance (ESG). Learn about how each department manages its own impact on your brand's reputation.

(Beerman, 2021)

Learning about and staying well informed of an array of business, economic, environmental, social, political, and ethical issues that affect cultures and communities other than your own is a smart step to understanding the intricacies of DEI and reputation management.

Bibliography

Alcorn, C. (2021, June 9). *Black-owned banks are booming, and they're pouring money back into their communities.* CNN Business. https://edition.cnn.com/2021/06/09/economy/black-owned-banks/index.html

Aratani, L. (2020, June 12) Starbucks reverses stance and allows staff to wear Black Lives Matter clothing. *The Guardian.* www.theguardian.com/business/2020/jun/12/starbucks-black-lives-matter-clothing

Baboolall, D., & Fitzhugh, E. (2021, June 11). *Black-owned businesses face an unequal path to recovery.* McKinsey Insights. www.mckinsey.com/featured-insights/sustainable-inclusive-growth/future-of-america/black-owned-businesses-face-an-unequal-path-to-recovery

Bank of America. (2022). *2022 Women & minority business owner spotlight.* https://newsroom.bankofamerica.com/content/dam/newsroom/docs/2022/Women%20+%20Minority%20Business%20Owner%20Spotlight%20ADA.pdf

Beerman, S. (2021, October 12). *Why a strong brand reputation starts with trust.* Forbes. www.forbes.com/sites/forbescommunicationscouncil/2021/10/12/why-a-strong-brand-reputation-starts-with-trust/

Ben & Jerry's. (2023). *Our values, activism and mission.* www.benjerry.com/values

Carstens, A. (2022, July 6). *Air France announces end to research monkey transport.* The Scientist. www.the-scientist.com/news-opinion/air-france-announces-end-to-research-monkey-transport-70198

Coombs, W. T. (2015). The value of communication during a crisis: Insights from strategic communication research. *Business Horizons, 58*(2), 141–148.

Davies, G., & Miles, L. (1998). Reputation management: Theory versus practice. *Corporate Reputation Review, 2,* 16–27.

Edelman Trust Barometer. (2022). www.edelman.com/news-awards/2022-edelman-trust-barometer-reveals-even-greater-expectations-business-lead-government-trust

Ettenson, R., & Gabrielle Klein, J. (2005). The fallout from French nuclear testing in the South Pacific: A longitudinal study of consumer boycotts. *International Marketing Review, 22*(2), 199–224. https://doi.org/10.1108/02651330510593278

Fink, S. L., Beak, J., & Taddeo, K. (1971). Organizational crisis and change. *The Journal of Applied Behavioral Science, 7*(1), 15–37.

Friedman, M. (2002). *Consumer boycotts: Effecting change through the marketplace and media.* Routledge.

Gundlach, G. T., & Murphy, P. E. (1993). Ethical and legal foundations of relational marketing exchanges. *Journal of Marketing, 57*(4), 35–46. https://doi.org/10.1177/002224299305700403

History.com. (2024). *Montgomery bus boycott.* www.history.com/topics/black-history/montgomery-bus-boycott

Hoffmann, S. (2011). Anti-consumption as a means to save jobs. *European Journal of Marketing, 45*(11–12), 1702–1714. https://doi.org/10.1108/03090561111167342

Holmes, P. (2005, January 1). *More than a third of world's consumers boycott brands.* Provoke Media. www.provokemedia.com/latest/article/more-than-a-third-of-world's-consumers-boycott-brands

Kam, C. D., & Deichert, M. (2020). Boycotting, buycotting, and the psychology of political consumerism. *The Journal of Politics, 82*(1), 72–88.

The Martin Luther King, Jr. Institute. (2023). *Montgomery bus boycott.* https:// kinginstitute.stanford.edu/montgomery-bus-boycott

Miller, A. (2021, September 16). Avoiding reputation risk by embracing DEI. *Risk Management Magazine.* www.rmmagazine.com/articles/article/2021/09/16/ avoiding-reputation-risk-by-embracing-dei

Mitroff, I. I., Shrivastava, P., & Udwadia, F. E. (1987). Effective crisis management. *Academy of Management Perspectives, 1*(4), 283–292.

National Park Service. (2023). *The Montgomery bus boycott.* www.nps.gov/articles/ montgomery-bus-boycott.htm

O'Dowd, N. (2023, June 19). The English land agent who inspired the buycott in 19th-century Ireland. *Irish Central.* www.irishcentral.com/roots/history/irish-invented-boycott

Segran, E. (2020, June 16). *Starbucks banned employees from wearing BLM t-shirts. Now it's designing its own.* Fast Company. www.fastcompany.com/90516865/ starbucks-banned-employees-from-wearing-blm-t-shirts-now-its-designing-its-own

Shi, D. (2021). *How Ben & Jerry's crafts its bold social media messaging.* Fast Company. www.fastcompany.com/90619448/how-ben-jerrys-crafts-its-bold-social-media-messaging

Sproutsocial.com. (2023). *Reputation management: The essential guide to protecting your brand.* https://sproutsocial.com/insights/reputation-management/

Stolle, D., & Micheletti, M. (2013). *Political consumerism: Global responsibility in action.* Cambridge University Press.

TAG TEAM Marketing. (2023). *Buy Black movement history.* www.buyblackmovement. com/about/history/index.cfm

Verlegh, P. W. J. (2023, June 26). Perspectives: A research-based guide for brand activism. *International Journal of Advertising.* https://doi.org/10.1080/02650487.20 23.2228117

Weber Shandwick. (2018, January 30). *Battle of the wallets: The changing landscape of consumer activism.* https://webershandwick.com/news/battle-of-the-wallets-the-changing-landscape-of-consumer-activism

Weber Shandwick. (2020, January 14). *The state of corporate reputation: Everything matters now.* https://webershandwick.com/news/the-state-of-corporate-reputation-in-2020-everything-matters-now

11 Communicating for Social Change

Lee Bush

As stated in the introduction and throughout this book, strategic communicators play a powerful role in shaping public perceptions. We are in essence cultural intermediaries, creating or recreating the narratives that help shape our societies (Aghazadeh & Ashby-King, 2022). When we become culturally proficient in diversity, equity, and inclusion (DEI) and begin to recognize the history and impact of social inequalities, part of our role in shaping public perceptions includes advocating for social justice.

While strategic communication as a profession has historically been conceptualized through the lens of corporate practice, the principles of strategic communications have been used throughout history to advance social movements. In more recent years, scholars have called for expanding our view of strategic communications beyond the lens of commerce to include the practices of social justice communications. And while the two practices are similar, there are also unique differences.

The purpose of this chapter is to serve as a brief overview of communications principles and practices used in social justice communications. Interested students are encouraged to investigate the topics further for more information. In this chapter, students will:

- Learn definitions of social justice, social change, and social movements
- Recognize the difference between activists and advocates
- Understand the broadening of our industry to include social justice
- Review theories and concepts that shape social justice communications
- Examine communications strategies and tactics used by activists

Defining Social Justice and Social Change

Before delving into the concepts and cases in this chapter, it's helpful to start with definitions: What do we mean by social justice and social change? Let's break down the terms into three parts: social, justice, and change.

DOI: 10.4324/9781003411796-12

The word *social* in relation to social justice, refers to a society – a collective of people and the systems and practices that govern them. That society could be the local community, a region or geography, or a larger society like the nation or even the world. Or it could refer to the policies and practices within societal institutions, like academia or healthcare. Systems and practices of a society can include economic, political, social, or cultural.

The word *justice* refers to just or fair treatment of people or groups of people within these societal systems. We often speak of justice in relation to the rights and privileges afforded to people in an equitable and fair society. The term ***social justice***, then, refers to *the fair treatment of all people and groups within a society and the equitable distribution of opportunities and privileges.* When conflict occurs, such as inequalities in race, class, or gender, groups of people come together to work toward social change (Soken-Huberty, n.d.).

The word *change* can be applied to many situations. We change our clothes, we change lanes while driving, or we change our attitudes. Change means we replace one thing with another or move from one area or state of being to another. Thus, in social justice terms, ***social change*** *refers to altering, replacing, or transforming an unjust practice, policy, attitude, or system to one that is more equitable.* Social change can seek to change institutions and practices, or change societal attitudes, like attitudes that privilege heteronormative identities over queer identities.

Beneath social change, we will often find ***social movements***, that is, *an organized effort or initiative by a group of people to create social change.* Social movements can be found throughout history, such as abolitionist movements to end slavery, the Civil Rights Movement, labor movements, LGBTQ+ rights movements, disability rights movements, the Anti-Apartheid movement in South Africa, etc. These movements were geared toward changing unjust societal norms, practices, or policies and employed many of the concepts of strategic communications. For example, activists in the suffragette movement in the early 20th century were pioneers in using branding, merchandising, celebrity endorsements, staged photo opportunities, fundraising events, and national publicity to secure the vote for women (O'Brien, 2019).

Advocates and Activists

Behind social movements you will find advocates and activists. But what is the difference, you might ask, between a social justice advocate and an activist?

While the terms are often used interchangeably, generally ***advocacy*** involves *"persuading or arguing in support of a specific cause, policy, idea, or set of values"* (Cox & Pezzullo, 2016, p. 177), while activism involves more direct and noticeable action. Scholar Robyn Gulliver refers to advocacy as an umbrella term for working toward societal change, and activism as the more active practice of advocacy that can take a variety of forms, such as protests, marches, or petitions (Watchmaps, 2021).

Aghazadeh and Ashby-King (2022) understand *social justice activism* as "*sustained resistance to and disruption of harmful inequities, norms, and practices that discriminate against and marginalize people to ultimately promote equity*" (p. 14). It's worth noting that you can be an advocate or activist either for or against certain societal policies or practices. For example, you can advocate for racial equality while activating against policies or practices that create or sustain racial inequity.

Many social justice organizations work at both the advocacy and activism levels. Throughout this chapter, we use the terms advocacy and activism interchangeably to mean both working and acting toward social justice and change.

Moving from Corporate-Centric to Societal-Centric Strategic Communications

While we have seen strategic communications used in societal movements throughout history, public relations and advertising as professions were developed and conceptualized in the Western world principally as tools for commerce. In this frame, activists were traditionally viewed as adversaries of organizations – as external publics that had to be "managed" or "dealt with" to achieve organizational success – rather than communications practitioners themselves (Benecke & Oksiutycz, 2015; Ciszek, 2015, p. 448). For example, in issues management and crisis communications, corporate PR practitioners often monitor issues elevated by activists to preempt them from becoming a crisis for the corporation. We can see the unequal power dynamics at play in this framing, with corporations using their resources and power to silence or circumvent the work of activists.

In more recent years, however, scholars have called for framing and teaching strategic communications as a means of creating change both within organizations and within society (Hou & Wang, 2022). We can begin to see this shift by looking at the rise of corporate social responsibility (CSR) and corporate social advocacy (CSA), where organizations are concerned with their impact on society and publicly advocate for social-political issues, as discussed in Chapter 1. However, the focus of these practices is still on the corporation, with the main concern being how they may benefit or harm the organization in the process of creating societal change (Ciszek & Logan, 2018).

Over the past decade or so, scholars have been grappling with a more fluid and expansive definition of strategic communications to encompass the many roles of its practitioners in society, including social justice (Coombs & Holladay, 2012). For example, Edwards (2011) redefines PR as "the flow of purposive communication produced on behalf of individuals, formally constituted and informally constituted groups, through their

continuous trans-actions with other social entities" (p. 21). While this definition is grounded in academic theories and concepts that are beyond the
scope of this chapter, it holds several practical implications for communications practitioners. For example, it describes PR as a dynamic (rather than
static) process, having a purpose or particular outcome in mind, and involving continuous transactions with other entities, which relates to how PR
practices interact with those of the larger society.

Moreover, the definition expands the entities for whom strategic communications is produced beyond corporations to include individuals (such as
politicians or celebrities) and both formally constituted and informally constituted groups. This is important because in social justice activism strategic
communications may occur within an organizational setting (such as in
nonprofits and nongovernmental organizations) but also in grassroots
movements organized outside of formal organizational settings (such as
community or activist groups). For example, Black Lives Matter, Occupy
Wall Street, and the March For Our Lives movements began with a small
group of people, or even a single social media post, that mobilized others to
act (Jasper, n.d.). In this way, grassroots movements are often spontaneous,
decentralized, and more democratic than formal organizations, with the
focus being on the success of the cause rather than the success of an organization (Kaplan, 2023).

Despite efforts to broaden the strategic communication definition to
include social justice, Weaver (2019) notes that these attempts might be of
more concern to theorists than the activists themselves. Because of the
industry's history as a tool for powerful corporations, activists often find
themselves in opposition to advertising and public relations practices and
therefore may resist being considered under the same umbrella (pp. 107–
108). At the same time, however, USC Annenberg's annual Global
Communication Report (2022) indicates that this divide may be shrinking:
the percentage of agency and industry professionals who proactively involve
activist groups in their initiatives and policy planning increased from 14% in
2020 to 46% in 2022, and 73% predict their engagement with social issues
will continue to increase.

Social Justice Concepts Relating to Strategic Communications

Below, we outline three concepts that can help us better understand the
underlying principles of social justice communications and how they differ
from conventional communications models.

Applying Critical Theories to Social Change

In Chapter 1, we discussed critical theories and their relationship to critiqu-
ing inequitable societal systems and structures. Embedded in this critique is

a review of the power structures that create, elevate, and maintain social inequalities. Likewise, social justice activism is focused on exposing, resisting, and dismantling the power structures that maintain the status quo. These power structures could be political, cultural, social, or economic.

Critical theory relates to social change in that theories such as critical race theory, feminist theory, and queer theory examine how these dominant systems impact marginalized identity groups and offer alternatives for more equitable structures. For example, when we look at the impact of social inequalities, we can see *what* is happening and to *whom* by examining the lived experiences of people with intersectional identities. If we then examine the underlying causes of social inequalities and ask *why* they exist, we often uncover historical contexts and power dynamics that privilege certain voices and identities and marginalize others. Social justice activists often work at both levels: intervening to lessen the impact of social inequalities on marginalized identities while also working to dismantle and offer alternatives to the systems and structures that led to the inequalities.

An example is The Bail Project (n.d.), an activist organization whose mission is to disrupt the racial and economic inequalities in the cash bail system in the United States. The Bail Project intervenes to lessen the impact of the inequitable system by providing bail assistance and community support to low-income individuals who have been deemed eligible for pre-trial release by a judge but who can't afford to pay bail. At the same time, through legislative advocacy they provide a policy road map for dismantling the cash bail system and creating a criminal justice system that is more just, equitable, and humane.

Social (Re)production and Communications

From a strategic communications standpoint, communication often produces or reproduces these dominant power structures. At its essence, communication is about creating meaning. From a cultural studies perspective, we can view communications itself as culture or as "a symbolic process where reality is produced, maintained, repaired and transformed" (Carey, 1989, p. 23). It is at the repair and transform stages where social justice communicators intervene to bring attention to injustices and ultimately transform the culture with new symbols and narratives. Strategic communicators are in essence cultural intermediaries, either (re)producing dominant social systems, expectations, norms, and beliefs; or, as with activists, providing alternative perspectives to intervene in social (re)production (Aghazadeh & Ashby-King, 2022, p. 24).

We can see the connection of identity, power, and social (re)production play out in the advent of artificial intelligence (AI) tools. With the emergence of machine learning, algorithms, and generative AI tools like ChatGPT, what has also emerged is the inherent bias embedded in these systems (see, for example, Nicoletti & Bass, 2023). Because of the power dynamics of the technology industry creating these systems, and because inequities like racism, sexism, and homophobia are already embedded in the content from which these databases are developed, existing societal inequalities are being reproduced in these newer technologies.

For example, in a podcast on NPR's Science Friday (2023), Drs. Jenna Lester and Roxanna Daneshjou discussed a study in which they found that harmful and previously debunked racist ideas in medicine (like false ideas about different pain thresholds in Black and White patients) were being repeated and perpetuated on four popular chatbots. This could lead to doctors misdiagnosing or mistreating patients. Activist organizations and initiatives such as the Algorithmic Justice League, the Tech Equity Initiative of the National Fair Housing Alliance, and the Distributed AI Research Institute are working to prevent and dismantle inequitable AI practices and intervening in these social (re)productions.

Consensus and Dissensus in Social Justice Communications

Traditionally, strategic communicators have been guided by consensus building. For example, the two-way symmetrical model of public relations (Grunig & Hunt, 1984) envisions communications as a means of conflict resolution and mutual understanding. However, the idea of symmetry assumes 1) that the entities in conflict have equal power, and 2) that consensus is the aim of communication for those in conflict (Ciszek, 2015). Because consensus often privileges those in power, it can lead to silencing alternative views, especially those of marginalized communities.

When it comes to changing social inequalities, the role of activism is often the opposite of consensus building. Rather than achieving consensus, the goal of social justice activism is to *disrupt* the existing social order and dominant logic and challenge oppressive systems and views (Ciszek & Logan, 2018). Thus, activists often use actions like public protests, boycotts, and marches to circumvent traditional power structures and bring widespread public attention to their cause. Unlike consensus, dissensus fosters plurality, elevates marginalized voices, values difference over sameness, and questions inequitable systems of power (Kennedy & Sommerfeldt, 2015).

In the area of communications, some scholars refer to this as dissent PR. Moloney et al. (2012) define **dissent PR** as "*the dissention of ideas, commentaries, and policies through PR techniques in order to change current, dominant thinking and behavior in discrete economic, political, and cultural areas of public life.*" For example, De Moya (2019) examined how Haitian and Dominican Diaspora in the United States successfully opposed a 2013 immigration ruling by the Dominican government that would revoke the citizenship rights of many Haitian immigrants. The Diaspora organized through social media, staged a series of protests and marches that brought media attention to the issue, wrote letters to newspaper editors, presented counterarguments to each of the government's messages, and mobilized the international human rights community to support their cause. We can see in this example where activism worked on two levels: dissensus in pressuring the government to revoke its ruling and consensus in building a coalition of like-minded supporters.

Next, we look at how these social justice concepts are carried out through strategic communications.

Communication Strategies for Social Justice and Change

Social justice communicators use many of the same strategies and tactics found in corporate and brand communications. For example, they conduct research on audience and issues, develop strategies for effectively engaging publics, employ media relations to build credibility and legitimacy, use persuasive strategies to motivate audiences and policymakers, develop creative concepts and slogans to gain attention and support, enlist influencers and spokespeople, and employ tactics such as social media campaigns, advertising, PSAs, events, websites, and email marketing.

Social justice communicators also use a similar planning process. For example, in a Communications Strategies for Social Justice workbook created for the American Public Health Association (APHA/Resonance, 2022), the consulting firm Resonance outlines a four-step planning process they call the GAME plan: set **G**oals, determine **A**udiences, identify **M**essages and stories, and develop **E**ngagement strategies to achieve goals.

However, there are also unique considerations to be aware of with social justice communications, outlined below.

Coalition Building

Societal issues are often too big and dynamic for one group or organization to tackle alone. Unlike the corporate world where organizations have access to larger economic, human, and material resources, social justice organizations are often working on shoestring budgets and have limited capacity. To make their work more effective and efficient, activists will often build coalitions with other like-minded individuals, groups, or organizations.

A ***coalition*** can be defined as "*a group of individuals and/or organizations with a common interest who agree to work together toward a common goal*" (Rabinowitz, n.d.). Coalitions can be built for several reasons, including to address an urgent situation (such as a piece of legislation coming up for a vote), to make advocacy more efficient and eliminate duplication of efforts, to leverage political clout, or to increase communications between groups, among others (Rabinowitz, n.d.).

For example, in 2015, the National Council of La Raza (NCLR) and the League of United Latin American Citizens (LULAC) coordinated a response to a speech by former President Donald Trump in which he disparaged Mexican immigrants (De Moya & Bravo, 2016). The organizations developed key messages to dispute his claims, posted official responses on their websites, and mobilized their members to show opposition to the statement on social media.

Communications practitioners play an important role in helping groups or organizations form and maintain coalitions, foster cohesiveness, and manage ongoing communication between groups.

Identifying and Segmenting Publics

Like other communicators, social justice advocates research and segment audiences, tailoring communications and outreach based on each audience's needs and intersectional identities. Smith and Ferguson (2018) identify two broad audiences for advocacy organizations. The first is comprised of the people, groups, or entities who are the target of the advocacy or are needed to achieve the activists' goals (such as legislators, policymakers, and industry leaders). The second are those who provide sustainable support to activists or organizations in carrying out their social justice mission (such as followers, volunteers, and donors) (p. 444).

The Opportunity Agenda (2019), a social justice communications lab, breaks down social justice audiences into six segments: base (those already with you but need to remain active), persuadables (those who could support you with the right motivation), opposition (those against your position; you need to neutralize these groups), decision makers (those who can achieve your policy goals), and influencers (those who can help persuade decision makers) (p. 9). They note that decision makers can be both members of your base (or persuadables) or members of the opposition. Identifying influencers to whom those in opposition are responsive (such as faith leaders or other legislators) can help move them in your direction.

Once you have segmented your audiences, you can then develop more specific audience profiles, examining the intersectional identities, values, and barriers to support for each audience, and developing messages and strategies to reach them.

Framing and Reframing the Issue through Narrative Analysis

A fundamental concept in strategic communications is message framing. Originally conceived by Erving Goffman (1974), a "frame" is how we make sense of the world or "the culturally determined definitions of reality that allow people to make sense of objects or events" (Shaw, n.d.). When we frame messages, we attempt to persuade audiences of a particular point of view. For example, environmental regulations could be framed as either bad for business or as protecting the environment, spurring innovation, and creating new jobs. In social justice work, the choices we make about how to introduce, explain, and frame an issue can "have the power to influence people's understanding of the issues we care deeply about—and to shape the public response" (FrameWorks Institute, 2020).

One of the underlying purposes of framing in social justice communications is to *change* the narrative; that is, to offer narratives that counter existing and competing dominant narratives. A narrative is a "system of stories" or a composition of "multiple stories that relate to one another" (Halverson, 2011). Dominant narratives are engrained in our societies, passed down through generations, and often work to marginalize communities or silence alternative views. Reinsborough and Canning (2017) assert that changing the narrative starts with deconstructing the existing narrative by examining "the underlying assumptions that allow it to operate as truth and devising a strategy to challenge and reframe those assumptions" (p. 80). For example, the narrative assembled around poverty often creates the assumption that poverty is the result of bad decisions rather than the outcome of economic and structural inequities.

As co-founders of the Center for Story-based Strategy (n.d.), Reinsborough and Canning (2017) developed an approach they call "narrative power analysis" to strategically examine dominant narratives and develop effective counter-narratives side by side. The model involves using the elements of storytelling to "identify elements currently being used and explore some new ways to tell the story" (pp. 60–61). These elements include:

- Conflict (who or what is the conflict between)
- Characters (who are the power holders, who are the victims)
- Imagery (what images, metaphors, or symbols show the story)
- Foreshadowing (how competing stories envision the future)
- Assumptions (the beliefs and values reflected in the story), and, ultimately
- Intervention (how and where underlying assumptions can be exposed)

Once you have conducted a narrative analysis, you can then develop a message framework and strategies for communicating your messages. In its structure for developing a message framework, Resonance (APHA/Resonance, 2022) recommends starting with the "Why?" – "Why should your audiences care about your efforts" and "How can you show the intersection between what they care about and what you care about?" (p. 7). The Opportunity Agenda (2019) calls this "leading with shared values" (p. 14). Leading with shared values – like fairness, equality, community – is particularly important when audiences have little knowledge of the issue or when assumptions about the issue are already deeply engrained.

The next step in developing a message framework is to identify the barriers standing in the way of your shared values and propose solutions (APHA/ Resonance, 2022, p. 7; The Opportunity Agenda, 2019, p. 20). For example, if the shared value is fairness, identify how a particular system (like the criminal justice system) isn't fair to everyone and the solution/s for making it more equitable. You can then communicate how your organization or initiative is making an impact on the problem. To illustrate messages, communicators use facts and statistics, familiar themes and metaphors, and storytelling (discussed in detail below).

Lastly is the call to action – what do you want your audience to do? Donate to your cause? Contact their legislators? Show up to a city council meeting? Attend a protest? Tell your audience what they can specifically do to be part of the social change your organization envisions (The Opportunity Agenda, 2019, p. 20).

Storytelling: Humanizing the Issue

An important part of communicating counter-narratives involves telling the stories of those impacted by the issue. Storytelling is one of the most powerful tools for social justice communications. While this is true for all communications campaigns, it's particularly important for social justice work. Stories humanize the issue beyond facts and statistics; elevate marginalized voices; help us better understand the direct impact of the issue on communities; invoke empathy, conversation, and personal reflection; and illuminate the problem for legislators and policymakers who are often far removed from the issue.

The Opportunity Agenda (2019) identifies three sources for social justice stories: enlightened insiders (those who have worked inside an inequitable system, like law enforcement); the affected change agent (those who have been impacted by the system and tried to change it); and experts (researchers, policy analysts, etc.) who can discuss the bigger picture and how it affects everyone (p. 18). However, there are special considerations for communicators when developing these stories.

As Chelsea Fuller of Blackbird Communications advises, "Being a steward of others' stories comes with a higher level of responsibility—one that requires you to communicate that story to the world in a way that mitigates harm to the people to whom those stories belong" (Fuller, 2021, p. 9). Those impacted by the issue need to tell their stories on their own terms, determining if and when they want to tell their stories, which stories to tell, and how to tell them. In addition, Fuller instructs communicators to understand that "increased visibility without increased support/protection makes folks more vulnerable to job loss, investigation or increased surveillance, and/or harassment or targeting from the opposition" (p. 10). Without being cognizant of these issues, social justice communicators can end up exploiting impacted communities and perpetuating the very inequities they're trying to dismantle.

Further, recounting stories of social injustices can bring up unsettling experiences or traumatic events. Communicators need to be careful not to retraumatize impacted communities through storytelling. For example, when students in a Strategic Campaigns class interviewed impacted communities for The Bail Project (mentioned earlier) one of the women shared that she wanted to tell her story but didn't want to be "relocked up" by telling it.

Lastly, communicators need to connect personal stories to the larger issue. If audiences interpret personal stories as only one person's narrative or an aberration from what they think is true, they may not understand it as illustrating larger social inequities.

Box 11.1 March For Our Lives: Engaging and Motivating Audiences to End Gun Violence

March For Our Lives (MFOL), one of the largest and most powerful youth-led movements in the United States, was born out of the tragic shooting at Marjory Stoneman Douglas High School in Parkland

Florida on February 14, 2018. The organization activates to end gun violence through a policy agenda and legislative advocacy, civic engagement, education, direct action, and its 300 chapters nationwide (MFOL Impact Report, 2022). In addition to gaining widespread visibility through protests in 2018 and 2022, MFOL uses a range of paid, earned, and owned media channels to achieve its goals. Below are just a few examples:

Mobile and Digital: In addition to its massive social media presence, MFOL uses peer-to-peer texting, SMS, and email marketing to mobilize audiences and build a community of supporters. For example, for its "Our Power" campaign in 2020 MFOL contacted thousands of young people to register them to vote, and helped them make a plan, check their registration status, and request a mail-in ballot (Shorty Awards, 2020). MFOL also uses its digital platforms to hold virtual rallies, train volunteers, and livestream events and conversations with legislators, artists, activists, and musicians to keep supporters informed and involved.

Advertising: MFOL launched its first TV ad campaign on Fox & Friends and Morning Joe in 2020, which also ran on digital and broadcast platforms in nine states and in airports across the country (Shorty Awards, 2020). In 2019, the organization launched a digital billboard campaign in Times Square with messages including "I saw my brother get shot" and "I saw my classmate get shot" and a number to text to get involved in the organization (Cook, 2019).

Media Outreach: Through its online "Press Center," the organization regularly develops news releases to build awareness of legislative initiatives, release official statements, promote upcoming events, and highlight voices and leaders within the movement. MFOL consistently appears in national print and broadcast media, and youth activists in MFOL chapters around the country gain publicity for actions and initiatives in each of their areas.

Creative Activism: MFOL uses creative activism to bring attention to and create cultural conversations around gun violence. The organization has worked with artists to create a library of shareable GIFs; launched art interventions in major cities to raise awareness of the systemic issues intersecting with gun violence; hosted a live artist video series; and partnered with Sankofa.org (n.d.), an organization founded by Harry Belafonte to activate artists and performers in service of grassroots movements. In 2022, MFOL installed 1,100 body bags spelling out "Thoughts and Prayers" on the National Mall to represent those killed by gun violence since Parkland (The Drum, 2022). A PSA accompanied the activation.

Organizing and Mobilizing in the Digital Age

A core activity of activism is organizing and mobilizing the public to action. While in previous generations it could take months to build organizing capacity, digital media has transformed how activists mobilize and bring attention to their causes. For example, Tarana Burke, the founder of the #MeToo movement, originally used the term in a MySpace post in 2006 describing her work with girls of color. Ten years later, the #MeToo hashtag went viral on Twitter, bringing global attention to the magnitude of sexual violence (Me Too Movement, n.d.).

In that timespan, social justice activists have become much more adept at using social media and technologies like Google Drive, Slack, WhatsApp, and Zoom to organize, collaborate, and build collective action. In fact, in a 2020 article in *The New Yorker*, journalist Jane Hu suggested we're seeing "the second act" of social media activism, in which "tools of the Internet have been increasingly integrated into the hard-won structure of older movements." For example, the difference between the BLM movement of 2013, when the hashtag was first tweeted, and the BLM of today is that the movement is backed by the work of organizations like BLM Grassroots, BLM Global Network Foundation, the Movement for Black Lives, and the networks these organizations have built around the world (Hu, 2020).

Sociologist Zeynep Tufekci (2017) explains that movements require a shift in tactics at different points in time, and often experience a "tactical freeze" after an immense networked event. She asserts:

> The ability to organize without organizations, indeed, speeds things up and allows for great scale in rapid time frames … However, the tedious work performed during the pre-internet era served other purposes as well; perhaps most importantly, it acclimatized people to the processes of collective decision making and helped create the resilience all movements need to survive and thrive in the long term.
>
> (Tufekci, 2017, p. xiii)

Activist and author Feminista Jones (2019) believes one of the greatest outcomes of social media activism is its ability to empower marginalized voices to share their stories. She affirms: "They are connecting with people across their cities and their states and their countries and other countries because we're realizing that people are experiencing the same kinds of things all over the world" (Gehr, 2021).

While social media activism has become mainstream, some think that people use it more for "virtue signaling" or "slactivism" rather than real political activism (University of Sussex, 2023). In a Pew Research survey (2023), 82% of Americans agreed with the statement "social media distracts people from issues that are truly important" and 76% agreed it "makes people think they're making a difference when they really aren't." Still, the majority of survey participants agreed that social media "highlights important issues that might not get attention otherwise," and "helps give voice to underrepresented groups."

In addition, hashtag campaigns such as #BLM, #MarchforOurLives, #TheWomen'sMarch, and #MeToo and the activists behind them have effected real social change. These include an increase in police reforms and gun safety laws, more women running for office (both Republican and Democratic) than ever before, and record numbers of young people turning out to vote. And, like Tarana Burke's movement that began in 2006, social media has empowered sexual assault survivors, who may not otherwise have shared their stories, to stand up and say, "me too."

Creative Activism: Tapping the Arts for Social Change

Another tool often used by social justice activists is creative activism. **Creative (or artistic) activism** can be defined as *"a dynamic practice combining the creative power of the arts to move us emotionally with the strategic planning of activism necessary to bring about social change"* (The Center for Artistic Activism, n.d.).

When we refer to "the arts," this encompasses a broad range of activities such as painting, graphic design, music, photography, film, dance, poetry, theater, the performing arts, and folk arts and crafts, to name a few. The use of creative activism is not new. For example, protest songs were used extensively during the Civil Rights era to express emotions, promote justice, and foster cohesion. In the 1980s, the AIDS Memorial Quilt brought attention to the lives lost to the AIDS epidemic. Each successive generation brings new artistic forms, technologies, and cultures to motivate action around social change. In the past decade, digital technologies and the use of memes have transformed how people express and share their support for a cause.

An example of creative activism is Ducks for Detainees (D4D). In 2016, Australian artist Maggie Cowling corresponded with a refugee being held on Manus Island in Papua New Guinea who missed his pet duck left behind when he fled his home. She and her neighbors painted ducks and sent them to the detainee via Facebook Messenger. This sparked the idea to use the duck symbol as a nonthreatening way to raise awareness and money for detainees. Thus, D4D was born. D4D subsequently held dozens of art exhibitions; hosted various children's duck-making events at community centers and schools; held a "Pop-Up Pond" event that included a film screening and musical performances; and staged a photo event with 1,300 hand-decorated ducks on the lawn of Parliament House in Canberra (Cowling, n.d.).

The benefits of combining art and activism include bringing greater attention to issues, reaching people in unexpected ways, fostering cooperation, establishing a sense of belonging in communities, and making social justice accessible to broader audiences (Sanz & Rodriguez-Labajos, 2021; The Center for Artistic Activism, n.d.).

Bibliography

Aghazadeh, S. A., & Ashby-King, D. T. (2022). Centering activism and social justice in PR education: Critical communication pedagogy as an entryway. *Journal of Public Relations Education, 8*(2), 11–41. https://journalofpreducation.com/2022/08/

APHA/Resonance. (2022). *Communication strategies for social justice*. Developed for the American Public Health Associate by Resonance. https://apha.org/Topics-and-Issues/Environmental-Health/EH-Council/ejta

Benecke, D. R., & Oksiutycz, A. (2015). Changing conversation and dialogue through LeadSA: An example of public relations activism in South Africa. *Public Relations Review, 41*(5), 816–824. https://doi.org/10.1016/j.pubrev.2015.06.003

Carey, J. (1989). *Communication as culture*. Routledge.

Center for Story-based Strategy. (n.d.). www.storybasedstrategy.org/

Ciszek, E. (2015). Bridging the gap: Mapping the relationship between activism and public relations. *Public Relations Review, 41*(4), 447–455. http://dx.doi.org/10.1016/j.pubrev.2015.05.016

Ciszek, E., & Logan, N. (2018). Challenging the dialogic promise: How Ben & Jerry's support for Black Lives Matter fosters dissensus on social media. *Journal of Public Relations Research, 30*(3), 115–127. https://doi.org/10.1080/1062726X.2018.1498342

Cook, L. (2019, April 15). *March For Our Lives launches 'Save Lives' billboard campaign in Times Square*. amNY. www.amny.com/news/march-for-our-lives-billboards-times-square-1.29846116

Coombs, T. W., & Holladay, S. J. (2012). Fringe public relations: How activism moves critical PR toward the mainstream. *Public Relations Inquiry, 38*, 880–887.

Cowling, M. (n.d.). *Ducks for Detainees: Interview about artivism*. The Commons Social Change Library. https://commonslibrary.org/ducks-for-detainees-interview-about-artivism/

Cox, R. J., & Pezzullo, P. (2016). *Environmental communication and the public sphere*. Sage.

De Moya, M. (2019). Protesting the homeland: Diaspora dissent public relations efforts to oppose the Dominican Republic's citizenship policies. In A. Adi (Ed.), *Protest public relations: Communicating dissent and activism* (pp. 106–127). Routledge.

De Moya, M., & Bravo, V. (2016). The role of public relations in ethnic advocacy and activism: A proposed research agenda. *Public Relations Inquiry, 5*(3), 233–251. https://doi.org/10.1177/2046147X16635225

Edwards, L. (2011). Defining the 'object' of public relations research: A new starting point. *Public Relations Inquiry, 1*(1), 7–30. https://doi.org/10.1177/2046147X11422149

FrameWorks Institute. (2020). *What's in a frame?* www.frameworksinstitute.org/article/whats-in-a-frame/

Fuller, C. (2021, July). Building a movement with powerful media relations. In *Digital power: Best practices for strengthening strategic communications for social justice documentary engagement*. Center for Media & Social Impact. https://cmsimpact.org/report/digital-power/

Gehr, E. (2021, February 25). How social media is shaping 21st century social justice movements and activism. *The Daily Campus.* https://dailycampus.com/2021/02/25/how-social-media-is-shaping-21st-century-social-justice-movements-and-activism/

Goffman, E. (1974). *Frame analysis: An essay on the organization of experience.* Harvard University Press.

Grunig, J. E., & Hunt, T. (1984). *Managing public relations.* Holt, Rinehart and Winston.

Halverson, J. R. (2011, December 8). *Why story is not narrative.* Center for Strategic Communication, Arizona State University. https://csc.asu.edu/2011/12/08/why-story-is-not-narrative/

Hou, J. Z., & Wang, Y. (2022). Creativity is key: Using creative pedagogy to incorporate activism in the public relations classroom and beyond. *Journal of Public Relations Education, 8*(2), 78–110. https://journalofpreducation.com/2022/08/

Hu, J. (2020, August 3). The second act of social media activism. Has the internet become better at mediating change? *The New Yorker.* www.newyorker.com/culture/cultural-comment/the-second-act-of-social-media-activism

Jasper, D. (n.d.). *Seven fundamental strategies for grassroots movements.* Street Civics. https://streetcivics.com/seven-fundamental-strategies-for-grassroots-movements/

Jones, F. (2019). *Reclaiming our space: How Black feminism is changing the world from the tweets to the streets.* Beacon Press.

Kaplan, E. A. (2023, July 28). How Black Lives Matter changed the U.S. *Yes Magazine.* https://blmgrassroots.org/how-black-lives-matter-changed-the-u-s/

Kennedy, A. K., & Sommerfeldt, E. J. (2015). A postmodern turn for social media research: Theory and research directions for public relations scholarship. *Atlanta Journal of Communication, 23*, 31–45. https://doi.org/10.1080/15456870.2015.972406

March For Our Lives. (2022). *2022 Impact Report.* https://impact.marchforourlives.com/

Me Too Movement (n.d.). *History and inception.* https://metoomvmt.org/get-to-know-us/history-inception/

Moloney, K., McQueen, D., Surowiec, P., & Yaxley, H. (2012). *Dissent and protest public relations.* The Public Relations Research Group, The Media School, Bournemouth University. www.academia.edu/69746209/DISSENT_and_PROTEST_PUBLIC_RELATIONS

Nicoletti, L., & Bass, D. (2023). *Humans are biased: Generative AI is even worse.* Bloomberg Technology. www.bloomberg.com/graphics/2023-generative-ai-bias/

O'Brien, M. (2019). Activists as pioneers in PR: Historical frameworks and the suffragette movement. In A. Adi (Ed.), *Protest public relations: Communicating dissent and activism* (pp. 45–64). Routledge.

Pew Research Center. (2023, June 9). *Americans' view of and experiences with activism on social media.* www.pewresearch.org/internet/2023/06/29/americans-views-of-and-experiences-with-activism-on-social-media/

Rabinowitz, P. (n.d.). *Section 5: Coalition building 1: Starting a coalition*. Community Toolbox, Center for Community Health and Development, University of Kansas. https://ctb.ku.edu/en/table-of-contents/assessment/promotion-strategies/start-a-coaltion/main

Reinsborough, P., & Canning, D. (2017). *Re:Imagining change: How to use story-based strategy to win campaigns, build movements, and change the world*. PM Press.

Sankofa.org. (n.d.). https://sankofa.org/about

Sanz, T., & Rodriguez-Labajos, B. (2021, April). Does artistic activism change anything? Strategic and transformative effects of arts in anti-coal struggles in Oakland, CA. *Geoforum*, *122*, 41–54. https://doi.org/10.1016/j.geoforum.2021.03.010

Science Friday. (2023, November 17). *How AI chatbots can reinforce racial bias in medicine*. Flora Lichtman interview with Dr. Jenna Lester and Dr. Rosanna Daneshjou. NPR. www.sciencefriday.com/segments/ai-chatbots-medical-racism/#segment-transcript

Shaw, E. (n.d.). *Frame analysis*. Britannica. www.britannica.com/topic/frame-analysis

Shorty Awards. (2020). *Our power: March For Our Lives 2020. From the 5th Annual Shorty Social Good Awards*. https://shortyawards.com/5th-socialgood/our-power-next-time

Smith, M. F., & Ferguson, D. P. (2018). Organizing for advocacy: Activist organizational rhetoric. In Ø. Ihlen & R. L. Heath (Eds.), *The handbook of organizational rhetoric and communication* (1st ed., pp. 439–451). John Wiley & Sons, Inc.

Soken-Huberty, E. (n.d.). *What is social change?* Human Rights Careers. www.humanrightscareers.com/issues/what-is-social-change/

The Bail Project (n.d.). *After cash bail: A framework for reimagining justice*. https://bailproject.org/after-cash-bail/

The Center for Artistic Activism. (n.d.). *Why artistic activism?* https://c4aa.org/2018/04/why-artistic-activism

The Drum, (2022, June). *March For Our Lives: Thoughts and prayers by McCann, NY*. www.thedrum.com/creative-works/project/mccann-ny-march-our-lives-thoughts-and-prayers

The Opportunity Agenda (2019). *Vision, values, and voice: A communications toolkit*.

Tufekci, Z. (2017). *Twitter and tear gas: The power and fragility of networked protest*. Yale University Press.

University of Sussex. (2023, July). *Is digital activism effective?* https://study-online.sussex.ac.uk/news-and-events/social-media-and-campaigning-is-digital-activism-effective/

USC Annenberg Center for Public Relations. (2022). *The future of corporate activism*. Global Communication Report. University of Southern California. https://annenberg.usc.edu/research/center-public-relations/center-public-relations-research

Watchmaps. (2021, July 12). *COMU3015: Activism and public interest interview with Dr. Robyn Gulliver* [Video]. YouTube. www.youtube.com/watch?v=xvl_2wmx2ko

Weaver, C. K. (2019). The slow conflation of public relations and activism. Understanding trajectories in public relations theorising. In A. Adi (Ed.), *Protest public relations: Communicating dissent and activism* (pp. 12–28). Routledge.

Glossary

Ableism   a type of social prejudice that devalues or ignores disabled people through normalizing ability.

Active listening   includes observing and processing differences in communication styles and body language before assuming or responding.

Advocacy   persuading or arguing in support of a specific cause, policy, idea, or set of values (Cox & Pezzullo, 2016, p. 177).

Ageism   discrimination, stereotypes, and prejudices that occur due to assumptions made about a person based on their age or generational category.

Alt text (short for alternative text)   a written description that appears in place of an image when the image cannot be loaded or recognized.

Ambivert   a person who is a combination of introvert and extrovert and can switch between the two personality types depending on the situation.

Americans with Disabilities Act (ADA)   the world's first comprehensive civil rights law that prohibits discrimination against people with disabilities in everyday life (ADA National Network, n.d.).

Applied communications research   primary research that can be applied to a specific client or organizational communications situation or challenge.

Audiences   those with whom you want to communicate.

Behavioral-based misunderstanding   occurs when an individual acts in a way that is contradictory or considered socially impolite than what you believe is acceptable in a social or workplace situation.

Belmont Report   the set of ethical principles and guidelines developed in the U.S. to protect human subjects of biomedical and behavioral research.

Belonging   suggests that individuals have a need to form meaningful relationships, social attachments, and experiences by being part of a group or community (Baumeister & Leary, 1995).

Blackfishing   describes the phenomenon of non-Black influencers, celebrities, entertainers, or public figures who change their appearance to look like what society considers Black identifying (Stevens, 2021; Thompson, 2018).

Boycott   an individual consumer's decision to respond to and participate in a collective call to refrain from purchasing from a specific company, brand, or engaging with a government entity for the explicit purpose of exerting pressure to achieve objectives related to social, environmental, or economic change.

Brainstorming   a technique where people in a group or team are prompted to spontaneously verbally share words, suggestions, or thoughts as a means of generating ideas or solutions.

Brand safety   the consideration and the practice of ensuring that an ad does not appear alongside inappropriate content that might be offensive, controversial, illegal, or unethical (World Federation of Advertisers, 2022).

Brand suitability   the practice of determining ad placement based on the unique criteria derived from a brand's own values.

Buycott   an individual or collective call for consumers to intentionally spend money in support of a brand or business with which they agree on social, moral, political, or environmental issues (Kam & Deichert, 2020).

Camel case   the practice of formatting a compound word or phrase by starting the first word with either an uppercase or lowercase letter and then capitalizing the first letter of all the other words (e.g., #noFilter or #NoFilter).

Categorization   typically a spontaneous cognitive process that humans use to identify and label groups, individuals, or objects based on observing or experiencing them (Crisp & Hewstone, 2007).

Coalition   a group of individuals and/or organizations with a common interest who agree to work together toward a common goal (Rabinowitz, n.d.).

Collaborative research approaches   research processes in which researchers and participants share equal power as co-creators of knowledge. These approaches share the common principle of researching with rather than on vulnerable communities (Gomez et al., 2019, p. 3).

Collectivism   relates to cultures in which the focus is more about actions that prioritize the greater good of society, a group, or family.

Corporate responsibility to race (theory of)   because corporations have historically perpetuated and profited from racial oppression, they have a responsibility to communicate in ways that advocate for racial justice, attempt to improve race relations, and support achieving a more equitable and harmonious society (Logan, 2021, p. 1).

Corporate social advocacy   institutions taking a stance on and advocating for sociopolitical issues, like racial and social justice, gun violence, LGBTQ+ rights, or immigration issues.

Creative (or artistic) activism   a dynamic practice combining the creative power of the arts to move us emotionally with the strategic planning of activism necessary to bring about social change (The Center for Artistic Activism, n.d.).

Crisis management   involves using proactive and reactive strategies to address untrue or negative occurrences, images, and messages that might threaten an organization's reputation and its relationship with its publics and stakeholders.

Critical theories   theories that analyze and critique societal systems and structures with an eye toward making them more just and equitable for all, such as critical race theory, feminist theory, and queer theory.

Cultural approach to audience segmentation   an approach where the unique needs, experiences, cultures, and intersectional identities of audiences are considered in campaign planning.

Cultural appropriation   where appearance, traditions, behaviors, languages, or cultural practices from diverse communities are used by those not belonging to a diverse social identity without giving proper acknowledgement or credit to the original diverse identity group.

Cultural context   learned societal behaviors, attitudes, and values of what is considered accepted or expected in given situations.

Cultural reductionism   being unable to view situations from a perspective other than our own (Krownapple, 2016, p. 131).

Culture   a set of shared meanings, norms, values, beliefs, symbols, and traditions among a specific social identity group

Digital accessibility   the design and creation of digital products, including both the interface and the content (e.g., website, social media, mobile application, electronic document, online campaign, etc.) to be available, approachable, or usable by people with disabilities and other special needs or functional limitations (Kulkarni, 2019).

Disaggregating data   to break data down into distinctive categories, often by social identity groups such as race, gender, or income.

Dissent PR   the dissention of ideas, commentaries, and policies through PR techniques in order to change current, dominant thinking and behavior in discrete economic, political, and cultural areas of public life (Moloney et al., 2012).

Diverse media channels   channels that are owned by and/or primarily serve underrepresented communities.

Diversity   the range of differences in identities, experiences, and perspectives between people and groups.

Equity   fairness, with the goal of eliminating disparities in treatment, access, or opportunity.

Ethnicity   a group of individuals who share the same cultural traditions, language, and ancestry.

Extroverts   people energized by verbally communicating or processing ideas out loud, working on teams, and meeting new people at an event.

Four principles of WCAG   perceivable, operable, understandable, and robust.

Gender identity   one's own internal sense of self and their gender, whether that is man, woman, neither or both (Wamsley, 2021).

Generation   a group of people born and living within a 15 to 20-year period.

Heading markup   the HTML and XHTML tags indicating heading levels.

Inclusion   the practice of creating an environment in which all voices within a society are included, respected, and supported.

Inclusive design   an approach born out of digital environments that aims to design and create products that understand and enable people of all abilities (Gilbert, 2019).

Inclusive leadership   involves behaviors by leaders that exhibit openness, accessibility, and authenticity in their interactions with followers that acknowledge the diverse characteristics and identities of their teams (Carmeli et al., 2010; Ospina & El Hadidy, 2011).

Inclusive research   seeking out, understanding, and considering the full spectrum of lived experiences of our audiences.

Inclusive research brief   a research brief that looks at the problem or challenge through different cultural lenses and approaches DEI with intentionality.

Inclusive style guide   a document that defines and demonstrates how to consistently and accurately use acronyms, words, phrases, and descriptors related to diverse audiences, employees, consumers, and publics.

Individualism   involves the belief that every person is self-reliant, self-motivated, and the focus is on achieving individual success.

In-groups   refers to people belonging to a group or team who share identity characteristics and possibly similar behaviors and opinions.

Intersectionality   acknowledges that individuals and groups experience discrimination differently based on their multiple, overlapping identities (Crenshaw, 1989; 2013).

Introverts   people who gain energy from solitude and become quickly drained when asked to constantly verbally communicate or interact without having time to think and process ideas.

Keyword blocklist (keyword exclusion list) a list of words or phrases that a brand desires to avoid having its advertisements displayed alongside due to safety concerns (Brand Safety Institute n.d.).

Language-based misunderstanding an unintentional error in comprehension by receivers due to the form of language employed by senders in communicating a message (Fiset et al., 2023).

LGBTQ+ people who identify as one or more of these categories lesbian, gay, bisexual, transgender, queer, and the plus sign is also used to signify inclusion of other identities (i.e., intersex, asexual) and orientations that words cannot yet describe.

Localization to effectively adapt messages, images, and behaviors to meet both the linguistic and cultural needs of the audience.

Neurodiversity describes the idea that people experience and interact with the world around them in many different ways; there is no one "right" way of thinking, learning, and behaving, and differences are not viewed as deficits (Baumer & Frueh, 2021).

Normalization occurs when we try to conform people or places to what we believe is an acceptable societal standard.

Optimal distinctiveness theory suggests that individuals have a desire to attain a balance of both inclusion and distinctiveness in social and team situations (Leonardelli et al., 2010).

Organizational culture assumptions, beliefs, habits, language, symbols, values, and accepted interactions that influence employee behavior in various workplace situations (Ravasi & Schultz, 2006).

Organizational values a set of core beliefs or words that govern a business, its philosophy, and how employees are expected to act.

Out-groups people who do not identify with the social identities and characteristics of the larger group or team in which they are participating.

Pascal case the practice of starting every word with an uppercase letter for a compound word or phrase (e.g., #MyBodyMyChoice).

Performative Allyship organizations and individuals who support marginalized groups on a surface level when it is convenient.

Person with a disability a person who has a physical or mental impairment that limits one or more life activities (ADA.gov, 2023).

Political consumerism the use of the market as an arena for politics to change institutional or market practices found to be ethically, environmentally, or politically objectionable and to reward companies for favorable practices (Stolle & Micheletti, 2013).

Psychological safety the feeling of being able to speak up, take risks, and make mistakes without fear of negative consequences (Edmondson & Lei, 2014).

Publics a group of people who share common interests and actively engage with a product, service, or idea. We sometimes interchangeably refer to publics as **audiences**.

Race the historic, socially constructed categories assigned to a group of individuals based on observable physical characteristics.

Rainbow-washing when brands use rainbow-themed symbolism in advertising, merchandise, or on social media to support LGBTQ+ people during Pride Month, but do not offer active, long-term support of their rights or identities beyond Pride Month.

Reappropriation to reclaim derogatory words to diminish the power of the word.

Relational leadership   highlights a leader's social influence in organizing, listening to, and understanding the needs of followers within the context of relational dynamics (Uhl-Bien, 2006).

Reputation management   involves creating and managing communication strategies designed to influence and build authentic relationships and elevate positive actions, beliefs, and opinions about an individual or brand (Davies & Miles, 1998; Sproutsocial.com, 2023).

Self-aware   to possess conscious knowledge of one's own character, feelings, motives, opinions, and desires in various social and cultural situations.

Slang   informal words associated with race, ethnicity, gender, ability, or other cultural traditions.

Social change   altering, replacing, or transforming an unjust practice, policy, attitude, or system to one that is more equitable.

Social identity   a person's self-concept that is derived from belonging to a group or category with similar beliefs, characteristics, experiences, or physical traits.

Social identity categories   most often refer to race, ethnicity, ability, gender, sexual orientation, religion, and age.

Social justice   the fair treatment of all people and groups within a society and the equitable distribution of opportunities and privileges.

Social justice activism   sustained resistance to and disruption of harmful inequities, norms, and practices that discriminate against and marginalize people to ultimately promote equity (Aghazadeh & Ashby-King, 2022).

Social justice advocacy   persuading or arguing in support of a specific cause, policy, idea, or set of values (Cox & Pezzullo, 2016, p. 177).

Social listening   the practice of monitoring and analyzing social media conversations about sentiment, opinions, trends about a brand, competitors, and industry at large (Newberry & Macready, 2022).

Social movement   an organized effort or initiative by a group of people to create social change.

Socially constructed   refers to the fact that racial categories are not scientific or biological and were the early creations of colonists to assign physical descriptions to groups of people.

Stereotype threat   the pressure to avoid being judged by negative group stereotypes.

Stereotypes   applying uneducated judgements or generalizations to everyone in a group.

Strategic communications   explores the capacity of all organizations, including corporations, not-for-profit organizations (including advocacy and activist groups), and government, for engaging in purposeful communication (Oxford Bibliographies, 2018).

Systemic inequities   inequities that are embedded and reinforced in societal policies, systems, and structures.

Tokenism   the practice of making only a perfunctory or symbolic effort to be inclusive, especially by recruiting a small number of people from underrepresented groups in order to give the appearance of equality (Hahn et al., 2017).

Traditions   social customs, religious practices, celebrations, and habits passed from generation to generation within a shared community.

Translation   interpreting and communicating spoken or written words into a different language.

Unconscious bias   prejudices that we may hold toward another person or group that we are unaware of.

User testing (also called usability testing)   a type of user research that evaluates the user's interaction with a digital interface to detect usability issues (Usability.gov, n.d.).

Visual accessibility   the practice of designing visual content in a way that can be easily accessed, understood, and used by people with disabilities, including those with visual impairments.

Visual storytelling   involves the use of graphics, images, pictures, and videos to engage with viewers in an effort to drive emotions, engage intercommunication, and motivate an audience to action (Content Marketing Institute, 2020).

Web Content Accessibility Guidelines (WCAG)   a set of guidelines on how to make web content more accessible to people with disabilities published by the Web Accessibility Initiative of the World Wide Web Consortium (W3C).

Woke   awareness of systemic injustices and prejudices, especially involving the treatment of historically oppressed individuals.

Woke-washing   when brands try to capitalize on social justice and identity themes in their advertising and social media campaigns without ongoing, identifiable support or immediate action.

Working agreement   a short written list of up to five items that a team agrees is acceptable behavior to create respectful interactions.

Writing in the disciplines   writing purposefully within the framework of specific professions/disciplines to practice formats and genres that are typical or popular in those areas (WAC Clearinghouse, 2023).

References

ADA.gov, U.S. Department of Justice and Civil Rights Division. (2023). www.ada.gov/

ADA National Network. (n.d.). *What is the Americans with Disabilities Act (ADA)?* https://adata.org/learn-about-ada

Aghazadeh, S. A., & Ashby-King, D. T. (2022). Centering activism and social justice in PR education: Critical communication pedagogy as an entryway. *Journal of Public Relations Education, 8*(2), 11–41. https://journalofpreducation.com/2022/08/

Baumeister, R. F., & Leary, M. R. (1995). The need to belong: Desire for interpersonal attachments as a fundamental human motivation. *Psychological Bulletin, 117*(3), 497–529.

Baumer, N., & Frueh, J. (2021, November 23). *What is neurodiversity?* Harvard Health Publishing. www.health.harvard.edu/blog/what-is-neurodiversity-202111232645

Brand Safety Institute. (n.d.). *Brand safety glossary.* www.brandsafetyinstitute.com/resources/glossary

Carmeli, A., Reiter-Palmon, R., & Ziv, E. (2010). Inclusive leadership and employee involvement in creative tasks in the workplace: The mediating role of psychological safety. *Creativity Research Journal, 22*(3), 250–260. https://doi.org/10.1080/10400419.2010.504654

Content Marketing Institute (2020, March 20). *#CMWorld 2019 – Visual storytelling at its best – Eric Goodstadt & Sacha Reeb* [Video]. YouTube. https://youtu.be/j83sKBN8pLk?si=3pUS76RpiQh3Dflv

Cox, R. J., & Pezzullo, P. (2016). *Environmental communication and the public sphere.* Sage.

Crenshaw, K. (1989). Demarginalizing the intersection of race and sex: A Black feminist critique of antidiscrimination doctrine, feminist theory, and anti-racist policy. *University of Chicago Legal Forum*, Vol. 1989, Issue 1, Article 8. https://chicagounbound.uchicago.edu/uclf/vol1989/iss1/8

Crenshaw, K. W. (2013). Mapping the margins: Intersectionality, identity politics, and violence against women of color. In M. A. Fineman & R. Mykitiuk (Eds.), *The public nature of private violence* (pp. 93–118). Routledge.

Crisp, R. J., & Hewstone, M. (2007). Multiple, social categorization. *Advances in Experimental Social Psychology*, *39*, 163–254.

Davies, G., & Miles, L. (1998). Reputation management: Theory versus practice. *Corporate Reputation Review*, *2*, 16–27.

Edmondson, A. C., & Lei, Z. (2014). Psychological safety: The history, renaissance, and future of an interpersonal construct. *Annual Review of Organizational Psychology and Organizational Behavior*, *1*(1), 23–43.

Fiset, J., Bhave, D. P., & Jha, N. (2023). The effects of language-related misunderstanding at work. *Journal of Management*, 01492063231181651.

Gilbert, R. M. (2019). *Inclusive design for a digital world: Designing with accessibility in mind.* Apress.

Gomez, A., Padros, M., Rios, O., Mara, L-C., & Pukepuke, T. (2019). Reaching social impact through communicative methodology. Researching with rather than on vulnerable populations: The Roma case. *Frontiers in Education*, *4*(9). https://doi.org/10.3389/feduc.2019.00009

Hahn, D. L., Hoffmann, A. E., Felzien, M., LeMaster, J. W., Xu, J., & Fagnan, L. J. (2017). Tokenism in patient engagement. *Family Practice*, *34*(3), 290–295. https://doi.org/10.1093/fampra/cmw097

Kam, C. D., & Deichert, M. (2020). Boycotting, buycotting, and the psychology of political consumerism. *The Journal of Politics*, *82*(1), 72–88.

Krownapple, J. (2016). *Guiding teams to excellence with equity: Culturally proficient facilitation.* Corwin Press.

Kulkarni, M. (2019). Digital accessibility: Challenges and opportunities. *IIMB Management Review*, *31*(1), 91–98. https://doi.org/10.1016/j.iimb.2018.05.009

Leonardelli, G. J., Pickett, C. L., & Brewer, M. B. (2010). Optimal distinctiveness theory: A framework for social identity, social cognition, and intergroup relations. *Advances in Experimental Social Psychology*, *43*, 63–113.

Logan, N. (2021). A theory of corporate responsibility to race (CRR): Communication and racial justice in public relations. *Journal of Public Relations Research*, *33*(1), 6–22. https://doi.org/10.1080/1062726X.2021.1881898

Moloney, K., McQueen, D., Surowiec, P., & Yaxley, H. (2012). *Dissent and protest public relations.* The Public Relations Research Group, The Media School, Bournemouth University. www.academia.edu/69746209/DISSENT_and_PROTEST_PUBLIC_RELATIONS

Newberry, C., & Macready, H. (2022, December). *What is social listening, why it matters + 14 tools to help.* Hootsuite. https://blog.hootsuite.com/social-listening-business/

Ospina, S., & El Hadidy, W. (2011). *Leadership, diversity and inclusion: Insights from scholarship.* National Urban Fellows Public Service Leadership Diversity Initiative.

Oxford Bibliographies. (2018, July 25). *Strategic communication – by Kjerstin Thorson.* https://doi.org/10.1093/obo/9780199756841-0007

Rabinowitz, P. (n.d.). *Section 5: Coalition building 1: Starting a coalition.* Community Toolbox, Center for Community Health and Development, University of Kansas. https://ctb.ku.edu/en/table-of-contents/assessment/promotion-strategies/start-a-coaltion/main

Ravasi, D., & Schultz, M. (2006). Responding to organizational identity threats: Exploring the role of organizational culture. *Academy of Management Journal, 49*(3), 433–458.

Sproutsocial.com. (2023). *Reputation management: The essential guide to protecting your brand.* https://sproutsocial.com/insights/reputation-management/

Stevens, W. E. (2021). Blackfishing on Instagram: Influencing and the commodification of Black urban aesthetics. *Social Media+ Society, 7*(3). https://doi.org/10.1177/2056305121103

Stolle, D., & Micheletti, M. (2013). *Political consumerism: Global responsibility in action.* Cambridge University Press.

The Center for Artistic Activism. (n.d.). *Why artistic activism?* https://c4aa.org/2018/04/why-artistic-activism

Thompson, W. (2018, November 14). *How White women on Instagram are profiting off Black women.* Paper. www.papermag.com/white-women-blackfishing-instagram-2619714094.html

Uhl-Bien, M. (2006). Relational leadership theory: Exploring the social processes of leadership and organizing. *The Leadership Quarterly, 17*(6), 654–676.

Usability.gov. (n.d.). *Usability testing.* www.usability.gov/how-to-and-tools/methods/usability-testing.html

WAC Clearinghouse. (2023). *What is writing in the disciplines?* https://wac.colostate.edu/repository/resources/teaching/intro/wid/

Wamsley, L. (2021, June 2). A guide to gender identity terms. *NPR.* www.npr.org/2021/06/02/996319297/gender-identity-pronouns-expression-guide-lgbtq

World Federation of Advertisers. (2022). *Diversity & representation guide.* https://wfanet.org/knowledge/diversity-and-inclusion/dei-in-media-guide/about

Index

#28DaysofBlackCosplay campaign 71–72
3Ps (presence, perspective, personality) framework 54–56

AARP (American Association of Retired People) 44
abbreviations/acronyms, as identity group descriptors 23, 44–45
ABC, *Shark Tank* panel 6
Abdel-Messih, I. A. 80
ability 21, 24–26, 63; teamwork and differences in 119–120; *see also* disabled people
ableism 25
accessibility: digital and social media 67–71, 76–77; healthcare 4–5, 41; inclusive leaders 125; internet connection 41; visual stories 59–61
Accessible Canada Act 68
Accrediting Council on Education in Journalism and Mass Communications x
accuracy 42, 46
ACLU (American Civil Liberties Union) 44
Act on Welfare of Persons with Disabilities in South Korea 68
action-based research 89–90
active listening 115–116
activism/activists 146–147, 147; *see also* social justice activism
Ad Council 85–86
ADA *see* Americans with Disabilities Act
Advertising Association (UK) 103

advocacy 146–147; corporate social advocacy (CSA) 10–11, 147
#AirieREAL campaign 71
African Americans *see* Black community
age 21, 26–27; and visual storytelling 62
age labels, avoidance of 45
ageism 27–28, 119
Aghazadeh, S. 89, 90, 145, 147, 149
AI *see* artificial intelligence
AIDS Memorial Quilt 158
Air France 140–141
Alcorn, C. 141
Aldoory, L. 89, 90
Algorithmic Justice League 150
alternative text (alt text) 60, 68
ambiverts 116
American Association of Retired People (AARP) 44
American Civil Liberties Union (ACLU) 44
American Dairy Association 30
American Heart Association, "The Heart Truth" campaign 19
American Public Health Association (APHA) 151, 153, 154
Americans with Disabilities Act (ADA) 24–25, 68, 86
ANA *see* Association of National Advertisers
Anders, G. 132
animal rights 140–141
anonymity, research 88
AP (Associated Press) Stylebook 43–44, 46
APHA *see* American Public Health Association

applied communications research
79–80

artificial intelligence (AI) 12, 81; and
bias 47, 48, 95, 149–150; and global
ethics 82; use in inclusive writing
47–48

artistic (creative) activism 156, 158–159

Ashby-King, D. T. 145, 147, 149

Asian American and Pacific Islander
(AAPI) community 72–73

Asian Americans 23, 95; and
COVID-19 pandemic 104

Asos 27

Associated Press (AP) Stylebook
43–44, 46

Association of National Advertisers
(ANA) x, 7; Alliance for Inclusive
and Multicultural Marketing 104

assumptions 79, 153

attention deficit hyperactivity disorder
(ADHD) 120

audience(s) 19; effects of COVID-19
pandemic on different 40–42;
engagement, digital and social media
76; internal 127–128; segmentation,
cultural approach to 100–101;
segmentation, and social justice
communications 152; understanding
your audience 54

audio description 60

authenticity, and inclusive leadership
125, 127, 131

autism spectrum disorder (ASD) 120

autonomy 80

AXIOS 105

Baboolall, D. 141

The Bail Project 149, 155

Bank of America 141

Bass, D. 47

Baumer, N. 119

beauty standards 56

Beerman, S. 142

behavioral-based misunderstanding 115

Belafonte, H. 156

Belmont Report 80, 87

belonging 3, 6, 21, 50, 126, 128

Ben & Jerry's 10, 129, 138

benchmark research 77

beneficence (research ethics) 80, 81

Beyoncé 25

bias 20; in artificial intelligence (AI)
tools 47, 48, 95, 149–150; checking
for 46, 48, 84, 113; conscious
(explicit) 13, 43; gender 107; and
research 79, 84; unconscious
(implicit) 13–14, 43, 102

big data 82

BIPOC-owned businesses: brands
promoting equity of 5–6; and
buycott campaigns 141

Black community 23, 39, 95, 97, 103, 105;
representation in communications
industry 7; *see also* BIPOC-owned
businesses; Black women

Black Girl Sunscreen 66–67

Black Illustrations 59

Black Lives Matter (BLM) Global
Network Foundation 157

Black Lives Matter (BLM) Grassroots
157

Black Lives Matter (BLM) movement
52, 139, 148, 157, 158

Black PR Wire 105

Black women: feminist activism 12;
health care inequity 4–5; workplace
discrimination against 9

blackfishing 24

blocklists 73–74

body language 116

body type, and visual storytelling 63

Bourne, H. 126

Boycott, C. C. 140

boycotts 139–141

brainstorming 42–43, 118

brand safety practices 73–75

brand style guides 46

brand suitability 74–75

Brandwatch 76, 137

Bravo, V. 152

Brown, V. 14

Bugis people, South Sulawesi 27

Burg, B. 52

Burger King UK 28

Burke, T. 157, 158

Burlew, K. A. 84, 85, 88

business case for DEI 7, 8, 94, 95, 97

#Buyblack campaign 141

buycotts 141

buying power 95

Camel case format (hashtags) 70
Campaign Against Living Miserably
    (CALM) 102
campaign planning 94–110; audience
    selection and strategy development
    100–101; client briefing 96–97;
    cross–cultural media planning
    104–106; defining the challenge
    and setting goals and objectives
    98–100, 107; elimination of
    stereotypes 102, 107; intentionality
    in research brief 97–98; measuring
    for equity and inclusion 106–107;
    preliminary research 96–98;
    representation and creative
    development 101–103; supplier
    diversity 103
Canning, D. 153
Carey, J. 149
categorization 18, 20; *see also* social
    identity categories
Center for Story-based Strategy 153
The Center for Artistic Activism 158
CEOs 61, 125; activism 128, 129, 138
#ChampionBlackBusinesses initiative
    5–6
change 146; *see also* social change
Chen, A. 100
Cheng-Tek Tai, M. 80
Chick-fil-A 10
Chief Communications Officers (CCOs)
    see strategic communicators
Chief Diversity Officers (CDOs) 132
children 103
Chinese culture 115, 120
Cision 137
Ciszek, E. 147, 150
citing sources 48
civil rights 7
Civil Rights Movement 139, 146, 158
climate change activism 129
Cloverpop 111
coalition building 151–152
collaborative research methods 88–91
collaborative work in teams 118–119
collectivism 113–114, 115, 119
Collins, P. H. 12
colloquialisms 114–115
colorblind society 11
colors, meaning of 30
Commisceo Global 115, 117

Commission on Public Relations
    Education x, 8
communication style, inclusive leaders
    130–131
community advocate relationships 137
community-based participatory
    research 90
competitive advantage 8
competitor analysis 77
complaint engagement, online 137
confidentiality, research 88
Confucian ethics 80
conscious (explicit) biases 13, 43
conscious marketing 95
consensus, in social justice
    communications 150–151
contacts, list of 43; using snowball
    technique to grow 43
content creation 136–137
Content Marketing Institute 51
copy-editing 42, 48
copyright 48
corporate responsibility to race (CRR),
    theory of 9–10, 95
corporate social advocacy (CSA) 10–11,
    147
corporate social responsibility (CSR)
    10, 147
corporate-centric communications 147
counter–narratives 153, 154
COVID Collaborative 85–86
COVID-19 pandemic 81; effects on
    different audiences 40–42; and Asian
    American community 104; vaccine
    hesitancy research 85–86
Cowling, M. 158
Cox, R. J. 146
CreateHER Stock 59
creative activism 156, 158–159
creative brief 102–103
Creative Equals 107
Crenshaw, K. 9, 11, 18
crisis communications 147
crisis management 138–139
Crisp, R. J. 20
critical race theory (CRT) 11–12, 149
critical theories 11–13, 148–149
cross-cultural media planning 104–106
cultural appropriation 23–24
Cultural Competence for Equity and
    Inclusion framework 13

cultural competency 7, 13–14
cultural context of team members 112, 113
Cultural Fluency methodology 95
cultural identity 13
cultural intelligence 121
cultural intermediaries 145, 149
cultural reductionism 8–9, 103
cultural sensitivity 67; *see also* culturally sensitive research
cultural stereotypes 112–113
cultural studies 149
cultural traditions 20, 31
culturally proficient communicators 1
culturally sensitive research 79–93; action-based research 89–90; analyzing and reporting results 87; collaborative research methods 88–91; consulting with community experts 85–86; disabled people as research participants 86–87; harm, avoidance of 87–88; inclusive research approach 82–88; language and terminology 84, 86; participant recruitment 85, 86; participants as co-creators of knowledge 89; participants' preferred self-identity 84; preliminary research and research questions 83–84; research ethics and geo-cultural contexts 80–82; research instruments: language and terminology 84
culture 20, 30; collectivist 113–114, 115, 119; individualist 80, 113, 114, 115; organizational 125–126
customer service satisfaction 142
Czymoniewicz-Klippel, M. T. 80

Dallis, I. x, 15
Daneshjou, R. 150
data: big data 82; disaggregation 87, 107
Daykin, J. 104
De Moya, M. 150–151, 152
Deloitte 120
Dentsu 95
digital accessibility 67–71, 76–77; definition 68
digital communication strategies 65–78; and accessibility 67–71, 76–77; brand safety practices 73–75; and engagement by audience segments 76;

ensuring representation and diverse voices 71–73; evaluating effectiveness of 75–77; goals and objectives 75; impact 76; inclusive design tips 69–71; key performance indicators (KPIs) 75; language considerations 67, 69, 71; and social justice activism 157–158; social listening 66–67, 76; user testing (usability testing) 66, 67, 76–77
digital technologies, and research 82
Digitas, "The Other Side" campaign 73
Dijksterhuis, A. 20
Disability Language Style Guide 86
Disability Pride Month 25
Disabled and Here 58
disabled people 8–9, 24–26; in communications industry 7; definition 25; and digital and social media 67–69; as research participants 86–87; and visual storytelling 63
disaggregating data 87, 107
discrimination 9, 20; housing 10, 39; structural/systemic 11; workplace 9
dissensus, in social justice communications 150–151
dissent PR 150–151
Distributed AI Research Institute 150
diverse media channels 104–106
diversity, definition 4
Diversity Action Alliance 7
diversity, equity, and inclusion (DEI) 3; addressing and overcoming fears in doing 14; business case for 7, 8, 94, 95, 97; definitions 4–7; evolution and importance of in strategic communications 7–8; moral case (fairness case) for 7–8, 10, 94, 95, 97; theories and concepts 8–13
Diversity Photos 59
diversity-washing 11
Dolce & Gabbana 120
Dominican Republic 150–151
Douyin 65
Ducks for Detainees (D4D) 158

Edelman, *Future of Corporate Communications Study* (2023) 127
Edelman Trust Barometer 125, 128, 135
Edmondson, A. C. 125
education, and COVID-19 pandemic 41

Edwards, L. 147–148
El Pollo Loco, "For Your Consideration" campaign 6
emojis 69–70
emoticons 70
empathy 42
employee engagement 127–128
employee resource groups (ERGs) 125, 45, 125, 128, 130
Equal Rights of Persons with Disabilities Act (Israel) 68
equality, equity versus 4, 5
Equality Act (UK, 2010) 68
equity 4–6; of BIPOC-owned businesses, brands promoting 5–6; definition 4; racial 10; systemic 4–5; versus equality 4, 5
ESPN 5–6
ethics: of care 39, 80; research 80–82
ethics dumping 81
ethnic diversity 7
ethnicity 21, 22–24; preferred identifiers 45–46; and visual storytelling 61
Eurocentrism 31
European Accessibility Act 68
European Association of Communications Agencies, "Addressing D&I in Brand Safety Guide" 74
extroverts 116

Facebook 65
Facebook Insights 76
fact-checking 42, 48
fairness: as rationale for practicing DEI *see* moral case for DEI; *see also* equity
faith *see* religion/faith
Fallon, J. 23–24
Farwell, T. M. 40, 100
fears: addressing and overcoming 14; sources of 14
feminist theory 12, 80, 149
Ferguson, D. P. 152
Fitzhugh, E. 141
Floyd, G. x, 27
focus groups 45, 85
FrameWorks Institute 153
framing and reframing 152–154
Frueh, N. 119
Fuller, C. 154–155

GAME plan, for social justice communications 151
Gay and Lesbian Alliance Against Defamation Media Institute (GLAAD) 27, 44
Geena Davis Institute on Gender and Media 102
Gehr, E. 157
GEM (R) (Gender Equality Measurement) 107
gender 12, 21; bias 107; fluidity 62; and humor 28; identity 27; "norms" 27–28; as social construct 12, 27; stereotypes 28; and visual storytelling 62
gender pronouns, preferred 45
Gender Spectrum Collection 58
generational categories 26–37; and teamwork 119
geo-cultural ethics 80–82
Getty Images: DEI Imagery Search Guide 59; "Inclusive Visual Storytelling" report 61
GLAAD *see* Gay and Lesbian Alliance Against Defamation Media Institute
Global Alliance for Responsible Media, Brand Safety Floor and Suitability Framework 75
global ethics 81–82
Global Initiative on Ethics of Autonomous and Intelligent Systems 82
goals: and campaign planning 98; digital and social media strategies 75
Goffman, E. 152
Gomez, A. 88, 89
Good Humor 72
Goodman, D. 13
Goodstadt, E. 51
Graham, E. 6
grassroots movements 148
green-washing 11
GroupM, Media Inclusion Initiative (MII) 105
Gulliver, R. 146–147
gun violence 155–156

Hahn, D. L. 56–57
Haitian Diaspora 150–151
Hallmark 66
Halverson, J. R. 153

harm, avoiding, in research 87–88
Harris, J. 119, 120
hashtags, user-friendly/inclusive 70, 73
heading markups 70
healthcare access: Black women 4–5;
  and COVID-19 pandemic 41
Henrich, J. 85
heteronormativity 12, 13
Hewstone, M. 20
Hispanic population 7, 23, 46, 95
Hispanic PR Wire 105
historic realities impacting
  communities, learning about 38–40
Hobby Lobby 10
housing discrimination 10, 39
Houston, E. 116
Hu, J. 157
Human Rights Campaign 28
human trafficking 12
humor 28, 31, 120
hyperlinks 70

IBM (International Business Machines
  Corporation) 126
IDEA Wheel 32
idea-mapping 43
identity 149; cultural 13; gender 27;
  heteronormative 12, 13;
  intersectional *see* intersectionality;
  sexual *see* sexuality/sexual
  orientation; social *see* social identity
immigrants/immigration 10, 38, 39,
  150–151, 152
impact: campaign 107
digital and social media strategies 76
implicit (unconscious) biases 13–14, 43,
  102
impressions (digital content) 75
in-groups 112, 113
inclusion, definition 6
inclusive design, web and social media
  69–71
inclusive language 6, 40, 44–47, 69
inclusive leadership 13, 124–134,
  137–138; and authenticity 125, 127,
  131; communication style 130–131;
  communications strategy 129–130;
  defining 125–127; and subject matter
  expertise 131; traits 132–133; and
  trust 127
Inclusive Market Group 85

inclusive style guides 46, 47
Indigenous communities: conducting
  research with 80–81; media outlets
  105; *see also* Native Americans
individualism 80, 113, 114, 115
influencers 72–73, 106, 136, 152
informed consent 81
Instagram 65
Instagram Insights 76
intellectual property rights 48
intentionality in a research brief 97–98
intercultural competence 13–14
internet: accessibility 41; user numbers
  65; *see also* digital communication
  strategies; social media
Interpublic Group 95
intersectionality 9, 12, 18, 31, 39, 45,
  100, 106; as strategic
  communications mindset 18–19, 20,
  21, 29, 31, 31–33, 40, 42; and visual
  storytelling 57–58
interviews, as research method 85
introverts 116
issues management 147

Jacquez, F. 91
Japan 7
Jenkins, M. 126
Jones, F. 157
Jopwell Collection 59
justice 3; definition 146; racial 9–10, 95,
  125; and research ethics 80, 81; *see
  also* social justice

key performance indicators (KPIs): for
  inclusive digital strategies 75–76; for
  measuring campaign success 107
keyboard accessibility 70
keyword blocking 73–74
Kirtzman, F. 132
Korn Ferry Institute 132
Krownapple, J. 8
Kuaishou 65

Lancôme, HAPTA device 26
language considerations 30–31;
  culturally sensitive research 84, 86;
  digital and social media strategies
  67, 69, 71; inclusive language 6, 40,
  44–47, 69; inclusive leadership 131;
  reappropriation of words 24; slang

and colloquialisms 24, 114–115; and teamwork 114–115; translation and localization 30–31, 32
Latin America, U.S. presence in 39
Latinx community 6, 7, 23, 39, 46, 105
leadership: relational 125; *see also* inclusive leadership
League of United Latin American Citizens (LULAC) 152
Lester, J. 150
Levi Strauss & Company 29
LGBT Foundation (UK) 88
LGBTQ+ community 7, 10, 13, 28–29, 106; buying power 95; and campaign planning 103; media outlets 105; and research 84, 88; and visual storytelling 62
LGBTQ Institute 90
LGBTQ Nation 105
LinkedIn 120, 132
listening 115–116; *see also* social listening
lived experiences, knowledge of 23, 38, 39, 43
Lizzo 25
local media outlets 105
localization 30–31
Logan, N. 9, 10, 11, 95, 147, 150
logos 30
LULAC (League of United Latin American Citizens) 152
Luttrell, R. 31

Mallick, M. 132
Manifest content marketing agency 51
March For Our Lives (MFOL) 148, 155–156, 158; "Our Power" campaign 156
marketing, conscious 95
Matterkind 95
MAVEN Media Framework 104
McDonnel-Horita, R. 8–9
Me Too Movement 157, 158
media monitoring 137
Meltwater 76
Mercedes-Benz 30
Meta 71
Mexican immigrants 152
Micheletti, M. 139
microaggressions 43
Micropedia of Microaggressions 43
Microsoft Advertising 95

mistakes, understanding and learning from 14
Moloney, K. 150
Montgomery Bus Boycott 140
moral case for DEI 7–8, 10, 94, 95, 97
Movement for Black Lives 157
Moy, C. 83
Mundy, D. 8

Nappy 58
narrative analysis 152–154
National Association for the Advancement of Colored People (NAACP) 44
National Association of Black Journalists (NABJ) 44
National Association of Hispanic Journalists (NAHJ) 44
National Association of Latino Elected and Appointed Officials (NALEO) 44
National Council of La Raza (NCLR) 152
National Fair Housing Alliance, Tech Equity Initiative 150
National LGBT Media Association 103
National Museum of African American History & Culture 22
Native Americans 95
navigation (website) 70–71
NBA (National Basketball Association) 5–6
Nembhard, I. M. 125
Neufeld, S. D. 82
neurodiversity 119–120
newswires 105
Nextdoor 65
Nickelodeon, #28DaysofBlackCosplay campaign 71–72
Nicoletti, L. 47
Nielsen 104–105
Nielsen Norman Group 60
Nike 27
Nooyi, I. 131
normalization 31
NPR (National Public Radio) 27, 150

objectification 55
objectives: and campaign planning 98–100, 107; digital and social media strategies 75; SMART+IE 75, 99–100, 107
Occupy Wall Street 148

Old Navy 27
Omnicom Media Group (OMG) 105; Diverse Content Creators Network 72
online complaint engagement 137
online education, and COVID-19 pandemic 41
operability (web content) 68–69, 76
Opportunity Agenda 152, 153, 154
oppression, racial 9, 10
optimal distinctiveness theory 111–114
organizational culture 125–126
organizational values 126, 137
out-groups 112
outcomes (campaign impacts) 107
outputs or outtakes (campaign impacts) 107

Parks, R. 140
participatory research 88–91
Pascal case format (hashtags) 70
patronization 46, 56, 61
People of Color Collective (POCC) 103
PepsiCo 52–53, 54
perceivability (web content) 68, 76
performative allyship 129
personality: 3Ps framework 56; and teamwork 116–117, 121
perspective (3Ps framework) 55–56
persuadables (social justice audiences) 152
PETA (People for Ethical Treatment of Animals) 140–141
Pew Research Center 40, 43, 157–158
Pezzullo, P. 146
POCC (People of Color Collective) 103
political consumerism 139–141
positivist research 88
power dynamics 147, 149–150
Pratt, B. 80
presence (3Ps framework) 55
Pride Month 28–29
Procter & Gamble 105
psychological safety 112, 113, 121
Public Health Foundation 98
Public Relations Society of America x
publics (stakeholders) 19, 37, 128–129; *see also* audience(s)
punctuality 117
purchasing power 95

QQ 65
qualitative research 79, 87
quantitative research 79, 87
queer theory 12–13, 149

Rabinowitz, P. 151
race 11–12, 21, 22–24; preferred identifiers 45–46; social construction of 22, 23; and visual storytelling 61
racial diversity 7
racial equity 10
racial justice 9–10, 95, 125
racial oppression 9, 10
racial stereotypes 10
racism 10, 11–12, 39, 125, 150
Rae, A. 23–24
Ragan 44
Ragan & HarrisX 128
rainbow-washing 11, 28
reach (digital content) 75
reappropriation of words 24
reciprocity, in research 80, 81, 82
Reeb, S. 51
regional ethics 80–81, 82
Reid, J. 14
Reinsborough, P. 153
relational leadership 125
relationship building, with community advocates 137
religion/faith 21, 29; and visual storytelling 62
representation of social identity groups, accurate and consistent 51–54, 61–63, 101–103
reputation management 135–144; definition 135; and political consumerism 139–141; proactive 136–138; reactive 138–139; role of strategic communicators 135–136; and trust 142
research: campaign planning 96–98; primary *see* culturally sensitive research
research briefs 97–98
"Research Manifesto for Ethical Research in Downtown Eastside" (Neufeld et al.) 82
Resonance consulting firm 151, 153, 154
resource library 43–44
respect for persons (research ethics) 80, 82
reverse ageism 26–27

robustness (web content) 69, 76
Roundel Media Fund 6

Sampson, P. 13
Sankofa.org 156
Schwarz, C. 12
Science Friday 150
search engine optimization (SEO) 137
SeeHer coalition 107
segregation 140
self-awareness 13–14, 112–113
sexism 28, 150
sexuality/sexual orientation 12–13, 21;
    and visual storytelling 62; *see also*
    LGBTQ+ community; queer theory
sexualization 55
Shalett, L. 130
shared values 153–154
Shaw, E. 152
Singer, J. 119
slang 24, 114–115
SMART+IE objectives 75, 99–100,
    107
Smith, B. 104
Smith, K. N. 53
Smith, M. F. 152
Snapchat 65
social change 145, 146; applying critical
    theories to 148–149; communication
    strategies for 151–159
social identity 13, 18, 20, 21, 102
social identity categories 20, 38–40;
    abbreviations/acronyms as
    descriptors for 23, 44–45; accurate
    and consistent representation of
    51–54, 61–63, 101–103; differing
    effects of circumstances on
    (COVID-19 pandemic) 40–42;
    gaining insight into 21–29;
    intersecting *see* intersectionality;
    language and terminology
    considerations when researching 84;
    visual storytelling and accurate
    representation of 51–54, 61–63; *see
    also* ability; age; ethnicity; gender;
    race; religion; sexuality/sexual
    orientation
social justice 8, 10, 13, 27, 52, 138, 145;
    definition 146
social justice activism 147, 148, 149,
    150–151, 155–158

social justice communications 145;
    coalition building 151–152;
    consensus and dissensus in 150–151;
    creative (or artistic) activism 156,
    158–159; and digital media 157–158;
    framing and reframing issues in
    152–154; storytelling 154–156;
    theories and concepts that shape
    148–151
social listening 66–67, 76, 137
social media activism 157–158
social media strategies 65–78, 136–137;
    and accessibility 67–71, 76–77;
    brand safety practices 73–75; and
    engagement by audience segments
    76; ensuring representation and
    diverse voices 71–73; evaluating
    effectiveness of 75–78; goals and
    objectives 76; impact 76; inclusive
    design 67–71; key performance
    indicators (KPIs) 75; language
    considerations 67, 71; monitoring
    137; search engine optimization
    (SEO) 137; social listening 66–67, 76,
    137; user testing (usability testing)
    66, 67, 76–77
social movements 146
social (re)production 149–150
societal-centric communications
    147–148
Sodexo 126
Sony PlayStation 25–26
sources 42, 43; checking 48; citing 48;
    diversifying 106
spokespeople, and campaign planning
    106
Sprout Social 76
Stable Diffusion 47
stakeholders *see* publics
Starbucks: and Black Lives Matter
    movement 139; logo 30; Race
    Together campaign 11
stereotype threat 88
stereotypes/stereotyping 4, 20, 50, 55,
    119; avoiding/checking for 43, 44, 46,
    48, 54, 56, 61, 84, 102, 107, 121;
    cultural 112–113; gender 28; racial 10
Stocksy 59
Stolle, D. 139
storytelling: and social justice
    communications 154–156; and

stereotyping 102; *see also* narrative analysis; visual storytelling
strategic communications: definition and purpose 37; social justice concepts relating to 148–151
strategic communicators 127–129; and external audiences 128–129; and internal audiences 127–128; and reputation management 135–136
structural discrimination 11
style guides 43–44, 46; brand 46; disability language 86; inclusive 46, 47
suffragette movement 146
supplier diversity 103
Sweden 7
SWOT-DEI analysis 98–99
systemic discrimination 11
systemic inequity 4–5

Talkwalker 76
Tapia, A. 132
Target Corporation 6
teamwork 111–123; and ability differences 119–120; and behavioral-based misunderstanding 115; body language considerations 116; and brainstorming 118; collaborative working to adapt to differences 118–119; and generational differences 119; and individualism versus collectivism 113–114, 115; and language-based misunderstanding 114–115; listening and learning to understand team member differences 115–116; and optimal distinctiveness theory 111–114; and personality types 116–117, 121; and psychological safety 112, 113, 121; and self–awareness 112–113; and time and punctuality 117; tips 121; and trust 113; and visualization 117; working agreements 118–119
TelevisaUnivision 105
terminology, culturally sensitive research 84, 86
TikTok 23–24, 65, 71, 99; "That Girl" trend 83
time, and teamwork 117
Tindall, N. T. 19
tokenism 56–57, 61, 99

TONL 59
trademark laws 48
traditions, cultural 20, 31
translation 30–31, 31
Travon 53
Trump, D. 152
trust 95, 126, 135; and inclusive leadership 127; and reputation management 142; and research 80–81; and teamwork 113
Tufekci, Z. 157
Tuskegee Experiments 41
Twitter/X 65
Twitter/X Analytics 76
two-way symmetrical model of PR 150

U.S. Asian Wire News 105
U.S. Bureau of Labor Statistics 7
U.S. Census Bureau 23, 39
unconscious biases 13–14, 43, 102
understandability (web content) 69, 76
UNICEF 103
UnitedWeDream 44
Unstereotype Alliance 43, 54
Urban One 105
URL blocklists 73–74
USC Annenberg Center for Public Relations 148
user testing (usability testing) 66, 67, 76–77

values: organizational 126, 137; shared 153–154
Van Edwards, V. 116
Van Knippenberg, A. 20
Vardeman-Winter, J. 19
Vaughn, L. M. 91
VICE, Gender Spectrum Collection 58
visual accessibility 60, 117
visual storytelling 50–64; 3Ps (presence, perspective, personality) framework 54–56; accessibility 59–61; accurate and consistent representation of social identity groups in 51–54, 61–63; definition 51; finding inclusive imagery for 58–59; and intersectionality 57–58; avoiding tokenism in 56–57, 61
visualization 117
voting rights 12
Voto Latino 44

W3C Web Accessibility Initiative 68
Wallace, A. A. 31
Wamsley, L. 27
Ware, K. 14
Waters, R. D. 99, 100
We Are Social report (2023) 65
Weaver, C. K. 148
Web Content Accessibility Guidelines
   (WCAG) 68–69, 76
WebAxe 60
Weber Shandwick 135–136
webpage load time 76
websites: responsiveness 76; search
   engine optimization (SEO) 137;
   useful 40, 43, 44
WeChat 65
Weinbaum, C. 81, 82
WEIRD research 85
WFA *see* World Federation of
   Advertisers
WHO *see* World Health Organization
woke-washing 27
wokeness 27
women: in communications industry 7;
   intersectional identities 19; rights of 7;
   voting rights 12; *see also* Black women
Women of Color in Tech 58
#TheWomen'sMarch 158

working agreements 118–119
World Economic Forum, Racial Justice
   in Business Initiative 95
World Federation of Advertisers (WFA)
   x, 73, 75, 102, 107; Global DEI
   Census 7
World Health Organization (WHO) 25,
   60, 67
writing in the disciplines 37
writing strategically 37–49; Step 1:
   Learn about history and social
   identities 38–40; Step 2: Consider
   how circumstances affect audiences
   differently 40–42; Step 3: Brainstorm
   topics and keep a resource library
   42–44; Step 4: Avoid stereotypes and
   use inclusive language 44–47
Wu-Tang Clan 72

X/Twitter 65
X/Twitter Analytics 76

Young, K. 116
Youth Participatory Action Research
   Hub (YPAR) 90

Zandan, N. 130
Zavala, M. 89

For Product Safety Concerns and Information please contact our EU
representative GPSR@taylorandfrancis.com
Taylor & Francis Verlag GmbH, Kaufingerstraße 24, 80331 München, Germany